THE LAST MILE

Creating Social and Economic Value from Behavioral Insights

Most organizations spend much of their effort on the first stages of the value creation process: creating a strategy, developing new products or services, and analyzing the market. They pay a lot less attention to the end: the crucial "last mile" where consumers come to their website, store, or sales representatives and make a choice.

In *The Last Mile*, Dilip Soman shows how to use insights from behavioral science to understand customer decision-making and close the gap between intentions and actions. Beginning with an introduction to the last mile problem and the concept of choice architecture, the book takes a deep dive into the psychology of choice, money, and time. It explains how to construct behavioral experiments and understand the data on preferences that they provide. Finally, it provides a range of practical tools with which to overcome common last mile difficulties.

The Last Mile helps lay readers not only to understand behavioral science, but to apply its lessons to their own organizations' last mile problems, whether they work in business, government, or the non-profit sector. Appealing to anyone who was fascinated by Dan Ariely's *Predictably Irrational*, Richard Thaler and Cass Sunstein's *Nudge*, or Daniel Kahneman's *Thinking, Fast and Slow* but was unsure how those insights could be practically applied, *The Last Mile* is full of solid, concrete advice on how to put the lessons of behavioral science to work.

DILIP SOMAN is a professor and the Corus Chair in Communications Strategy at the Rotman School of Management at the University of Toronto. A behavioral scientist with a PhD from the University of Chicago Graduate School of Business, he is director of the University of Toronto's India Innovation Institute and the coordinator of the Behavioural Economics in Action research cluster.

THE LAST MILE

Creating Social and Economic Value from Behavioral Insights

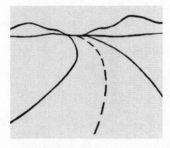

Dilip Soman

With illustrations by Yue Zhuo

UNIVERSITY OF TORONTO PRESS
Toronto Buffalo London

© University of Toronto Press 2015
Rotman-UTP Publishing
University of Toronto Press
Toronto Buffalo London
www.utppublishing.com
Printed in the U.S.A

Reprinted in paperback 2017

ISBN 978-1-4426-5043-5 (cloth)   ISBN 978-1-4875-2182-0 (paper)

♾ Printed on acid-free, 100% post-consumer recycled paper.

Library and Archives Canada Cataloguing in Publication

Soman, Dilip, author
The last mile : creating social and economic value from behavioral insights /
Dilip Soman; with illustrations by Yue Zhuo.

Includes bibliographical references and index.
ISBN 978-1-4426-5043-5 (bound) – ISBN 978-1-4875-2182-0 (softcover)

1. Economics – Psychological aspects.   2. Economics – Sociological aspects.
3. Human behavior – Economic aspects.   4. Human behavior – Social aspects.
5. Choice (Psychology) – Economic aspects.   6. Decision making –
Psychological aspects.   I. Title.

HB74.P8S66 2015   330.01'9   C2015-903005-6

University of Toronto Press acknowledges the financial assistance to its
publishing program of the Canada Council for the Arts and the Ontario Arts
Council, an agency of the Government of Ontario.

Canada Council   Conseil des Arts
for the Arts   du Canada

ONTARIO ARTS COUNCIL
CONSEIL DES ARTS DE L'ONTARIO
an Ontario government agency
un organisme du gouvernement de l'Ontario

Funded by the   Financé par le
Government   gouvernement
of Canada   du Canada

Canada

Contents

Acknowledgments

The material in chapter 3 is drawn from two sources where it originally appeared: (1) A report entitled *An Overview of the Behavioural Sciences* that I prepared for Industry Canada as part of work undertaken with the Canadian partnership for Public Policy Oriented Consumer Interest Research (PPOCIR); (2) D. Soman, "Option Overload: Dealing with Choice Complexity," *Rotman Magazine* (Fall 2010): 43–7. I thank Carmen Cayouette of Industry Canada and Karen Christensen of *Rotman Magazine* for permission to use the materials. To subscribe, visit: www .rotmanmagazine.ca.

Chapter 5 includes material that originally appeared in chapter 12, "Hang On: The Psychology of Time and Implications for Designing Queues," in David Soberman and Dilip Soman (Eds.), *Flux: What Marketing Managers Need to Navigate the New Environment* (Toronto: University of Toronto Press, 2012).

Chapter 6 is an extended and updated version of an article that first appeared in *Rotman Magazine*; see D. Soman, J. Xu, and A. Cheema, "A Theory of Decision Points," *Rotman Magazine* (Winter 2010). I thank Karen Christensen of the Rotman School of Management and my collaborators Jing Xu and Amar Cheema for permission to use the materials. To subscribe, visit: www.rotmanmagazine.ca.

Chapter 10 is based on the following report, which was published online by the Rotman School of Management: K. Ly, N. Mazar, M. Zhao, and D. Soman, *A Practitioner's Guide to Nudging*, Behavioural Economics in Action Research Report Series (Rotman School of Management, University of Toronto, 2013). I thank Kim Ly, Nina Mazar, and Min Zhao for permission to use materials from the report in this chapter.

INTRODUCTION: AT THE LAST MILE

Every organization that I know of is in the business of changing somebody's behavior. A for-profit company will try to convince consumers who currently purchase their competitor's products to switch to theirs. A government might want to convince citizens to pay their taxes on time or to renew their driver's licenses online where it can be done more cost effectively and quickly. A public welfare organization might want to encourage eligible families to sign up and receive aid or tuition support for their children's education. In fact, I do not know of any organization that is *not* in the business of changing behavior.

If you think about what people in organizations typically do, a lot of their efforts are spent on what I call first mile problems. These are efforts devoted to developing strategy, coming up with new products and services, designing processes of innovation, and thinking through the competitive landscape. However, very little attention is paid to the last mile. The last mile is where the rubber meets the road. The last mile is where consumers come to your website, or to your retail stores, or talk to your sales representatives, and make a decision to switch to your product. The last mile is the place where citizens interact with a welfare organization and decide whether or not to sign up for a program. The last mile is where an individual goes to a government office in order to get access to a service and either chooses to stay or throws up his hands in frustration and goes home.

When one thinks about the last mile and listens to stories from consumers and citizens who have not had a great experience there, one realizes that it is not the big things that matter. It is the small things that matter. At the last mile, little things like the manner in which a decision was presented, the ambiance of the room, the phrasing of the question that people were asked, the color of the paper on which a form was printed, or the pleasantness of the agent with whom the consumer interacted are all determinants of the decision to buy products, open accounts, or, more generally, consume services. As a society in general, and as business schools in particular, I would argue, we have spent a disproportionate amount of time and energy thinking about first mile problems when in fact we should be thinking about the last mile problem. The last mile is what makes or breaks organizations, and yet many organizations tend to outsource the last mile to service providers. In my mind, this is a mistake.

Where does a good theory of the last mile come from? Any theory of the last mile has to include a theory of behavior change. I have been studying behavior change for many years. I am an engineer by training, and my first job involved sales and service for heavy earthmoving machinery. I realized that the attributes of my products made very little difference to customers, but the small things at the last mile made a big difference. After completing a stint in sales and service, I went out to get an MBA, and then a PhD at the University of Chicago's Graduate School of Business.

At Chicago's Center for Decision Research, I got a chance to work with some of the brightest minds that I have ever met. After finishing in 1996, I subsequently worked at the University of Colorado in Boulder, the Hong Kong University of Science and Technology, and then the University of Toronto's Rotman School of Management. During all these years, I have had a chance to think about decision making with an academic and theoretical lens as well as a practical lens, and with a behavioral lens as well as an engineering lens. My research interests can be described by the following simple sentence: I'm interested in interesting human behaviors and in identifying ways in which we can use those interesting behaviors to help people help themselves.

Over the last few years, there has been a surge of interest in the behavioral sciences, largely because of the publication of books such as Dan Ariely's *Predictably Irrational*, Richard Thaler's and Cass Sunstein's *Nudge*, and Daniel Kahneman's *Thinking, Fast and Slow*. These and many other books present great ideas. I had been thinking about ways in which these ideas – the interesting findings in the behavioral sciences – could be harnessed to help people and organizations make better choices. This led to the formation of a research cluster at the Rotman School (called Behavioural Economics in Action, or BEA@R) that works with partners in industry, government, and welfare organizations to conduct research that is rigorous yet applicable to real-world situations. More recently, I decided to teach a massive open online course, a MOOC. The stated goal of my course, *Behavioral Economics in Action*, was not only to expose students to the practices of what has come to be called behavioral economics but also to help them think (and act) like behavioral scientists. To do so they needed the ability to read and critically examine research in the area of the behavioral sciences and, and, more importantly, the ability to look at real-world situations and identify interventions to help people make better choices. In the process of developing the MOOC, I was able not only to improve my own approach to teaching but also to develop a much more nuanced approach to what I knew about the behavioral sciences. When you are in the trenches doing research, or you are in an organization looking to address a specific behavioral problem, you tend to look at the ground level and at specific details germane to that problem. You tend to look at the trees and not the forest. Teaching allowed me to take a much bigger perspective on the problem. I was able to rise above the narrow tree-level interest of any particular research or consulting project and look at the proverbial forest – the big picture.

This book covers the materials that I have taught as lectures and in discussions not only at the MOOC but also at the University of Toronto's Rotman School of Management. I initially started out trying to develop a book that was a companion piece for my courses, but in its gestation phase the book took on a life of its own and is now a complete, stand-alone set of ideas. My former students will recognize some of the content here, but I am confident they will find many new insights to take away. As in my course, the goal of this book is not just to present the next big idea but to help you think through what you will be able to do with the ideas you come up with and how you might be able to get behavioral science to work for you.

What needs to happen for you to be able to master the last mile? First, you need to understand what happens at the last mile: "How do your stakeholders (consumers or citizens) make choices and what affects these choices?" That is the focus of the first six chapters. I begin with a description of what the last mile is (chapter 1) and a definition of "choice architecture" (chapter 2). The next three chapters take a deep dive into the psychology of choice, money, and time (chapters 3, 4, and 5). Chapter 6 presents a theory of decision points – a theory that sets the stage for understanding how people can modify their own consumption behaviors. Second, you need to understand the methods that are best suited to study behavior at the last mile. Chapters 7 and 8 discuss behavioral experiments (or trials, as they are often called) and approaches to understanding preference. Finally, you need to take all these ideas and address the "So what?" question. The final six chapters tackle different aspects of the last mile, including a broad framework for choice repair (chapter 9), a process of designing nudges (chapter 10), decision crutches (chapter 11), a behavioral lens on disclosure (chapter 12), a deep dive into retailing (chapter 13), and finally some prescriptions for how to master the last mile (chapter 14).

I would like to thank a large number of my former students and teachers for providing feedback and suggestions on the classroom materials that have helped me sharpen my own thinking in this area. I would like to thank four people from whom I have learnt not just the nuts and bolts of research but also the knack of developing research that is rigorous yet relevant. Richard Thaler, Steve Hoch, Chris Hsee, and Sanjay Dhar were my thesis committee members at the University of Chicago, and I owe them almost everything in terms of my intellectual development. I was also fortunate to learn from (and in some cases, work with) several fantastic fellow graduate students at the University of Chicago: John Gourville, Klaus Wertenbroch, Jack Soll, Craig McKenzie, and Radhika Puri. I have learned a lot from each one of them. In addition there were several other scholars from whom I learned a lot, though we were not affiliated in any formal capacity. These include Josh Klayman, Elke Weber, Robin Hogarth, Itamar Simonson, Bob Meyer, Joel Huber, John Lynch, Jim Bettman, Peter Ayton, Hal Arkes, George Loewenstein, Drazen Prelec, George Wu, and Rick Larrick.

I would also like to thank a number of individuals for pushing my thinking through intriguing and challenging conversations, questions, and collaborations. In particular, my former doctoral students Catherine Yeung, Amar Cheema, Xiuping Li, Maggie Liu, Heekyung Ahn, Jaewoo Joo, and Yanping Tu have done a wonderful job of questioning almost everything that I have said in a very nice, intellectual, and constructive manner.

At the University of Toronto, I have been fortunate to work with several colleagues who are not only smart and talented but also highly energetic and enthusiastic. Together we have formed the research cluster that I wrote about earlier. I am deeply indebted to Min Zhao, Nina Mazar, Tanjim Hossain, Avi Goldfarb, Pankaj Aggarwal, Claire Tsai, and Glen Whyte.

The materials in this book draw on research done both by others, which has been cited, and by me, ably assisted by several research assistants, including Kim Ly, Sandesh Kulkarni, Stew Lawrence, Michael Walker, Vivian Lam, Neuri Park, Christine Lim, Yue Zhuo, Silu Liu, Lynda Liu, and Janice Cha. In addition, some of the materials covered in this book are based on research conducted in collaboration with a number of amazing individuals. An acknowledgment of the original research is made at the appropriate places in the book, and I thank all my collaborators for their contributions not just to the book but to my own intellectual development. Special thanks are due to Felice Lai, the manager of this book project, and to Yue Zhuo, who created the illustrations for the book. I also thank Rory Sutherland, George Wu, Kyle Murray, and Simona Botti for comments and suggestions on earlier drafts of the manuscript.

Finally, I thank my wife, Teesta, my son, Neel, and my daughter, Meera, for being with me throughout my journey, from the first mile to the last!

Dilip Soman
Toronto

THE LAST MILE

Creating Social and Economic Value from Behavioral Insights

PART ONE

The Theory of the Last Mile: Principles and Ideas from the Behavioral Sciences

1 The Last Mile

In chapter 1
You will find answers to questions such as:

1 What is the last mile in the value chain and why is it critical to the success of organizations?

2 Why is human behavior so central to the last mile?

3 What are the three pillars of human behavior?

4 Why is the medium cup of coffee the most popular size?

5 Why do people not do things in their best interest despite knowing what to do?

6 What are the three sets of activities that organizations need to engage in to master the last mile?

It was a beautiful summer's day in the middle of 1997. I was on a road trip across the United States, and the last leg of my trip took me from upstate New York to Boston, Massachusetts. These were the days before Google Maps and also, of course, before GPS. I had been told that the drive was going to take about six and a half hours. Imagine my surprise when, at the end of six and a half hours, I got to a sign by the highway that said, "Boston, 1 mile," and very quickly after that, a sign saying "Welcome to Boston." I was feeling pretty pleased with the fact that my drive time actually matched the prediction and the expectation that I had, and I thought I was home. But I was wrong.

Some of you may remember that at that time Boston was undergoing a major road construction and renovation program known as "The Big Dig."[1] Roads were being dug up. Elevated highways were going to be reconstructed underground. The map of Boston was going to be altered. There was construction equipment all over the place.

In fact, the road network kept changing on a daily basis. There were some roads that allowed one-way traffic in one direction on one particular day and one way in the other direction on the next day. When I got off the expressway to go to my destination in downtown Boston, I was stuck in a maze of construction, one-ways, and slow earthmoving equipment. It took me a full fifty minutes from the time I got off the highway to arrive at where I wanted to be. I was the victim of what is called the last mile problem.

When I look back and think about the journey I made back in 1997, I was struck by the two parts of the journey and the differences between them. In the first part, I zipped along the highway from upstate New York to Boston. In the second part, I left the highway and then had to make my way to a precise address in the heart of downtown Boston. This story is not unique to Boston. If you're zipping along the motorways in England and exit toward a destination in London, you've experienced the same sense of frustration as I did; or in India, when it takes you three hours to get to Bombay from the end of the Pune-Bombay expressway, you know exactly what I mean by the last mile problem.

This situation mimics many other situations in the real world. Think about a system of distribution of physical goods. Suppose you are a company that is looking to distribute your products across the nation. Think about the difficulty of transporting goods from upstate New York to Boston and then, once they've arrived in Boston, the cost involved with transporting those goods to individual stores or individual households.

As you might imagine, the cost of the second part of this distribution system is going to be significant compared to the first part. It is just like my drive. The time and energy I spent in the first part seemed to pale in comparison to the time, energy, and frustration experienced in the second part of the journey. It is a classic illustration of the last mile problem.

The Last Mile Problem

The term "the last mile problem" came from the very early days of the telegraph.[2] This was an old technology where people used to send messages to each other through wires that were strung all across the county. It was an amazing piece of technology. Before then, the only way you could communicate with others was through letters, and letters took a long time to reach the recipient. The telegraph was fantastic, because with a few simple keystrokes, the person at the other end of the telegraph line would get a message within a matter of hours. Messages could be sent thousands of miles almost instantly. Of course, there was a last mile problem with the telegraph. While it was easy for messages to zip from the place of origin to the end of the telegraph line, somebody had to get on a horse or a bicycle and carry that message over that last mile to the right person.

Since then, the "last mile" is a phrase used by telecommunications, cable television, and Internet industries generally to refer to the final leg of the telecommunications network delivery process. In particular, it refers to the end of the delivery process where these companies have to provide connectivity to retail customers. The last mile of any communication network is the part that actually reaches the customer.

The last mile problem shows up in many different industries. While the term is used primarily in telecommunications, it is relevant elsewhere. I live in Toronto, and we recently had an election for a new mayor. One of the big issues in this election was public transit. Public transit is important for ensuring connectivity and for reducing the burden on the roads in any major city. It is something that every city in the world should push for, because we know that it cuts down on the use of gas, it reduces congestion, and it makes connectivity easier. However, there is one interesting problem that designers of transit have to think about. It is the idea that while it might be easy to transport people from point A to point B – say two stations on a transit network, we need to worry about how people get to point A from their homes and how they get to their workplace from point B. One big barrier to using public transit is the cost (in money, time, and psychological stress) of getting to and from the transit station. How do we solve this last mile problem?

There are a number of solutions. In Toronto, for example, a lot of the buses are equipped with bike racks so that people can actually ride their bicycle up to the bus station, attach their bicycle to the bus rack, get onto the bus, and then hop back onto the bicycle when they get off the bus to get to their final destination.[3] In Europe, there is a solution called Hiriko City Car.[4] This is a two-person electric vehicle that bridges the gap between your home and your public transit station, and between your public transit station and your place of work. There are yet other solutions. There is a folding electric motor scooter called a RoboScooter,[5] and an electric-assisted bike called the Green Wheel.[6] These are all simple solutions that facilitate the overcoming of the last mile problem, thereby making it easier for consumers to use public transit.

Let me step back a bit and think more broadly about the last mile problem. The examples we've touched on thus far suggest that the last mile problem applies only to situations where there is some element of physical transportation, or some element of physical distribution. But it's not as narrow as that. The last mile is a challenge in many situations. Let me offer three different examples.

First, let's look at the world of new products. Depending on which survey you read and depending on how that survey has defined the term "success," you'll learn that new product success rates are typically in the region of 1 percent to 25 percent. In other words, more than 75 percent of new products that are launched fail.[7]

Why does this happen? One could come up with many different reasons for why that might be the case. Perhaps, if the product is technologically sophisticated, it might have some features that are difficult to use and that consumers just don't understand. Or, it could be that the marketing communication was problematic. Perhaps the advertising wasn't done well, or the consumer wasn't aware of the product or didn't understand what the product did.

Alternatively, it could also be that the pricing was wrong. While consumers would have purchased the product at a lower price, somehow the manufacturer got the pricing wrong and the people who would truly have appreciated the product still would not purchase it.

There is a simpler behavioral story that might explain the failure. The behavioral story has to do with the fact that, while the product was being developed, the developer didn't really think about the last mile – about the effort that was going to be needed to get people to adopt and use the product. I would argue that, as organizations, we spend a lot of time and energy thinking about creating a product and making it the best possible product that we can, and even selling the product. But we don't think as much about the usage of the product. How do we get consumers to actually use and engage with the product? Often, the answer to that problem isn't technological. It is psychological.

A second example comes from a different domain – government programs. In Canada, the federal government introduced a new initiative called the Canada Learning Bond, the CLB. The CLB is a wonderful program that gives eligible low-income families $500 that they can use to educate their children. While there are obviously some details in terms of what the money can and cannot be spent on, you could think about this as $500 worth of free money that the government gives to all eligible families to use for educating their children.

If you were an economist and you looked at this particular arrangement, you would say, "Wow, $500 free, who would not take the money?" As an economist your prediction would be that the take-up rate of this Canada Learning Bond would be close to 100 percent. Yet, in the first year when the bond was introduced, the take-up rates were as low as 16 percent.[8] Why were 84 percent of eligible families not taking the "free money"? The reason had nothing to do with the quality of the program – indeed, it was a generous program. However, there was a last mile problem.

The last mile problem was that in order to benefit from the program, an eligible family needed a bank account. A lot of the families that were eligible for this particular bond didn't have the time to go and open a bank account. They were low-income families where the parents were juggling multiple jobs. They had children to look after. They had to make childcare arrangements for the evenings, and hence lack of opportunity to get to a bank to open a bank account provided to be the primary reason why this program didn't succeed. It wasn't a problem with the program design. It was a last mile problem.

The last mile problem also shows up in the area of public policy. Think about the importance of disclosures. Let's imagine that you're buying a new house or a financial product and you don't understand the risks associated with that product. Governments all over the world try to protect consumers by mandating the disclosure of important pieces of information.[9] This could be information relating to risks, to product features, or to potential fees and charges that the consumer might need to incur.

The belief behind requiring mandatory disclosure is simple. The belief is that the more information people have in making a choice, the better their choices will be. In fact, the term "better informed choices" has come to be synonymous with better choices. In a similar vein, policymakers and marketers alike believe that providing people with more choice is a good thing, because it allows them to align their preferences better with what is available in the marketplace. Consequently, what we've seen happening in the world of policy and in the world of marketing over the past few years is a growth in the number of options available to consumers, as well as a growth in the amount of information available to consumers. But does disclosure always work, and does it always make sense to offer people more choices?

Research in the behavioral sciences suggests that the answer to these two questions is an emphatic "no." Human beings are limited processors of information. The more options you give them and the more information you present to them, the more likely they are to undergo some sort of cognitive paralysis. For instance, giving people excessive amounts of information – disclosing too much at the back of a credit card statement, for example – might lead people to ignore that information altogether. Likewise, providing people with too many options increases the likelihood that they will actually switch to a product category or a brand that doesn't offer so many options.[10]

This is yet another classic example of the last mile problem. The logic behind offering lots of information and lots of choices is compelling, but the manner in which that information and those choices are presented can create a last mile problem, resulting in choice deferral and the ignoring of the presented information.

The First Mile and the Last

In general, keeping in mind these examples and many, many others, I believe that as business schools, as policy schools, and as schools of governance, we make a distinction between strategy – the first mile – and tactics – the last mile (figure 1.1). We have spent a disproportionately large amount of effort and resources on strategy, and much less on tactics.

Let's think about the specific examples we looked at. In a marketing context, thinking about strategy involves thinking about the "what"

Figure 1.1 Comparing First Mile and Last Mile Problems

First Mile	Last Mile
• Strategy • Focus on the *what*: played out in boardrooms, research and development facilities, and planning committee sessions • New product development • Policy development • Welfare program design	• Tactics • Focus on the *how* and *when*: played out in retail spaces, customer service locations, webpages, and online/telephone support • New product adoption and use • Policy implementation and delivery • Welfare program adoption and take-up

question. What needs to be done? Thinking about tactics pushes us to the "how and when" questions. How is it going to be done? Likewise in the world of policy, setting up a policy is a strategic question. Delivering the policy is a tactical question. Coming up with the idea for a new product is a strategic question. Taking the product to market is a tactical question.

One of the first people to use "the last mile problem" to describe a failure of adoption in the domain of government programs was Sendhil Mullainathan, a professor of economics at Harvard University.[11] In describing scientific innovations to help combat diseases (such as diarrhea) that are the biggest causes of child mortality, Mullainathan made a distinction between the scientific discovery and affordable distribution of drugs, on the one hand, and the proper adoption and use of these drugs, on the other.

The last mile problem is one of understanding human psychology and harnessing the insights. It is not a problem of technology or product and program design. The last mile is tricky because it relies on behavioral insights, and there is a large variation in behaviors! The last mile problem is something that we as businesses, as policymakers, and as governments need to think a lot more about, because while we have wonderful theories of strategy, we do not have as many good theories of tactics. Can we, for example, develop a good theory that allows us to predict how we can get people to open more envelopes? How can we get people to read (and understand) information at the back of their credit card statements? How can we get people to try new products? How can we get people to make choices that we believe are good for them? We simply lack the tools to help organizations accomplish these ends.

I would not be the first author to write about the notion of behavioral insights, or behavioral economics, as it has come to be known. I like the term behavioral insights, or behavioral science, more because behavioral economics represents a very narrow part of the entire spectrum of behavioral insights. Many authors have written about the fact that human decision making is not rational and that people make choices that are not predicted by the standard economic model of decision making. For instance, in a 2008 book called *Nudge*, Richard Thaler and Cass Sunstein make a distinction between econs and humans.[12] Econs are the unicorns of the decision-making world – they are mythical beasts that inhabit the pages of economics textbooks. Econs are forward-looking, they have infinite computational ability, they are unemotional, and they have this uncanny ability to assign something called a utility to every product or service they consume, and to each attribute of that product or service. On the other hand, real people – humans – are myopic and impulsive. Emotion guides their decision making. They seemingly make decisions quickly without thinking too much. A lot has been written about the fact that if these basic principles of economics are not adhered to, we're going to end up calling humans irrational.

My take on irrationality is slightly different. If people are not obeying the laws of economics, I don't think they're being irrational. I just think they're being human. In fact, any theory that tries to put in a structure on decision making that is different from what humans do is perhaps not the best theory to use as a descriptive theory of human behavior.

Irrationality 1.0: When Our Expectation of Others' Behavior Is Incorrect

There are two forms of irrationality that we need to think about a bit more carefully. The first form is the difference between what people actually do to make decisions versus what policymakers and marketers think they do. The more we educate our policymakers and our business students about the notion of economic rationality, the more they expect everybody else to behave like the rational model. Policymakers might be surprised to learn that disclosing a lot of information could backfire. Likewise, a marketer who offers a superior product might be surprised to learn that consumers don't rush to the stores to buy that product. One form of irrationality arises when there is a mismatch between what consumers actually do and what we expect them to do. In particular, people might not be as strongly influenced by features of a product or program as marketers or policymakers expect them to be. Conversely, they might be influenced by factors that might, a priori, not have been deemed relevant to their decision.

Here are three examples that highlight this form of irrationality. The first example is based on research done by two fantastic researchers at Columbia University, Eric Johnson and Dan Goldstein.[13] In a paper published in the journal *Science* in 2003, these researchers explored the world of organ donations.

In their article, the authors presented a chart that showed the effective consent percentages – that is, the percentage of people saying that they're willing to donate organs – as a function of several European countries. What they found in that chart was interesting. There were some countries where the effective organ donation rates were very low. Denmark, for example, had 4.35 percent; Germany, 12 percent; and the United Kingdom, 17 percent.

But there were other countries where the effective consent rates were incredibly high. Austria had 99.98 percent. France had 99.91 percent. Hungary had 99.97 percent. What might explain the differences between countries that were geographically not very far away from each other but had dramatically different organ donation rates?

The simplest answers that might come to mind turned out not to explain these patterns of data. For example, it wasn't the case that Belgium or France or Austria was spending significantly more per capita than Denmark or Germany. It wasn't the case that the advertising programs – or the penetration of the advertising programs – was different in one set of countries than in the other.

The only difference across these two sets of countries was what is called the default option. Think about the organ donation process in North America. In Canada, for example, a person who wants to consent to donate organs needs to go to the Department of Motor Vehicles and obtain a form. The form is fairly long and complicated, and it is typically given to you at the end of whatever work it is that you came to do. For instance, after renewing your driver's license, you might be handed the form and asked whether you would consider being an organ donor.

The implicit assumption is that if you do not complete and hand in the form, you will not be an organ donor. This is what we would call an *explicit consent* (or an opt-in) process. In an explicit consent process, anybody who wants to register to be an organ donor needs to actively take steps to say that they want to be an organ donor.

In a country like Austria, the default is different. Austria is what is called a *presumed consent* (or opt-out) country. You retain the freedom of choice about whether (or not) to donate organs, but the assumption is that unless you fill out and hand in a form, you do want to donate organs. The default is that you will donate your organs. That simple difference between an explicit consent process and a presumed consent process can push organ donation rates from, let's say, 4.25 percent in Denmark to 99.98 percent in Austria.

Defaults are tremendously powerful because of two reasons. The first reason for why they work is that several years of research has shown us that human beings are supremely lazy, both physically and cognitively.[14] This laziness implies that people stick to the default because if they have to exercise their right of choice to move away from the default, they actually need to make an effort. We know that people are averse to effort, so unless the default option is something they are particularly averse to, people tend to stick with the default.

The second reason for why defaults work is that they tend to signal some sort of a social norm. If the default is that everybody is a donor, people might think that perhaps they should be donors as well. If the default is that nobody is a donor, then they might take that as a suggestion.

The default shapes choices in a very significant manner in a number of different domains. When I lived in Hong Kong, my credit card application form had an opt-in box that I needed to tick and sign if I wanted my contact information to be shared with partner merchants. In North America, it had an opt-out box, and hence I received significantly more solicitation messages. Default effects show up in other places where they can help people make better decisions. In a project that I was involved in a number of years ago, I was interested in seeing how we can get people to go to their doctor for an annual physical checkup. In this particular population, the percentage of people who went in for their annual medical checkups was as low as about 16 percent.

I tried to understand why people didn't go for a physical checkup. When I asked people, the most common excuse I heard was, "I'm really very busy." They claimed that they had every intention of going but just could not find the time. These same people found the time to go on vacations, read books, watch TV movies, and have relaxing barbecue get-togethers.

The reality of the situation was simpler. Some of them felt busier than they were. More importantly, there was some effort required to pick up the phone, make an appointment, and then arrange to be available for the hour of the appointment. The economic costs of doing this were very small, yet it seemed like a nuisance and the "hassle costs" were high.

We tried something that sounds incredibly simple in hindsight. We used a random date generator to randomly assign people to doctors' appointments. A mailing to one of the members might say, for example, "John, thank you for enrolling in a health plan. As part of the plan you're entitled to an annual health checkup with your doctor. You have been assigned the time-slot of 10 AM on June 26th. Should you not be able to make it, please give us a call. Otherwise, we look forward to seeing you then."

The simple act of changing the default resulted in an increase in the number of people going for their annual health checkups. In this particular sample, the number went up from 16 percent to about 64 percent. Again, changing the default had a very dramatic effect on changing people's behavior. This is a classic example of a simple solution to a last mile problem.

Here's a second example. This has to do with what is called the medium effect, or, as it was called first, the compromise effect. Coffee shops all over the world sell coffee in three sizes, small, medium, and large. Yet it turns out that the most popular size of coffee all over the world is the medium size of coffee. I asked the managers of several coffee shops in six different countries for their best estimates of the distribution of coffee sales across these three sizes, and found out that 74 percent of the coffee sold in these coffee shops was in the medium-sized cups.

I also asked these managers to tell me the volume of coffee in each of the three sizes. Interestingly, it turned out that the amount of coffee in the medium-sized coffee cup was different in different countries. In some countries it was twelve ounces, in some it was eight, in some it was fourteen. It did not matter how much coffee was in the medium

cup of coffee – the fact that it was the medium size increased the likelihood of its purchase. This phenomenon was first documented by Stanford professor Itamar Simonson.[15] According to his research, it wasn't simply a matter of calling the medium size "medium"; as long as there was a bigger and more expensive option and a smaller and cheaper option, the one in the middle was likely to get selected. This is called the compromise effect because the one in the middle is not extreme on any dimension – it is a compromise. And people tend to choose compromises when options are difficult to evaluate and when they have no strong preferences or aversions.

In order to further test these ideas, I actually did a simple study in a coffee shop that was in the atrium of an office complex in Hong Kong. The majority of the clientele at this coffee shop were repeat visitors – people who worked in the office buildings. We checked to see which of these three different sizes was the most popular. Not surprisingly, the most popular size was the medium size. A research assistant and I stopped people who were leaving the coffee shop and asked them why they had picked the size they chose. People who had purchased the medium size provided a response that was something along the lines of a Goldilocks story; we heard that the small coffee had too little, the large size had too much, and the middle one was just right.

At this point, the three sizes of coffee were eight ounces, ten ounces, and twelve ounces. After a period of three or four weeks we increased the size of each cup by two ounces. Now, the small size had ten, the medium had twelve, and the large had fourteen. Lo and behold, the new medium size became the most popular size. When we again stopped people and asked them about their choice, we heard the same kind of Goldilocks response; that the small size had too little coffee and the large one had too much! People who were previously claiming that twelve ounces of coffee was too much were now consuming it!

The point of this example is that most people did not know how much coffee was in their medium cup of coffee. They also clearly did not have any clear preference as to how many ounces of coffee they actually wanted to drink. But what they were doing was making sense of the environment; they were looking at the context and making an inference about what they should be choosing based on what was available.

These examples illustrate the fact that changing the default can change preferences, and putting something in the middle of two extreme choices can increase the choice of that middle option. This leads to the insight that preferences depend dramatically on the context in which those preferences are made. The context not only allows people to make judgments about products and programs in relation to other offerings, it also allows people to make inferences about what is popular and what is not. This is an important insight, because in economics we assume that people are able to assign some sort of a utility to products that might be independent of the context. But that is not true. It is important to understand decision making in a particular context. Changing the context can often change the decision.

When we think about market research companies, we notice that often the questions that are asked of consumers are devoid of context. This is important to keep in mind when we interpret the results of market research. We have often heard the question, "Why is it that consumers who are satisfied with a product don't end up buying it?" Or "Why is it that the opinion polls told me candidate A was going to win the election, but candidate B actually won?"

These kinds of discrepancies between predictions based on market research and reality can be explained by the fact that the data were collected in a context that is very different from the context in which the actual choice was being made.

The Three Pillars of Human Decision Making

In my opinion, the fact that context influences our decision making is one of the three big pillars of understanding human decision making.

The second pillar is something that can be easily explained by Sir Isaac Newton's laws of motion.[16] A body at rest will continue to be at rest unless it is given an external push, and a body that is moving will continue to move unless some external force slows it down. Human decision making is a lot like that. As we saw in the example of defaults, people will continue to do whatever it is they are doing unless they are pushed to do something different, and so changing defaults can often change decision making. Likewise, research has shown that people often mindlessly continue to eat (or spend) unless there is some external force that gets them to stop.[17] Throughout this book we'll see more and more examples of this particular principle.

The third pillar for understanding human decision making is based on something called intertemporal choice. The American author Augusten Burroughs wrote one of my favorite books, *Magical Thinking*, published in 2004.[18] The back cover of the book says that the book is full of true stories that give voice to thoughts that we all have but don't express. I think that's a very good characterization of the book. Of particular interest to our topic of decision making is Burroughs's comment, "I myself am made entirely of flaws stitched together with good intentions."[19] This is a fascinating statement, because it describes human behavior perfectly.

Think about all the decisions we think people should take but don't – the fact that people don't exercise as much as they should, don't eat healthy food as much as they should, don't take public transit, work too hard, and don't spend enough time with their families. It isn't that people don't want to do these things. Everybody intends to be good, everybody intends to eat healthy food, everybody intends to exercise, and everybody intends to save more for the future. It is just that life gets in the way and they don't act on their good intentions. That's captured beautifully by Augusten Burroughs.

Irrationality 2.0: The Intention–Action Gap

We need to think more about this second kind of irrationality – the fact that there is a gap between what people think they would like to do and what they actually end up doing. In other words, there's a big gap between intention and action.[20] There are many domains in which there is awareness but no action. The solution to these problems at the last mile isn't so much about creating awareness as it is about facilitating action.

Think about financial well-being. Governments all over the world have reacted to lower savings rates by investing more in financial literacy initiatives, and I think that's great. But financial literacy alone is not enough. A lot of the people who don't save as much as they should know that they don't save as much as they should. In order to supplement their financial literacy, we need to think about a last mile solution that encourages people to act and open bank accounts.

To sum up: there are two forms of irrationality that we should be concerned about. The first is the idea that sellers of products and makers of policy believe that end users use a decision-making process that is different from what they actually do.

The second is the mismatch between people's intentions and their actions. At the last mile, if we can close these two gaps we will end up with a world where the last mile problem isn't as big a challenge as it is today.

So What's an Organization to Do?

If you have made it this far and agree with me that there is a last mile problem, and that the problem is primarily one of psychology, you're probably getting ready to ask, "This is all very fine, but what should an organization do to master the last mile?"

The goal of the rest of this book is to equip you with the answer to this question, but for now I present a very simple framework that captures the basic elements. There are three sets of activities that an organization needs to engage in, and I refer to them as translation, application (or auditing), and intervention (figure 1.2). Three separate teams could each take responsibility for one of these activities.

In the *translation* activity, the organization needs to monitor the academic research in the behavioral sciences and translate the academic findings into business insights and practical guidelines. The first six chapters of this book do exactly that! In particular, these chapters provide a framework for behavior change and choice architecture and review research on the psychology of money, time, and consumption behavior. Appendix 1 presents a summary of the key findings, with examples, and endnote references to the original research.

In the *application* activity, the organization needs to understand specific touch points at the last mile that are susceptible to the kinds of last mile issues we have highlighted here. Several chapters in the book focus on specific applications. Chapter 8 provides a broad understanding

Figure 1.2 Mastering the Last Mile

Mastering the Last Mile

Translation	Auditing	Intervention
Translating academic research into digestible insights	Monitoring efficiency of processes	Designing nudging interventions
Coming up with prescriptive advice	Identifying bottlenecks and areas for improvement	Piloting interventions, running controlled trials, and monitoring success
Thinking through areas of application	Using tools from psychology to identify opportunities	Iterating and identifying longer term success factors

of the manner in which people – consumers and stakeholders – form preferences. Chapters 11, 12, and 13 each dive deep into one specific area – respectively, how organizations can help consumers make better choices, how they can disclose information in a behaviorally informed manner, and how they can use behavioral insights in the retail environment. In each of these domains, the organization needs to actively monitor and audit what happens at the last mile. The questions they need to ask include the following: What stages do consumers/stakeholders go through as they make decisions? What information, emotions, and decision contexts are relevant at each stage? Which stage is the bottleneck and which stage can be improved? Appendix 2 provides some useful questions to ask as organizations audit the last mile.

In the *intervention* activity, the organization actively changes the context in which decisions are made at the last mile and measures the success of these changes. The tool for doing this is controlled trials – or experiments as they are called in the world of the behavioral sciences (chapter 7). Chapter 9 presents a broad framework for how to think about choice repair, while chapter 10 describes a process for choice architecture – a process for designing nudges to steer people toward a particular choice.

There are two quick comments I'd like to make about these three activities. First, while I write about them as three distinct sets of activities, the overlaps should be obvious. For instance, without *translation* it would not be easy to audit the *applications*. Likewise, auditing identifies potential *interventions*, but the interventions need to be followed by ongoing auditing to ensure that they have had the desired impact. Second, the reader will notice that the chapters in the book are not cleanly categorized into these three activities – for two reasons. The first reason relates to the inherent overlaps between the three activities, and the second has to do with the development of an appropriate vocabulary. For example, many of the applications may not make sense unless we know what an experiment is and what the different forms of experiments are.

Nanos Gigantum Humeris Insidentes

Before we start our journey on the last mile, I want to take time to acknowledge the intellectual shoulders on which I stand. The field of behavioral sciences has benefited immensely from the wisdom of several researchers.

In particular, some of my academic heroes include Richard Thaler and Cass Sunstein, authors of the influential book *Nudge* that I mentioned earlier. That book made a simple and compelling point. If we know that context affects choice, can we change the context to steer people toward making better choices?

The other legend in the field is Nobel laureate Daniel Kahneman. Daniel Kahneman, along with Amos Tversky, did a number of studies in the 1970s, 1980s, and 1990s that have completely changed the way we think about human decision making. In the research they start off by documenting empirical generalizations – facts that describe how people make decisions. Some of the most commonly used terms in our field today – for example, "loss aversion" or "prospect theory" – were coined by Kahneman and Tversky. A lot of Daniel Kahneman's thinking has been captured in a recent book called *Thinking, Fast and Slow*. The book makes a very important distinction between two styles of decision making that humans use.[21] The first system, "system one," makes decisions quickly, intuitively, and emotionally. The second system, "system two," is slow, deliberative, uses more information, and is typically considered more logical.

But again, I would make the argument that we as a society have tended to overvalue the benefits of system two, when in fact system one can be very effective. System one allows us to learn from the environment, be intuitive, and make some important decisions quickly without spending too much time on the intricate decision-making process that system two calls upon.

In addition to these scholars, there are many more who have influenced my thinking. In the pages that follow, you will read about research by a number of other intellectual giants. The insights of these scholars form the basis of much of my own thinking about behavioral science. As we walk through the journey of the last mile, I will highlight some of their research, as well as that of many other people, in building a framework for understanding how we solve that last mile problem.

The solution is, very simply, that we need to think through the behavioral insights that prevent people from making the right choices. We need to think about how we could use context and the manner in which we ask questions to overcome those obstacles. And then we need to make sure that making the decision is easy and fun. Making it easy to make a choice and making it fun to make the right choice can then steer decisions toward the right option.

2 Choice Architecture and Nudging

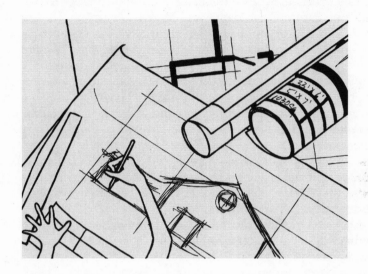

In chapter 2
You will find answers to questions such as:

1 *Why is every organization in the business of changing behavior?*

2 *How would a lawyer, an economist, a marketer, and a behavioral scientist solve the same behavior change problem?*

3 *What is a nudge and what is choice architecture?*

4 *How would a choice architect get more people to engage in the following behaviors – eat healthy food, be organ donors, get flu shots, be more honest, and be more productive?*

When I was a student in business school in the 1990s, one of the first things I was taught was to create elevator pitches – the art of saying things precisely and in one sentence. Elevator pitches are useful in all kinds of situations. You could use an elevator pitch to introduce yourself to other people, but also to introduce your business – to talk about what it is that your company does or sells. For example, The Walt Disney Corporation could say, "We are in the business of making people happy," or a manufacturing company might say, "We are in the business of manufacturing and selling widgets." If we think more broadly about elevator pitches and their relevance to all kinds of businesses and, in fact, all kinds of organizations, I believe there is one simple elevator pitch that captures everything about what organizations all over the world do.

That most generic and widely applicable elevator pitch is this – my organization is in the business of changing other people's behavior. These other people could be your customers. They could be other stakeholders, your suppliers, or your vendors. If you were a government, they could be your citizens. If you were a public welfare organization, they would be people whose welfare you were trying to improve. In general, perhaps the most fundamental last mile challenge is in the area of behavior change.

The Business of Behavior Change

Let us imagine that you are a for-profit company – in particular, a marketer. What you want to do is to get people to switch from using somebody else's product to choosing your product. That is an example of a behavior change. Alternatively, you might want to get people who have never purchased in your product category before to now make a purchase. As well, you probably want your customers to use cheaper channels of communication with you. For example, if you were a retail bank, you want consumers to use an ATM or online banking instead of going to talk with a physical teller. That is another example of a behavior change.

You might want your customers to recommend your products and services to other people. You might want them to stockpile your product or service. Finally, you might actually want customers to make repeat purchases of your product over time. These are all specific behaviors that you, as the marketer, are looking to influence.

If you are a government, you might also have a specific set of behavioral objectives in mind. One set of objectives might have to do with compliance. For example, you want to get people to pay their taxes or their dues on time. You want new parents to register their children's births on time. You want people to renew their passports on time. Compliance, or getting things done, is something that governments are always looking for citizens to do on time.

You might also want to ensure the compliance not just of citizens but of other stakeholders. If you are a government, you want to get corporations to file their papers on time, to pay their taxes on time, and, indeed, to comply with other requirements, such as workplace safety regulations and labor certification documentation. And while ensuring compliance is a big part of what governments want to do, governments could also want to make processes more efficient. For example, if you were a government agency that ran a motor vehicle licensing center, you might want to get people to renew their licenses online rather than physically showing up, because it is more efficient for all parties concerned. For the citizen, it is easier to get errands done from the comfort of home, and for the agency, it is cheaper to deliver that service online rather than at a physical location. You can no doubt think of other examples of governments looking to change the behavior of citizens, vendors, or other stakeholders to improve efficiency.

Finally, as a government, you might also want to use "mandatory disclosure" requirements to enable people to make better choices. For example, if there is a domain in which there is some sort of product risk – say, in the financial markets – governments seek to ensure that investors are provided with the right information, so that they can make well-informed choices. Or, governments want to make sure that there are laws in place to ensure that patients who consume certain medications can make well-informed choices about risks and side effects.

If you are a doctor, you might want to encourage your patients to make a number of behavior changes, such as eating more healthy food, or eating three regular meals instead of snacking throughout the day. You perhaps want them to exercise more instead of sitting on the couch. You might want to promote more attention to physical activity in schools, or encourage people to get their annual health checkup and get the flu shot in flu season.

If you are a public welfare organization whose goal is to help people save more, you might want to get people to open bank accounts, or retirement accounts, or special accounts for their children's education, and you would also want to encourage them to make regular contributions to these accounts over time.

No matter who you are, whether you are selling soap or shampoo, whether you are a government looking after the welfare of citizens, or an agency promoting financial well-being and better health, or an institution that is responsible for collecting taxes, you are definitely in the business of changing people's behavior.

A Lawyer, an Economist, a Marketer, and a Behavioral Scientist Go into a Bar....

Now let us try and put a structure on the problem of behavior change. Let us imagine that one of your stakeholders is a person who has chosen Option A, but you want to get them to choose Option B. A and B could be anything – products, services, or behaviors. What are the different tools or approaches that are available to us as we encourage or think about how to get people to switch from A to B?

There are a number of reasons why we might want people to choose B instead of A. Perhaps it is in our interest for the other person to choose B – perhaps B is the product we sell. Or perhaps we can recognize that B is a better choice than A, but the decision maker has failed to see that. Perhaps B is something that the consumer knows she wants to do but just can't get down to doing. We spoke earlier about the fact that people who don't save enough (i.e., who choose Option A) wish they had saved more (Option B). B could be a situation where people wish they could set more money aside in their bank accounts rather than going to a coffee shop every day, but they simply aren't able to do that.

This sounds like a perfect opportunity to bring in one of these lawyer and economist jokes where they all go to a bar. While they're in the bar, the bartender poses the following simple problem – the exact same problem that we talked about. The bartender says, "There was this guy in the bar a little while ago. He asked me a simple question: 'If I want to get people to move from Option A to Option B, how can I do that?'"

The lawyer says, "That's very easy. The answer to that question is simply to ban Option A. You make it illegal to choose Option A. If you do that, then people will choose Option B, assuming there is nothing else to choose."

It turns out that the lawyer is right. Banning or placing a restriction or introducing some legislation that forces compliance is a very handy

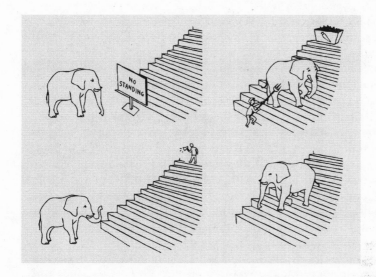

strategy for changing behavior. If you were a marketer, you could place a restriction simply by making Option A unavailable. We see this happening a lot in the marketplace. When a new version of an electronic gadget is introduced, the older version is taken off the market and people now have to buy the new version. Likewise, in the world of public welfare and governments, there was recently much debate about then Mayor Bloomberg's ban on large-sized soda drinks in New York.[1] This action would be an example of the first kind of behavior-change strategy, the idea of bans and restrictions.

Next, it is the turn of the economist to try and solve the puzzle. The economist says, "No, we don't need to ban anything. Instead, why don't we simply use incentives, i.e., the carrot-and-the-stick strategy?"

The carrot-and-the-stick strategy is simple. It basically argues that if you want to get people to move from A to B, you either impose some kind of economic tax on choosing A, making it expensive to choose A, or give people some kind of economic benefit for choosing B, making it economically attractive to choose B. In the world of consumer marketing, you could provide a carrot by simply offering a discount or a buy-one-get-one-free offer or some kind of promotion where people earn loyalty points and are essentially rewarded economically for choosing Option B. Or in the field of public welfare, think about a government that is trying to get farmers to adopt the latest technology or use a high-yielding variety of a particular crop. To make Option B attractive they might offer some sort of subsidy or impose a higher tax on the behavior that they are looking to avoid. A carbon tax – a tax imposed on certain products that leave large carbon footprints[2] – is another example of an economic approach to promoting behavior change.

The third person to answer the question is the marketer. The marketer says, "Let's not think about banning. Let's not think about offering economic restrictions. People are probably not choosing Option B either because they don't know about Option B, they don't understand why it is a superior option, or they simply need to be persuaded in order to choose Option B." The marketer's approach to behavior change would be one of advertising. It would be one of providing more information. Disclosures act in this particular manner. The rationale behind disclosures is very simple. The rationale is that if you provide people with more of the information they need to make better choices, they *will* make better choices. The whole advertising industry works on the premise that if you provide people with the right information and a good, compelling reason to purchase Option B, they will in fact do so.

Finally, it is the turn of the behavioral scientist. The behavioral scientist says, "We don't need to do any of the above. Instead, what we should do is simply make it easy for the person to choose Option B rather than Option A."

"We create a world in which Option B is the easy choice. There is some sort of effort, some sort of cognitive load, involved with choosing Option A. That is the right way of getting people to choose Option B instead of Option A."

What the lawyer, the economist, the marketer, and the behavioral scientist have proposed are essentially four ways to think about behavior change: the restriction approach, the incentive approach, the persuasion approach, and the nudge (or choice architecture) approach.

What exactly is a nudge? Here is a formal definition of a nudge from the authors of the book *Nudge*.

> A nudge is any aspect of the choice architecture that alters people's behavior in a predictable way without forbidding any options, or significantly changing their economic consequences. To count as a mere nudge, the intervention must be easy and cheap to avoid. Nudges are not mandates. Putting food at eye level to attract attention, and hence to increase the likelihood of getting chosen, counts as a nudge. The banning of junk food does not.[3]

Let us think about this in the context of an example that was mentioned in *Nudge* and also in *A Practitioner's Guide to Nudging*.[4] Think about two cafeterias that want to help students consume less junk food. One of them decides to attack the problem by imposing a tax on junk food, so they just increase the price of junk food. Or, as an alternative, they consider banning the sale of junk food altogether.

The other cafeteria decides to change the way in which food is displayed so that junk foods will be less likely to be chosen. Specifically, they place the fruits and vegetable snacks at eye level right at the front of the shelves, so it is easy for customers to reach out and pick those snacks. Junk foods, on the other hand, are placed on higher, harder-to-reach shelves, so that it is not very easy to pick them. Both cafeterias are trying to reduce the consumption of junk food, but as the example shows, they are using very different methods.

The first cafeteria is trying to influence behavior using the incentives option, or by imposing restrictions, which of course will eliminate freedom of choice completely. The second cafeteria does neither of these, but uses a nudging strategy.

Now while I make the distinction between these four different strategies for behavior change, we need to keep in mind that this is just a helpful taxonomy to get us to think about different approaches to tackling the problem. It is important not to get fixated on deciding whether an intervention is purely a nudge or purely an economic incentive. In fact, the most efficient methods of creating behavior change could have a bit of both elements.

For example, a fitness center/health club, which is trying to get people to exercise more, tries the tactic of reminding people how much they have paid for their membership. There is a classic finding called the *sunk cost effect*, which is discussed later in chapter 4. The sunk cost effect says that when people are aware of how much they have paid, they feel that they need to consume that particular product or service.

The health club could nudge people to exercise more frequently by framing their $600 annual membership as a $50 per month or perhaps a $12 a week expense. As you might imagine, framing something in narrower terms – $12 a week – is likely to create more of an incentive to use that particular service. It makes people realize that every week they do not use the health club, they are letting $12 go down the proverbial drain.

This is an example of an intervention that is based on an economic consideration – the fact that people have paid for a service. But the nudge has been added on through the manner in which that payment has been framed. It's a classic example of a situation where you have an intervention that is both economic as well as nudging in nature.

Consider a second example. A call center for a public organization found that the number of people who called in and then subsequently decided not to stay on the line was significantly high. People who called into the center and were put on hold until an operator was available to answer their call heard nothing from the other end of the line while they were waiting.

Research has shown that the time that is spent as a pure wait without any intervention, without any filling of the time, is considered to be more aversive than filled time.[5] And so one simple intervention that the call center could think of was to either play music during the wait,[6] or to have a message at the beginning that said something along the lines of, "Your call is important to us, but we are experiencing a high volume, so please be patient."

However, these interventions did not seem to work very well, primarily because the underlying process for answering the calls itself was sub-optimal.[7] Each call took its place in the queue, and the six available agents answered calls using the next-in-line heuristic. However, some of the calls to this service center were more urgent than others; in fact, some were actual emergencies while others could have been dealt with by a person with less expertise than the counselors answering the phone.

A better process was one in which all incoming calls were answered by one particular counselor, who could then triage the calls appropriately, pushing the more urgent calls to the head of the queue, and dealing with some of the easier calls immediately, allowing callers to avoid queuing up. Once this new and improved system was added, the intervention became more effective in keeping people on the line.

The point is that, to nudge people and get behavioral interventions to work for you, you need to make sure that the underlying process is as clean and as efficient as possible. If the process itself is not very efficient, or if the product that you're selling is not very good, or if the benefit that you're promising isn't very high, then no amount of nudging will help you change behavior.

In thinking about the four strategies for changing behavior, the most important question is: What is the right kind of strategy to use in which situation? I would argue that although there are no correct answers, there are three or four criteria that we need to think about to help us decide which type of strategy to use.[8]

The first criterion is whether enforcement is feasible and cost-effective. This is particularly relevant when we are using regulations and restrictions, as well as incentives, as our tools to change behavior. When we use these particular strategies, we need to think through whether monitoring and enforcement are actually possible. Is it easy to monitor who engages in a particular behavior? Is it easy to then sanction people and punish them appropriately, or reward them with the right incentives? If the cost of monitoring behavior is very high, then these strategies are perhaps not very cost-effective.

A second criterion is whether freedom of choice is an important consideration. As we mentioned earlier, one possible option for businesses to engineer behavioral change is to eliminate Option A and make Option B the only choice in the marketplace. Although this might be seen as acceptable from a business point of view (and note that recently we've seen examples from companies such as Facebook and Apple where consumers have actually rebelled against such a strategy), it is clearly not very appropriate if we are thinking about behavior change in the social welfare domain.[9]

For example, if Option B enhances an individual's standard of living, or if Option A leads to serious consequences for society or the individual, the policymaker should also consider whether eliminating choices results in a negative response from the community or from government.

A third criterion is the possible response from the marketplace. Policymakers working in domains such as financial services and consumer protection should consider how businesses will respond to their policies. For example, requiring them to ban certain products or requiring them to withdraw certain products from the marketplace might leave the door open for businesses to introduce new products. Likewise, providing an incentive for the choice of Option B could lead the business to provide a more attractive incentive for choosing Option A. That is why it is important to keep in mind that any lever that is pressed into service might result in a response from the marketplace.

Finally, a fourth criterion is the potential outcome of the intervention above and beyond the short-term goal. While any intervention is designed with particular attention to the immediate consequences of the intervention, it's also important for policymakers to think about secondary and longer-term effects.

One example of a secondary effect that might not be desirable is from the so-called research on the licensing effect.[10] The licensing effect shows that when people engage in one good behavior, they are likely to follow it up with a bad behavior. For example, research shows that people who conserve water tend to use more electricity.[11] Likewise, people who use paper towels that are ostensibly made from recycled materials are more likely to consume a larger number of paper towels.[12]

These are both situations in which a good action – conservation – results in a negative downstream outcome – increased usage. Clearly, policymakers need to think through the longer-term consequences of any intervention.

Keeping all of these factors in mind, table 2.1 gives us some guidance for thinking through when specific policy tools are useful and when choice architecture or nudging can be used to complement or enhance a particular strategy.

Nudges: Illustrative Examples

In order to think through what exactly a nudge is, let us look at some specific examples of nudging. The first example comes from the world of organ donations. Many support the idea of organ donations but fail to follow through on their intentions. As mentioned in the first chapter, one way of increasing organ donations is to change the default option in an organ donation setting.

However, there are simpler nudges that can be used. In many countries donors need to sign up to be an organ donor at the department of motor vehicles. But the burden of asking for the forms lies with the potential donor. In other words, potential donors who are visiting the motor vehicles facility have to know and remember that they need to ask for a form with which to indicate their willingness to donate their organs.

If we change the system so that there is a prompted choice in which applicants for driver's licenses are actively asked whether they would like to donate organs, research has shown that that simple nudge has increased organ donation rates from 38 percent to 60 percent in the U.S. state of Illinois.[13] Simply prompting the choice about making organ donations, making it more salient that there is a choice to be made, increases the likelihood that people will choose to donate.

A second example of nudging is in the domain of public health – in particular, flu shots. I wrote the first draft of this book in September, the start of the flu season in Canada and many parts of the northern hemisphere. In September and October, one often see signs in public places,

Table 2.1 Tools for Behavior Change

Regulations	
(Bans, Compliance Rules, Mandates)	
Useful When	• Behavior has consequences that are a high risk to society or take advantage of others *(e.g., crime, intentional fraud, pollution)* or violate society's values or ethics *(e.g., racial discrimination, freedom of speech)* • Third-party effects are present and the consequences of the behavior are not entirely absorbed by the individual or corporation. • Establishing standards that enhance standard of living or protect individuals *(e.g., minimum wage requirements, product safety)* • Enforcement is feasible and cost-effective.
Avoid When	• Regulation is perceived as overly restrictive or intrusive. • Individuals would likely respond with defiance or by undermining regulation.
When Choice Architecture Can Help	• Enforcement is in place but may not be working effectively. Choice architecture may help increase compliance.
Economic Incentives	
(Taxes, Penalties, Grants, Subsidies)	
Useful When	• Behavior is motivated by costs and benefits, and hyperbolic discounting does not take effect *(i.e., benefits are felt up front; losses are painful)*. • Incentives are salient to the individual. • Market is in line with the incentives and does not work against them *(e.g., subsidies for energy efficient products are in direct competition with cheaper products; "green" taxes on computers must work against marketing efforts to sell the latest and greatest products)*.
Avoid When	• Behavior is motivated by fairness, altruism, or social norms *(e.g., organ donations)*. • Taxes and penalties create "licenses" to engage in behavior.
When Choice Architecture Can Help	• Behavior is affected by cognitive influences *(e.g., loss aversion, status quo)*. Choice architecture can help highlight incentives or reduce particular barriers to accessing incentives.

Table 2.1 Tools for Behavior Change (*continued*)

Information and Persuasion	
(Advertising, Disclosures, Promotion Materials)	
Useful When	• Combined with other policy tools.
	• Encourage learning and can improve decision-making skills over time.
Avoid When	• Information is presented in a complex manner.
	• Message conflicts with what is being presented in the media or by other influencers such as peers.
When Choice Architecture Can Help	• When information is overly complex, choice architecture can help improve information processing using nudge techniques such as salience and simplification.
Nudges and Choice Architecture	
(Defaults, Simplification, Opt-in versus Opt-out)	
Useful When	• Freedom of choice is important and individual preferences vary.
	• Economic incentives or penalties are not appropriate.
	• Behavior is affected by cognitive influences and individuals struggle with turning intentions into action.
	• Aligned with current regulations or incentives.
Avoid When	• Context can be changed by businesses or other institutions in the marketplace. Additional regulation may be needed to set boundaries for market behavior. Or, incentives may need to be changed to improve alignment with policy goals.
	• Intended outcome of the nudge may go against individual intentions

including hospitals and clinics, encouraging people to go to a physician, pharmacy, or clinic to get a flu shot Yet it turns out that many of us don't get a flu shot. The question is, how can we design an intervention to get more people to protect themselves from the seasonal flu?

Professor Punam Anand Keller and her colleagues at Dartmouth University worked with a company that offered an annual flu shot as part of their medical benefits.[14] Not only did the company offer an in-house clinic to give flu shots to their employees, they also provided those employees who got a flu shot with an incentive of $50. Even under these (very attractive) circumstances, there were a large number of people who did not get a flu shot. What Professor Keller and her colleagues did was to experiment with three different ways of asking people whether they wanted to get a flu shot.

In the standard approach, this company (like many others that offer a similar health benefit) e-mailed all of their employees in September or early October informing them that flu season was here, and that there would be a clinic set up where they could get a free flu shot. This was a lot like the organ donation example we just looked at – while the e-mail conveyed information, it was incumbent upon every particular employee to make an active choice to go and get a flu shot.

In a variation on this basic procedure, a second group of employees not only received the information about a flu shot, but were also presented with a card or a short questionnaire that asked about their intention of getting a flu shot. They saw the same message as before, and were then asked to make a choice by checking one of two boxes. The first read, "Yes, I want to get a flu shot this fall"; the second read, "No, I do not want to get a flu shot."

There was a third version of the basic procedure. This is what the authors called an enhanced active choice version. The card provided the same information and it also gave employees two options, but the options were written out slightly differently. One option said, "Yes, I will get the flu shot to reduce my risk of getting the flu, and because I like the $50 incentive." The second option read, "No, I will not get a flu shot this fall because I don't care about my risk of getting the flu and I don't care for $50."

In this experiment, there was no change in economic incentives across the three versions. There was also absolutely no change in the content of the message, and, finally, no legislation requiring every employee to get a flu shot. There was only a simple change in the manner in which the question was presented.

What did they find? They found that in the standard (opt-in) case, the condition in which people were being given information but had to proactively make a choice to get a flu shot, 42 percent of employees expressed a desire to get a flu shot. When the employees were presented with a yes versus no active choice, that number went up from

42 percent to 62 percent. But even more interestingly, when they had an enhanced active choice, the number of people saying they wanted to get a flu shot went up to 75 percent.

These authors present to us a very simple idea. The first thing that they recommend is to make the choice salient to users. As we drift through life in daze of habit, many of us fail to recognize that we have an opportunity to make choices. We don't have to drive every day; we could take public transit. We don't need to drink an expensive latte; we could simply drink a glass of water. We do have the option of getting a flu shot or signing up for a gym class. However, these choices are not salient to us, and so simply making it salient to people that they are making a choice could be a successful nudge. The second recommendation is, in presenting the choice, to highlight the benefits of making the right choice and the costs of making the bad choice by using appropriate language.

Here is a third example based on research in the domain of dishonesty done by my colleague Nina Mazar and her co-researchers.[15] Nina and her colleagues make the argument that when it comes to self-reporting numbers when there might be economic consequences, people are often prone to fudging those numbers. People aren't being outright dishonest. We don't really want to cheat, but we do tend to fudge numbers once in a while, particularly if fudging those numbers can benefit us in the short run. For example, when we write tax returns, we tend to overestimate the expenses that can be written off for a tax credit. Or when we fill out insurance forms for our car, we tend to under-report how much we drive that car.

Nina and her colleagues had participants come into a lab to do an experiment. At the end of the experiment, participants had to report how much they thought they had earned in the lab using a simple form. The form looked much like a standard tax form. Participants wrote their name on the top. They wrote down all of the information that was asked of them. They were asked how much they had worked and how much effort they had put in, in order to price the contribution they had made to the experiment. Then they signed the declaration at the bottom of the form saying that everything that they had reported on that sheet of paper was true.

When people respond to questionnaires like these, their perception of themselves as an honest person – their identity as an honest person – is in the background. So by the time they sign the declaration their natural tendency to fudge numbers has already come into play.

The researchers asked themselves: "How can we make a subject's self-identification as an honest person more salient?"

They came up with a second version of the form which looked pretty much like the first except that the signature panel was now at the top. The first thing the subjects did was to sign a declaration saying, "Everything I'm going to report on this form is the honest truth to the best of my knowledge," after which they went on to report all the numbers as they had done in the first version.

What did this simple nudge do to people's level of honesty? Nina and her colleagues found that the rate of fudging declined dramatically. In fact, the data showed that only 39 percent of people misreported when they signed at the top compared to about 79 percent when the signature was at the bottom.

A fourth example of nudging comes from the work of yet another colleague at the University of Toronto, Philip Oreopoulos. Philip is interested in addressing the following important question: How can we raise the percentage of high school graduates who choose to go to college?[16] As Philip puts it, the process of going from elementary school to middle school and from middle school to high school is relatively easy. There is a default by which if you do nothing you will get transferred from grade six to grade seven. But there is no such default in grade twelve. You have to do something active to apply to college.

Access to higher education is an important issue, especially among lower-income families. In the United States there have been a number of financial aid programs developed to alleviate the burden of tuition costs. One of them is called the United States Free Application for Federal Student Aid or FAFSA. Unfortunately, applying to FAFSA is a long and tedious process. It frustrates many students and their families, and yet it is an important piece of documentation that must be completed in order to qualify for many states and for many different educational grants.

Philip and his colleagues decided to partner with a tax filing company, H&R Block, to design an intervention to reduce the complexity of the application process. What was interesting was that a lot of the information that went into tax forms was also relevant to filling up the FAFSA form. When an eligible family went to H&R Block and signed up to get their tax forms done, some of them were randomly asked if they would be interested in spending an extra ten minutes to get help with completing the FAFSA form. As a result, most of the information on the FAFSA form was automatically prepopulated at H&R Block.

Only about one-third of the form remained to be completed after the family left the H&R Block offices.

Results showed that 40 percent of families who accepted the H&R Block offer were likely to submit a FAFSA application as compared to 30 percent who had no access to the H&R Block service. It didn't matter how much information was given to families; that didn't seem to change the success rates. But Philip and his colleagues found that simply making it easy to fill in the FAFSA form by prepopulating that form and making people believe that they had already made progress in completing the form increased the likelihood that they would apply. It also increased the applicants' chances of being admitted and staying in college!

The final example of a nudge comes from the work of yet another colleague, Professor Tanjim Hossain. Tanjim and his colleagues were interested in the important question of how we can motivate people to work.[17] There is a lot of research in information economics suggesting that the easiest way of doing that is to provide contracts that reward people for doing more work. However, most of these contracts are fairly complicated and don't always work well in practice. These contracts also don't take into account the fact that people are motivated not just by monetary considerations but also by non-economic factors such as how the work is presented. In his research, Tanjim and his colleagues looked for different ways to frame the information in identical contracts to see if the differences had an effect on workers' productivity.

They ran a series of field experiments in a high-tech electronics manufacturing factory in China. All the workers in this factory were offered a weekly bonus for reaching a productivity target that was determined beforehand, and this was done for four weeks. One of the groups was presented with this bonus offer as a reward. For example, each worker was offered an extra 80 renminbi, which is about 25 percent of their weekly income, for reaching the target for each of these four weeks.

The second group were actually promised 320 renminbi at the end of four weeks, but were told that, for each week that they failed to reach the target, 80 renminbi would be deducted from the 320 that they were promised. There was always an economic incentive, but one incentive was presented in the form of a gain, the other as a potential loss. Otherwise the two contracts were exactly the same.

Tanjim and his colleagues found that although both these bonus schemes improved productivity, the increase in productivity was higher for workers who had received the bonus under the "potential loss" frame. The difference in productivity between these two groups was 1 percent. It doesn't seem very large, but recall that this difference came simply from changing the language of the contract. Also, a 1 percent increase in productivity, if persistent, can mean a dramatic increase in total revenues. As Tanjim puts it, a 1 percent productivity increase could make the difference between a developed country and a developing country.

This is another example of the difference made by a simple nudge. There was no difference in the persuasive techniques used, and there was no banning or restriction, yet there were significant changes in behavior.

These five examples collectively show that you can get people to donate more organs, get a flu shot, be more honest, apply to study in college, and work harder in a factory setting just by using simple nudging interventions. These results were achieved without the use of bans, without the use of significant economic incentives, and without providing a great deal more information or using extraordinary persuasive techniques. These are elegant last mile solutions to vexing problems.

Nudging is powerful technique that is applicable to a number of different domains. While there are many subtleties and nuances associated with developing effective nudges, it is possible to create a general framework for thinking through what the process of nudging and choice architecture should look like.

The chapters that follow first spend a fair bit of time examining the underlying psychology. How do people make choices? What sort of mistakes do they make? How do we think about money, and what phenomena can be observed about people's relationship with their money? What about time? Why are people impatient? Why are people willing to accept a smaller reward if it comes sooner rather than later? What can we do to overcome some of these weaknesses that human decision making has demonstrated?

These are some of the questions that will be addressed over the next four chapters. These four chapters are an example of the *translation* activity that organizations need to perform. Each chapter takes an important area of academic research, reviews the key findings, and presents insights that are relevant to a practitioner.

3 Choice

In chapter 3
You will find answers to questions such as:

1 *What are the three approaches to studying decision making and choice?*

2 *What are the "axioms" of rational choice?*

3 *Why is people's estimate of 1 × 2 × 3 × 4 × 5 × 6 × 7 × 8 × 9 × 10 smaller than their estimate of 10 × 9 × 8 ... × 1?*

4 *Why are people less likely to try new entrees at restaurants with long menus?*

5 *What do marshmallows teach us about human decision making?*

6 *Why do we all want to lose weight, exercise, save more money, be better people, and work hard – but only tomorrow? How can we therefore use precommit-and-lock to help people make better choices?*

Some of the most fundamental questions tackled by social scientists relate to the motivation behind human behavior and the processes used to make decisions. How *do* people make a choice? How *should* they make choices? These questions are central not only to academics in the behavioral sciences but also to the development of a broader theory of the last mile!

A Brief History of the Research on Choice

The research on judgment and decision making is thought to have been precipitated by the publication of a book in economics called the *Theory of Games and Economic Behavior*.[1] In addition to launching the field of game theory, a discipline that seeks to understand strategic decision making, the book also provided a mathematical theorem for the measurement of utility. Broadly speaking, the book postulated that choice is driven by the motivation of utility maximization, and went on to specify a set of axioms – rules that "rational" decision makers who exhibit a consistent pattern of choices must follow. This formed the basis of expected utility theory, which was followed by three waves of responses.

The first wave represented a series of empirical experimental tests that demonstrated that the axioms were often violated,[2] while the second represented process-based arguments for why utility theory might not explain choices.[3] These researchers showed that decision making is rational under the constraints of a limited cognitive apparatus and introduced the notion of *bounded rationality*. A third, more substantial wave responded to the criticisms of utility theory by providing alternative models of decision making.

One set of models incorporated new ways in which utility could be gained – for instance as a function of the sequence in which decision makers saw options or the rank of the option[4] or the value gained (or lost) presented as a well-defined function.[5] A second set of models introduced the notion of psychological representation. Researchers in this paradigm argued that it is essential to study the manner in which consumers frame – or mentally represent – decision problems, in addition to studying how they make the choices. For instance, researchers might ask experimental participants to make choices between two uncertain outcomes, each with a probability (p) of an outcome (V). However, people might mentally represent those problems along additional variables. These psychological representations might include risk (the fact that some probabilities appear to be inherently risky while others might not),[6] regret (the fact that the decision maker might anticipate that he might have wished he had chosen the other option),[7] ambiguity (a feeling that the data might be interpreted in multiple ways),[8] gain versus loss framing,[9] and mental accounting or categories of outcomes.[10] A third set of models proposed decision strategies that were very different from utility theory. Examples of these strategies included elimination by aspects (in which decision makers eliminated options that failed to meet certain criteria till they were left with one option),[11] or lexicographic decision making in which the option that was the best on the most important consideration (attribute) was chosen. More recently, interest has shifted away from the processes and models underlying decision making to the manner in which these insights can be harnessed to positively influence judgments and choice.[12] The reader interested in a more comprehensive historical perspective on the evolution of the behavioral sciences is referred to an outstanding chapter in a book by Bill Goldstein and Robin Hogarth[13] for a thorough analysis.

As is apparent, decision making can be studied using a number of different approaches. An understanding of the predominant four approaches is useful because it allows the reader to interpret findings in the context of the larger theoretical frameworks.

The Economic Approach

The economic approach treats decision making as an optimization problem in which people maximize something called utility. What is utility? Broadly speaking, the utility of an object or outcome refers to its usefulness, its ability to satisfy a particular need. In the economic approach, consumers are assumed to have the ability to assess the utility of various products (on various attributes) and to be able to compute the overall expected utility of an option. The expected utility theory posits that when consumers are faced with a choice between options, they choose the option that provides the highest expected utility.

The theory requires that behavior should be consistent with a number of axioms or beliefs. Three axioms – each of which appears to be perfectly logical at first blush – have come under scrutiny.

Completeness – In a choice between x and y, a decision maker should be able to choose x over y, or y over x, or be perfectly indifferent to which of the two is chosen. In other words, a consumer must have a definite preference (or indifference) and is not allowed to not know what she wants. We can all think of situations where this axiom is violated; often we don't have enough information about the alternatives or are simply not motivated enough to compute the utilities. Every reader will probably recall dozens of choice situations in which he has said, "I just don't know which one to choose." If this has happened and you have been unable to express a preference, you have violated the completeness axiom yourself.

Transitivity – If a decision maker chooses A over B, and B over C, he should choose A over C. Again, this sounds perfectly logical but may not always be true. Consider the following situation. Imagine you are a researcher and you are looking to hire a research assistant. You look for information on two attributes – the years of work experience the candidates have, and how intelligent they are (as measured by their IQ scores). That said, let's say that you also know that IQ scores come with some variability and that you need greater than a 15-point difference between IQ scores to reliably claim that one person is smarter than another. Your decision rule is simple: choose the more intelligent person and, if two people are not that different on intelligence, choose the one with more experience. You have three finalists (with IQ scores and years of work experience respectively) – Andy (100, 3), Beth (110, 2) and Chris (120, 1). If you compared Andy versus Beth, you'd conclude that there was no difference in intelligence and Andy had more experience. So Andy would trump Beth. Using the same chain of logic, Beth would trump Chris. If you choose Andy over Beth and Beth over Chris, you should be choosing Andy over Chris. But hang on – when you make the comparison between those two, the difference in intelligence is large enough, and by your rule, Chris would trump Andy. You've just violated transitivity even while sticking to the same decision rule!

Substitution – If a decision maker is indifferent between x and y, she should also be indifferent between two gambles that offer x and y with the same probability. A corollary of this axiom is the so-called cancellation principle,[14] which posits that the removal of an identical feature from two options should not change the relative preference between the two. The first violation of this axiom was documented by the French economist Maurice Allais and is widely referred to as the Allais Paradox (figure 3.1).[15] Think about two separate experiments. In the first experiment, you are offered a

Figure 3.1 The Allais Paradox

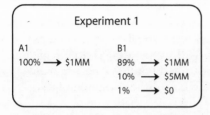

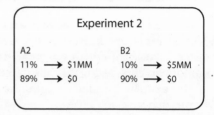

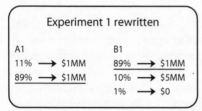

choice between two options. Option A1 offers you a million dollars for sure. Option B1 is a lottery with an 89 percent chance of getting $1 million, a 10 percent chance of getting $5 million, and a 1 percent chance of getting nothing. If you were like the vast majority of people, you would pick A1. After all, why take even a very small chance of going home with nothing when a million dollars could have been yours for the taking. In the second experiment, Option A2 is a lottery with an 11 percent chance of winning a million and an 89 percent chance at nothing; while Option B2 is another lottery with a 10 percent chance of winning $5 million and a 90 percent chance at nothing. Now you're probably thinking – $5 million is a lot more than $1 million, 89 percent and 90 percent sound about the same – and you'll choose B2.

While these preferences seem perfectly normal, you have just violated the substitution axiom. Take a moment to look at the rewritten version of Experiment 1 in the illustration above, and focus on the two items – one a part of Option A and the other a part of Option B – that have been underlined. Each is an 89 percent chance of winning $1 million, and if I simply replace "$1 million" with "0" I would be canceling an identical feature from both options. And if I did that, my Experiment 1 is identical to Experiment 2. If I chose Option A1, I should be choosing Option A2. Clearly, the seemingly obvious axiom isn't always valid.

With each demonstration of the violation of these axioms, the original expected utility model has been revised and updated several times. Each variant of the basic model features a modification that allows the model to be more consistent with consumer behavior. Unfortunately, in doing so it has become complicated and has lost the elegance of its original simplicity.

The Cognitive Approach

The cognitive approach treats decision making as a series of information-processing operations. One of the lynchpins of the cognitive approach to decision making is a stream of work that was developed by Duke University professors Jim Bettman and John Payne and Columbia University's Eric Johnson. This work is collectively called *contingent decision making* or *adaptive decision making*.[16] The theory acknowledges that consumers have two distinct motivations in making choices – accuracy and effort – and further acknowledges that choices that are high in accuracy will likely involve a high degree of effort.

Payne and colleagues identified a number of decision-making strategies that required varying levels of cognitive effort to execute. Consider a consumer choosing between many alternatives that are each described on multiple attributes or features. Let us also assume that the consumer is able to assign a number that captures the relative importance of each attribute. Also, the value of each alternative on each attribute can be expressed numerically. Payne, Bettman, and Johnson[17] identify a number of decision strategies that people could use to choose (there are additional variations of these basic strategies).

The first strategy is called the weighted additive decision rule (WADD). In the most cognitively effortful strategy, consumers assign importance weights to each attribute and then compute an overall score for each alternative by summing up the product of the importance weight and the score of that alternative. The alternative with the highest overall score is chosen. From a computational perspective, this rule requires multiplication, addition, and comparisons.

The second strategy, the equal weight rule (EQW), is simpler than WADD. The overall score is computed by simply adding the scores of each alternative across the attributes. This rule requires addition and comparisons. The third, satisficing (SAT), allows for the selection of any alternative that meets minimum criteria or aspiration levels (e.g., attains a minimum score on each attribute). This rule requires comparisons. The fourth, elimination by aspects (EBA) requires consumers to identify the most important attribute, eliminate options that do not meet the aspiration level on that attribute, proceed to the next important attribute, and continue eliminating options till there is one alternative left. This rule requires several comparison processes.

The final strategy, lexicographic (LEX), prescribes the selection of the alternative that has the highest score on the most important attribute. This rule requires two comparison processes – one to identify the most important attribute and the other to identify the best alternative.

This approach to decision making also recognizes the level of cognitive resources required to complete each particular decision task. That effort can be expressed in terms of a new unit called the EIP – elementary information process. Each EIP represents one unit of cognitive resource required to perform one cognitive comparison. For a given set of alternatives, the WADD strategy consumes a lot of EIPs while the LEX strategy consumes very few.

The idea of contingent decision making suggests that a consumer first forms some judgment of how accurate she wants her choice to be. The required accuracy might be a function of many factors – for instance, purchase frequency and price (accuracy matters more for high-priced, infrequently purchased items like cars and condos than for chewing gum or soap), involvement (accuracy matters more for personally expressive products like clothes), or context (accuracy matters more when a choice needs to be justified, or when choice comes under the scrutiny of others). Once the consumer has a sense of the level of accuracy she seeks, she then picks an appropriate decision strategy. This framework thus kicks up the research on decision making by one notch – consumers now not only need to make explicit choices between products or alternatives but also need to choose the manner in which they will make the choice. In some cases, the choice of a decision strategy may occur intuitively, based on a lot of experience and practice; but the key point is that a decision needs to be made. A professor from my days as an MBA student loved to quote Confucius: "Never use a cannon ball to kill a mosquito." In the world of choice, Confucius would probably say that it would be unwise to use a WADD strategy to choose between two brands of gum or to make other relatively trivial decisions. Figure 3.2 captures the mechanics of the cognitive approach to decision making.

Figure 3.2 The Cognitive Approach to Choice

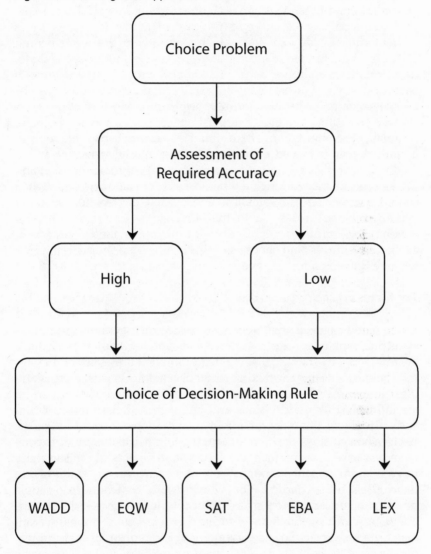

The contingent decision-making framework can also help explain the notion of bounded rationality, a term first introduced by Nobel laureate Herbert Simon,[18] as well as the adaptive use of decision shortcuts.[19] This concept can best be explained by thinking about the human mind through the metaphor of a computer-processing unit. Imagine that a user provides a computer with a task that requires a large volume of computational resources. In one of two situations, the computer will be unable to complete the ideal form of the computation and either (a) return a sub-optimal outcome to the user or (b) take a very long time to complete the computation. These situations occur when (1) the computational demands exceed the capacity of the computer (i.e., for an exceedingly complicated decision requiring a large number of EIPs) and (2) the computer is working on other tasks at the same time (e.g., when cognitive resources are somehow constrained or depleted by other decision-making processes). In the language of contingent decision making, the consumer might still optimize under the constraints of available resources, and choose simplifying decision shortcuts because they are functional under adverse cognitive-capacity conditions.[20]

The Social Psychology Approach

As its name suggests, the field of social psychology aims "to understand and explain how the thought, feeling and behavior of individuals are influenced by the actual, imagined or implied presence of other human beings."[21] While the field of social psychology is vast, there is ample evidence that the decisions and judgments of individuals in a group are influenced by the decisions and judgments of other group members.[22] In one of the most famous demonstrations of social influence, Asch[23] showed lines of different lengths to participants in an experiment and asked them which was longer. Participants did this exercise in groups of what they thought were other participants. Unknown to them, these "other participants" were actually confederates – people hired by the researcher to play a specific role. In some cases, the confederates provided an (obviously wrong) answer before the participant had a chance to respond. Asch found high levels of social conformity – people chose to go with the majority despite the existence of a clearly correct response to the question and despite the fact that the majority were obviously wrong. Researchers subsequently have broken down these social effects into two types. First, people conform because they want to be like the reference group and to be liked by them. Second, they conform because the responses of the group give them additional information and knowledge that they otherwise would not have on their own.

A large number of findings in the behavioral sciences demonstrate the effect of social others on choices. In his pioneering work on reasons-based choice, Itamar Simonson[24] proposed and demonstrated that consumers select options that are supported by the best reasons or justifications, rather than the options that maximize utility. An important corollary of his theory is this – asking people for justification for their choices changes the choices they make.

A second set of findings has to do with the effect of one person's choices on other consumers in a group setting. Dan Ariely and Jonathan Levav[25] proposed that consumers in a group setting need to balance two kinds of goals – the goal of maximizing their own well-being and a second set of goals triggered by the existence of the group (these may include self-presentation, increasing group variety, or compliance resulting in group uniformity). The latter sometimes results in choices that undermine personal satisfaction and increase the potential for regret. For instance, in one of their studies, the two researchers showed that real groups (tables) of lunch eaters at a cafeteria choose more varied dishes than would be expected by a random sampling of the population of all individual choices across all tables. Their results showed that in a group setting "people take the road less traveled and point to group variety seeking as a consistent and stable outcome when individuals order food and drinks in group settings."[26]

Finally, in a separate study, Stephan Meier and his colleagues[27] found support for the idea that consequential decisions made by consumers changed in a group setting – these included decisions to cooperate, to save money, and to be altruistic. These researchers assigned low-income individuals in Chile to self-help groups and found that membership in a group enhanced savings. Furthermore, these effects occurred even in situations in which the groups were randomly assigned and when the groups were minimal (i.e., groups that had been given an affiliation label).

Predominant Themes in the Field of Choice and Decision Making

Now that we have looked at some of the theoretical approaches to studying choice, let's take a walk through some of the dominant themes in the research – answers to big questions such as, "What do we really know about how people make choices?" In the rest of this chapter, I highlight four broad sets of findings – decision making by heuristics, the effect of context on choice, choice overload, and choice over time. In the next chapter, I cover research on the role of time and money, and the manner in which people perceive, earn, save, and use these important resources. I would not be the first person to write about these findings. In particular, Daniel Kahneman is the pioneering researcher on decision heuristics and has written extensively about them in *Thinking, Fast and Slow*.[28] Dan Ariely has written extensively about context effects as well as about the economic approach to irrationality in his book *Predictably Irrational*.[29] Sheena Iyengar and Barry Schwartz, respectively, write about choice overload in their books *The Art of Choosing*[30] and *The Paradox of Choice*.[31] And George Loewenstein and Jon Elster have edited a collection of essays entitled *Choice over Time*.[32] I cover some broad themes and findings relevant to the last mile here and refer the reader interested in more details to these excellent books.

Theme 1: Decisions by Heuristics and Resulting Biases

This stream of research pioneered by Daniel Kahneman and Amos Tversky[33] identifies a number of decision-making "shortcuts" that consumers typically use to make decisions. This research was initially developed to counter the utility theory model of decision making but has subsequently evolved as a legitimate field of research in itself.

Perhaps the most famous demonstrations of the use of heuristics (and resulting biases) were the representativeness heuristic, the availability heuristic, and anchoring and adjustment. Suppose the following question was posed to you:[34] You have picked a word at random from an English language text. Is it more likely that it begins with the letter K or that it has K as the third letter? In fact, there are many more words that have K as the third letter than words that begin with K, yet most respondents believe that they are likelier to encounter a word beginning with K. The authors argue that this happens because it is easy to think of words that begin with K but not as easy to think of words with K in the third place – the former are more accessible to memory. Similarly, people (incorrectly) believe that there are more deaths from causes that are more likely to occur in news reports and hence that are more noticeable (e.g., fires, natural disasters, and accidents) than from more mundane causes (e.g., illness).

Consider next the following scenario from Tversky and Kahneman:[35]

Linda is 31 years old, single, outspoken, and very bright. She majored in philosophy. As a student, she was deeply concerned with issues of discrimination and social justice, and also participated in anti-nuclear demonstrations.

Which is more probable?

1. Linda is a bank teller.
2. Linda is a bank teller and is active in the feminist movement.

While any student of probability (and indeed most logical thinkers) would point out that a more general outcome (1) is more likely than a more specific subset of that outcome (2), results suggested that the majority chose 2 as more likely. The authors argued that most respondents used the representative heuristic – Linda seemed more representative of a teller who was a feminist rather than just an average bank teller.

Tversky and Kahneman[36] asked two groups of participants to estimate the answer to an identical problem. One group was asked to estimate the answer to $1 \times 2 \times 3 \times 4 \times 5 \times 6 \times 7 \times 8 \times 9 \times 10$ and came up with a median estimate of 512. A second group estimated $10 \times 9 \times 8 \ldots \times 1$ and their median estimate was 2,250. These estimates are significantly different from each other (and from the correct answer, 40,320) and are explained by the anchoring and adjustment heuristic – the common human tendency to rely too heavily on the first piece of information offered (the "anchor") when making decisions. Table 3.1 provides a list of some of the more prevalent heuristics and related phenomena that emerged from this stream of research.

In many cases, these heuristic shortcuts are adaptive – beneficial to the decision maker – because they make decision making more efficient. On the flip side, as illustrated in the examples above, they could sometimes result in systematic biases. The three biases reported above can have significant consequences in many consumer contexts. For instance, Barber and Odean[37] test and confirm the hypothesis that investors are more likely to purchase attention-grabbing stocks (those that have been in the news) because their availability makes them more likely to get selected and because the alternative decision strategy – processing a very large amount of information on thousands of stocks

Table 3.1 Heuristics and Behavioral Influences

Behavioral Influences	
Status Quo	A tendency of individuals to maintain their current state even if a change in their circumstances would provide better options
Endowment Effect	The inclination to value and pay more for an item that is already in one's possession than for an item that has yet to be attained
Loss Aversion	A tendency of individuals to be more attuned to losses than to gains
Confirmation Bias	A predisposition to accept information that confirms one's opinions or conclusions rather than information that is contradictory
Mental Accounting	Mentally allocating money to several "accounts" such as clothing or entertainment rather than perceiving it as fungible
Willpower	The fact that individuals only have a certain amount of willpower at any given time and that willpower needs to be replenished periodically
Hyperbolic Discounting	Valuing benefits that are reaped now more than benefits reaped in the future. Consequently, costs that are paid in the future are not felt as deeply as costs that are paid now.
Choice Overload	The presence of too many choices for a particular decision, making it difficult to evaluate and decide.
Information Overload	The presence of too much information in the environment, preventing the individual from evaluating and making a good decision
Availability Bias	Using information that readily comes to mind to make a decision rather than using a comprehensive set of facts that evaluates all options
Representativeness	Using similar attributes to judge the likelihood that an event will occur. This is in contrast to using a more comprehensive approach that would utilize statistics (e.g., base rates) to determine likelihood
Anchoring and Adjustment	Making an estimate by applying adjustments to a particular reference value (i.e., the "anchor").
Social Proof	Looking to the behavior of peers to inform one's decision making, and tending to conform to the same behavior one's peers are engaged in.

– is cognitively too demanding. The anchoring heuristic posits – and evidence exists to confirm – that the asking price for property in a real estate market (presumably not a true indicator of the value of the property) influences the final transaction price.[38] Further, Uri Simonsohn and George Loewenstein[39] predicted and found that families who moved from more expensive cities to cheaper ones would rent pricier apartments than those arriving from cheaper cities. And in unrelated domains, Dan Ariely, George Loewenstein, and Drazen Prelec[40] showed that consumers' willingness to pay for products might be affected by seemingly irrelevant anchors that they might encounter in the environment.

Theme 2: The Effect of Context on Choice

One implication of the economic approach to decision making is the idea that the choice between two alternatives should be independent of the presence of other alternatives in the choice context. However, a large body of research has shown that this is not the case. Context can affect both the perception of the alternatives, by changing the way in which a problem is framed, or their evaluation, by providing the consumer with information that could change preferences.

Perhaps the earliest demonstration of context effects was done by Duke University researchers Joel Huber, John Payne, and Chris Puto.[41] These researchers studied choices between two alternatives that varied on two attributes. Assume that Option A is better on attribute 1 (say, quality) while Option B is better on attribute 2 (say, price). The choice between these options would depend on the relative importance that any given consumer assigns to these two attributes. Now imagine that a third option is made available – B* that is worse than B on both attributes, but better than A on price and worse than A on quality. B* is dominated by B and not by A, and hence this situation is referred to as asymmetric dominance. The result of adding B* is intriguing – not too many people choose B* (after all, B dominates it on all dimensions), but the relative preference as between A and B now shifts toward B. This occurs because now there is a compelling reason to choose B while there is no such reason to choose A (the *attraction* effect), and the new entrant B* is referred to as a decoy product because it simply serves to make one of the existing products look more attractive.

A second well-demonstrated finding is the *compromise effect*.[42] We've read about this in earlier chapters through the example of the coffee cups. The effect states that objects that are priced in the middle of choice sets – or are generally in the middle of a three-item choice set on multiple attributes – are looked on more favorably. The middle choice seems like a good compromise between choices that may be viewed as too extreme.

In both the attraction and the compromise effects, the presence of other products in the choice set provides additional information and potentially changes the encoding of the stimulus. Indeed, a more provocative claim first made by MIT professors Drazen Prelec, Birger Wernerfelt, and Florian Zettelmeyer[43] posits that consumers actually infer what they want from what is available. This work suggests that preferences are ill-formed and malleable enough that the context can actually help consumers construct their preferences. For example, the presence of a larger number of options in, say, laptop computers versus desktop computers could result in an inference that laptops are generally more preferred than desktops and hence a preference for laptops. Indeed, many researchers now believe that inferences made by consumers on seeing (a) retail displays, (b) informational displays, and (c) popularity ratings of different products can actually influence their own choices significantly. With mobile technology, this information is easier to share and hence might have significant implications for preference structures in markets.

Theme 3: Overchoice

In most Western societies, the concept of choice – including the ability to exercise it – is seen as fundamental to people's sense of autonomy and well-being. The disciplines of economics and public policy have been shaped by the notions of freedom of choice. In economics, the standard assumption is that the provision of more choice allows individuals to find alternatives that are more closely aligned to their true preferences; and in public policy and governance, the rights and the ability of individuals to choose what is best for them is the foundation of libertarianism.

As a result of this "choice is good" thinking, the number of offerings in a wide variety of product and service categories has increased significantly over time. Compared to just ten years ago, the range of products available in a typical North American supermarket has increased by 55 percent. Assortment sizes in almost every product category have gone up. In an informal study, my colleagues and I went to several drugstores to count how many different types of pain and fever medications were available and found that the number ranged from 55 to 211 varieties. Not only did headache medicines come in different ingredients and sizes, they also differed in physical format (syrups, capsules, tablets, and caplets), strengths, and additional active ingredients. As one of my research team members once remarked, "I guarantee that a consumer would end up with a headache making the choice even if they didn't have one to begin with."

The example of headache medications is not an isolated one. A number of popular writers and academic researchers have recently written extensively about the negative effects of choice. John Gourville and I conducted several experiments on what we called "overchoice." In essence, we found that under some conditions, offering people additional choices creates confusion and cognitive overload. As a result, we found that people were more likely to switch to brands that offered a small number of branded variants because it was easier to choose within that smaller set.[44]

There are a number of other recent demonstrations. Perhaps the most famous was by Columbia University's Sheena Iyengar and Ross Lepper, who conducted an experiment in a supermarket where they set up tasting tables for jams.[45] They found that when shoppers are given the option of choosing among smaller and larger assortments of jam, they show more interest in the larger assortment. But when it comes time to pick just one, they are ten times more likely to make a purchase if they choose among six rather than among twenty-four flavors of jam. Clearly, it became difficult for shoppers to sift through all the information when choosing from among twenty-four jams, so they simply decided not to buy.

In another example, I was once asked by the owner of a Chinese takeout restaurant about a phenomenon that he found very puzzling. He showed me his menu, which had 155 different items listed, bemoaning the fact that, "about eighty percent of my sales come from only five or six of these items." Inspired by this comment, I conducted a simple field study in several restaurants in a U.S. city and in ice cream parlors in a Canadian city. The idea was simple: I wanted to assess the effect of menu length on the variety of food ordered in a given restaurant over a period of time. For a given restaurant, I simply collected data on the number of unique entrées ordered in a given month and computed the market share of each entrée. I then calculated a market concentration index for each restaurant – higher numbers of which suggest that a smaller number of options dominate the choices.

Interestingly, I found a larger concentration index for restaurants with longer menus. The differences were not very large, but they were revealing. As particular examples, consider two Italian restaurants: Restaurant A had six entrée options; Restaurant B had fifteen. The data showed that choices were spread roughly evenly across the six options in Restaurant A. On the contrary, four options accounted for about 80 percent of the share in Restaurant B. When faced with a larger menu, diners tended to be conservative and stick to familiar entrées.

In a related finding, new patrons of coffee shops like Starbucks often report feeling overwhelmed by the menu board and end up choosing only regular coffee. The psychology underlying this pattern of data can be better understood by spending some time in an ice cream parlor and observing kids choosing the ice cream they want. The first problem they face is simple cognitive overload: by the time they reach the end of a long display, they have forgotten about the first few flavors they saw. The second problem relates to what John Gourville and I called "non-alignable tradeoffs": if I want chocolate, I can't have a fruit flavor, and if I want sprinkles, I can't get the sundae. These non-alignable tradeoffs create the potential for anticipated regret, where the consumer thinks that if he orders strawberry, he might feel bad that he didn't choose chocolate. The third problem is preference uncertainty. For instance, one child deliberated that she was "quite sure she liked caramel more than pistachio, but the last time I tried pistachio it was actually quite good." The "analysis-paralysis" resulting from this ends up with most kids choosing a tried-and-tested flavor, or in rare instances, asking for a rain-check on the ice cream.

In many situations, choice overload can also be worsened by information overload. Think about the information that average individual investors see when they are choosing which stock to invest in; or the innumerable track record details available to an individual who wants to place a bet on a race horse. Further, some situations are inherently more stressful and are associated with negative emotions (for instance, deciding between surgery and therapy for a serious medical condition), and that alone can increase the complexity associated with the choice.

While these results are interesting, perhaps they occur for relatively inconsequential products like take-out dinners and jams. Perhaps if the decision was really important and consequential, people would be more likely to benefit from additional choice. It turns out that this is not the case, and two sets of evidence stand out in this regard. The first is a study by the University of Chicago's Henrik Cronqvist and Richard Thaler on the Swedish social security system.[46] This plan, introduced by the Swedish government at the turn of the century, allowed participants to form their own portfolios by selecting up to five funds from an approved list. Funds were allowed to advertise themselves and to determine their own fee structure; individuals were encouraged to make their own choices; and any fund meeting certain fiduciary requirements was allowed to enter the market. In the end, individuals had a list of 456 approved funds from which they could choose. The researchers found that participants consistently made sub-optimal choices, and that they tended to choose default options. Further, their analysis revealed that people who made active choices for themselves did not necessarily end up with portfolios that did very well.

A second piece of evidence comes from research by Sheena Iyengar and her colleagues,[47] who analyzed retirement-fund choices ranging from packages of two to fifty-nine choices among more than 800,000 employees at 647 companies. The so-called 401(k) plans give people incentives to participate through tax shelters and employer matches. A thoughtful economic analysis on the part of individuals should suggest that the option of participating in these plans dominates the option of not participating. However, the researchers found that more options led people to act like the jam buyers: when given two choices, 75 percent participated in a 401(k) plan, but when given fifty-nine choices, only 60 percent did. The analysis also suggests a parallel with the restaurant study: when faced with many options, investors tended to be a lot more cautious in their investment strategy.

As is apparent from the examples above, choice complexity arising from too many options has a number of significant consequences. The first is simple deferral and non-participation; people simply decide they do not want to make a purchase now. The second consequence has to do with the nature of choices made: a smaller choice set encourages varied and perhaps aggressive and/or risky choices, while a complex choice might result in a smaller number of conservative choices with a view to minimizing regret. The third has to do with reliance on the status quo and the increasing role of defaults and suggestions. When choices are too complex, people simply prefer to go with a default option. And finally, people also tend to use others' choices as a heuristic to what they should choose. For instance, employees in matching retirement programs tend to have fund allocations that are close to the median of their peer group.

In the domain of marketing, choice complexity can have two specific effects on the aggregate pattern of choices. John Gourville and I made a distinction between choice assortments that are alignable versus those that are non-alignable. We defined an "alignable assortment" as a set of brand variants that differ along a single dimension, such that each variant has a specific quantity of that attribute. Examples would be several bottles of Advil-brand ibuprofen that vary in tablet count; air conditioners that vary in cooling capacity; and milk that varies in fat content. Such assortments require tradeoffs of a single attribute versus price.

In contrast, we defined a "non-alignable" assortment as one in which the brand variants vary along multiple, non-compensatory dimensions, such that while one alternative possesses one desirable feature, a second alternative possesses another desirable feature, with these features being "all or nothing" in nature. Examples include restaurant entrées (salmon versus steak versus lasagna) and college majors (biology versus philosophy), where choosing one alternative delivers a level of features not available in another. We showed that while increasing choice sets can actually benefit consumers (and hence brands) in an alignable assortment condition, it can be quite harmful when the assortments are not alignable. In summary, we reported that brands providing a large but non-alignable assortment may end up losing share to brands with smaller assortment sizes.

In ongoing research, we have conducted additional experiments to test the effects of choice complexity on within-brand choices. When a friend of ours was buying a car in Colorado many years ago, the dealer gave him the following options:

a) a basic version;
b) a basic version plus a ski package: features that added value to a frequent skier;
c) a basic version plus a winter package: features for people living in a region with a long winter;
d) a basic version plus an off-road package: features that added value to people who drove off the beaten track; and
e) a fully loaded version with all the features included.

Our friend was suitably confused. He wasn't quite sure if he was more of a "ski person" or an "off-road" person, and whether he really wanted to forego any of the features from the winter package. He ended up purchasing the fully loaded package.

Taking the cue from this conversation, we conducted experiments in several product categories. In each case, participants in our studies were asked to make a choice between a basic version, a fully loaded version, and one or more intermediate versions that were combined to create a non-alignable assortment. We studied cable television services (with versions varying in the type of premium channels), digital cameras (with versions varying on the type of lens), mobile phone plans (with versions varying in types of downloads available), and vacations (with versions varying in the destinations visited). Some participants saw three options (the two extreme options plus one intermediate), some saw four and others saw five. We were interested in the following question: as assortment sizes go up, are people more likely to choose one of the extreme (basic or fully loaded) versions of the product? Our results showed that this was indeed the case. When faced with three options, 49 percent of the respondents chose one of the two extreme options; implying that 51 percent chose the intermediate one. However, when an additional intermediate option was added to the mix, the percentage of respondents choosing one of the extreme options jumped to 61 percent. This meant that adding a second intermediate option *reduced* the choice of an intermediate option from 51 to 39 percent. And finally, when there were three intermediate options, the extreme options were chosen 67 percent of the time. We call this phenomenon "extremeness seeking." Unsurprisingly, we also found that when the assortment was alignable in nature, extremeness seeking did not arise.

Despite this research, it appears that people would like to have a choice, even in situations in which they might not be equipped to make a good choice. There is something personally satisfying about having the right to choose, rather than having an option foisted upon us. In sum, choice complexity is here to stay. The relevant question is, "What can providers of choice do to help people make better decisions that allow them to harness the benefits of large choice sets?"

We propose five strategies. *First,* streamline choices. A number of organizations – in domains ranging from packaged goods to financial services – have streamlined choices in response to the concerns about choice complexity. *Second,* help individuals understand their own preferences and tradeoffs. Perhaps the single fundamental reason for choice complexity has to do with the fact that most humans are limited cognitive processers of information. They can make tradeoffs between a small number of attributes and products, but with increasing options, these computations become intensive and beyond the capabilities of the human brain. Technology and the Internet provide one set of solutions: the development of web-based intelligent software applications that can help online shoppers find products and services that best fit their needs. Known as "shopping agents" or "shopping bots," these tools allow individuals to specify their needs and preferences at the level of an attribute, and then develop models of the buyer which are applied to available options in the marketplace to make recommendations. Other agents are simple price-comparison agents that allow the individual to better understand the tradeoffs inherent in the available choice sets. In other situations where individuals might find it difficult to express their preferences as tradeoffs (e.g., art objects, music, literature), collaborative filtering agents are now able to make recommendations to users based on information about the current consumption patterns of the individual. As an example, Amazon.com might recommend a book based on its knowledge of your reading pattern, and the Genius feature in iTunes could recommend new music based on its analysis of your current playlists.

Third, organize and eliminate options. Rather than having all options in a complex choice set being presented simultaneously, they could be categorized into different groups, and some of these groups could be eliminated sequentially as a function of the individual's stated preference until the choice set is narrowed down to a manageable number. For instance, rather than presenting a prospective new home buyer with the full MLS listing of 200 available houses, a real estate agent might group them by location, age, proximity to the subway, and school district. By gauging the importance of each of these underlying attributes, the agent can then start eliminating options from the choice set until it is down to a manageable set of options.

Fourth, encourage attribute-based decision making. A close look at a typical Chinese take-out menu shows that most of the very large number of options available can be generated by considering permutations of a number of simple attributes. These may include the protein being cooked (beef, chicken, pork, or tofu), the style of cooking (stir-fried, boiled, grilled), the type of sauce used (sweet and sour, chili, nut) and the type of noodles or rice requested (white rice, fried rice, vermicelli). Rather than presenting a patron with the resulting 154 options – each with a brand name like "General Tso's chicken," it might make more sense to ask the patron four separate questions about what protein they want, how they want it cooked, what sauce they would like and what type of rice/noodle they want with it. In a field study with a family-owned Chinese take-out restaurant, I found that the strategy of replacing the menu with these four questions resulted in (a) an overall increase in sales, (b) a greater tendency to seek variety, and (c) more participative and enthusiastic consumers.

Fifth, outsource decision making. Perhaps the simplest form of outsourcing of choice is choosing a recommended or default option. In this case, an individual relies on the presumed expertise of the recommendation provider and essentially allows this expert to make choices for him. A more active form of choice happens, for example, when individuals approach a wealth manager and task the adviser to manage their investment portfolio and make suitable buy, hold, and sell decisions. Alternatively, a patient deferring to the opinion of a doctor on a treatment plan is another example of an outsourced choice.

All signals indicate that choice complexity will only increase with time. Given this trend, one suspects that it is only a matter of time before individuals will want to outsource choices to agents. Perhaps we might see the advent of professional shoppers who, for a fee and broad guidelines on household patterns, undertake the task of keeping a family's pantry and refrigerator stocked with appropriate items. In the end, making the choice to *not* make a choice might turn out to be the optimal strategy in many product and service categories.

Theme 4: Choice over Time

People often need to make choices between options that will occur at different points in time. Empirical research shows that consumers are myopic (i.e., they value present outcomes disproportionately) and inconsistent (i.e., their choices change as they get closer to one of the options). As a result, consumers often need to exert self-control.[48]

Readers of this book may be familiar with the marshmallow experiments by Walter Mischel and his colleagues.[49] The experiments were conducted along the following lines. A child was offered a marshmallow on a plate but was then told that if she could wait for fifteen minutes without eating the marshmallow, she would receive a second marshmallow. If you were the child in this experiment, you had a choice to make – eat now and get just the one treat, or eat after fifteen minutes and get two treats. Mischel and his colleagues presented further evidence that children who were able to delay gratification went on to have better life outcomes – better SAT scores and educational accomplishments, body mass index scores, and other outcomes.

The Mischel experiments provide a handy metaphor for a large number of choices that people make day in and day out. Should I cash in on a savings fund today (one marshmallow) or wait for it to grow and cash it in later (two marshmallows)? Should I buy that $5 cappuccino at the local café today (one marshmallow) or add it to my retirement fund for later (two marshmallows)? Should I eat an unhealthy dessert with my dinner tonight (one marshmallow) or eat fresh fruit and enjoy a disease-free life later (two marshmallows)? Should I watch a movie tonight (one marshmallow) or catch up with work that is getting out of hand and have a work-free weekend (two marshmallows)? If you think about it, a very large fraction of all the choices that we make are choices over time!

A number of principles have emerged from the research on choice over time. The first is the simple realization that future outcomes are discounted. Supposed you offered people $100 now and then asked them the following question – How many dollars do I need to give you three months from now to make you indifferent to receiving $100 now? The number will surely be greater than $100. Let's say it is $120. You could now think of the additional $20 as the price that is demanded for having to be patient.

The second principle has to do with the idea that this discounting – the dollar worth of every day of patience – is not a constant. For example, I might demand $20 for waiting for three months, but will perhaps only demand an extra $30 for waiting for six months. Discounting is steepest around the time that the event is supposed to happen, and then becomes a lot more gradual. There is a precise mathematical equation that can be used to show the shape of the discounting. We won't worry about the math here, but will use the name of the function to describe the nature of discounting. In hyperbolic discounting, outcomes are discounted steeply around the time of the event but more gradually at further points of time.

The third principle is a consequence of the hyperbolic nature of discounting. Just as we thought about the future value of today's outcomes, you could think about the present value of future outcomes. Following the principles of hyperbolic discounting, the future outcome appears smaller now but then grows gradually in size with every passing day. However, when you get really close in time to the outcome, it shoots up in value to its full value. Think about the value of your next vacation. It starts off at the back of your mind, gradually builds up over time, and then reaches a peak a day or two before you actually depart. Conversely, think about the pain associated with doing work – say, completing a report at work. It starts off as a "to-do" list on your calendar, the dread associated with doing the work gradually builds up, and then as you approach the actual day, the full impact of how much work is going to be needed finally hits you. Both these patterns in time are hyperbolic in nature.

Imagine that you are presented with a choice between a shorter-but-sooner outcome (SS) – say, one marshmallow – and a larger-but-later outcome (LL) – say, two marshmallows. Figure 3.3 shows SS and LL that will happen respectively at times t_{SS} and t_{LL}. It is now $t = 0$, and imagine that you are standing at the extreme left of the figure looking to the future, which is on the right. The solid curved line represents the discounted value of LL as seen at different points in time, and the dotted curved line represents the discounted value of SS. These curves were obtained by using the hyperbolic function discussed earlier.

Standing at $t = 0$, it is easy to see that two marshmallows are better than one; after all the solid curved line is above the dotted curve. This is also true as time passes: you start moving along toward the right, and for much of the journey, LL looks bigger than SS. But notice what happens when you get to t^*, the indifference point. This is where the two curves cross over and the SS is very near. Once you get past t^*, you are like a child in Mischel's experiments. You knew all along that LL is better than SS, but now that SS is in front of you, you give in and eat the one marshmallow. There is a formal term for this change of preference – it is called dynamic inconsistency.[50] But in simple English, it refers to the tendency of people who know that they should choose LL to actually end up choosing SS. People who know they need to save more but don't are dynamically inconsistent – as are people who plan to exercise but watch TV instead. Being dynamically inconsistent is a hallmark of being human, most of us having displayed this behavior at one time or another.

The fourth principle explains the effectiveness of a certain class of incentives that promise people a cash benefit (say, a refund, or a reduced price to a consumer, or a wage to a part-time employee) in the future in exchange for the performance of some effort (say, accumulating information or points or filling in forms by the consumer, or doing a tedious job) also in the future. In my thesis research, I used the term "delayed incentives" for this class of incentives.[51] Since the rate of

Figure 3.3: Preference Reversal

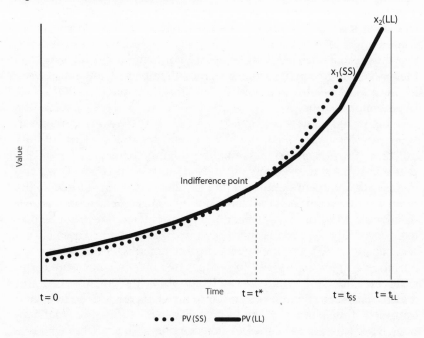

hyperbolic discounting is steeper for effort than for money (in other words, people underestimate future effort drastically) these transactions look attractive when they are in the future but not when it comes time to actually perform the task. This explains the extremely low redemption rates of mail-in rebates or delayed-benefit programs. The fifth principle relates to the idea that people generally believe they will have more time available in the future relative to the present.[52] For example, I recently gave a talk at a conference to which I had been invited several months ago. At that time, I was incredibly busy, juggling my teaching, research, other administrative jobs, and, of course, the loves of my life – my family and cricket! However, the conference was many months away, and I anticipated that I would have a lot of free time not only to prepare for the conference but also to learn something new. So I responded with an enthusiastic "Yes!" On the morning of the conference, I woke up and saw that my calendar was packed with ... you guessed it, teaching, research, administrative jobs, and the loves of my life – and I asked myself, "Damn, why did I say yes?" Now, I'm confident that most of you have had what John Lynch and Gal Zauberman would call *Yes-Damn* moments in your life. In fact, if you haven't ever had one, you're not human. But this is the important conclusion – despite my saying "Damn" I had to go to the conference. My name was on the schedule, I had made a public commitment, and there was no way for me to back out.

People plan to act on all of their good intentions, but only in the future. And when the future rolls around, they look to the next future. Perhaps one way of getting them to actually act is to get them to commit to doing something in the future and then design a mechanism where they are locked into that action. In my case, the locking mechanism was the public commitment. Perhaps we could use this tactic – the "precommit and lock" approach – to help people exercise more, eat healthier food, or save more for the future.

Imagine that you asked employees who worked in a given firm whether they would like to save more. Most would probably say yes, but that there was no way they could save more. They had bills to pay and were used to a certain consumption level, so to save more would feel like a loss. But if you then asked, "But would you commit to setting aside a portion of every future salary increase for savings?" most people would say yes, it makes perfect sense to do so. Now you have the commitment, you need a lock. Suppose the lock came in the form of an opt-out mechanism – employees were automatically enrolled into such a savings plan but could opt out whenever they wanted. Further, when their salaries actually went up, they would never see the full salary increase, as the pre-determined portion would automatically be swept into a separate account. No one would experience a loss. If this sounds like a fictional savings plan, it is not. UCLA professor Shlomo Benartzi teamed up with Richard Thaler to design exactly this program – they called it *Save More Tomorrow*.[53] Not only did this plan increase savings rates, but it also outperformed savings by people who had advice from the very best experts (wealth managers).

This is an excellent last mile solution to a major problem. It involves no economic incentives and no restrictions. No large-scale information campaign or persuasive effort is required. It merely uses very simple insights about human decision making to help people help themselves!

4 Money

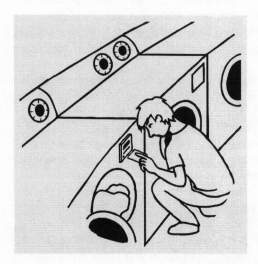

In chapter 4
You will find answers to questions such as:

1 *How do restaurant servers vary their spending depending on whether the money comes from salaries, bonuses, or tips?*

2 *How does your decision to let a prepaid ticket go to waste depend on the format of the ticket?*

3 *Why are monthly-paying health club members more likely to exercise each month than once-a-year-paying members?*

4 *How does your laundry behavior differ as a function of whether your laundromat accepts prepaid cards or cash?*

5 *Why would Italian consumers be more likely to choose a cheaper private label product over a more expensive brand when paying in liras than in Euros?*

For about 400 years, versions of the proverb "a penny saved is a penny earned" have been encouraging humankind to set aside money under the premise that a unit of money that is saved is identical to a unit that has been earned. In both economics and written English, there is a more formal concept that describes this idea. The word "fungibility" refers to a property of a resource whereby units of that resource can be mutually substituted for each other.[1] When applied to money, the term essentially means that a dollar is a dollar, no matter how you earn it, no matter where you save it, and no matter what currency or form it takes. The fungibility property has the following implications:

1) A penny saved is the same as a penny earned.
2) Cash in the form of a single $100 bill has the same properties as cash in the form of five $20 bills.
3) Cash in the form of paper bills should be perfectly interchangeable with an equivalent amount in the form of coins.
4) The evaluation of a payment for a product should not be influenced by the method of payment – for example, by whether the payment will be made in cash, by check, by a debit or credit card, or using electronic or mobile payment methods.

Admittedly, all of these statements are true – but typically only within the four walls of a bank or when the money is in the hands of a professional investor. A long stream of research originating in the 1980s shows that fungibility in money is repeatedly violated! People – consumers like you and me – spend money differently as a function of how we earn it, what we plan to spend it for, what physical form it takes, and what payment method we use. Since money is often a fundamental resource that is exchanged at the last mile, a thorough understanding of its psychological properties is at the heart of understanding behavior at the last mile.

Mental Accounting

Let me start by throwing out a simple example based on the early work of Richard Thaler.[2] Imagine that you love classical music and that the symphony orchestra is playing some of your favorite selections this weekend. Tickets to the symphony are $50 apiece, so you and your spouse decide to go. Now, let's create two versions of the story – two parallel universes if you will!

In the first universe, you go to the symphony hall and spend $100 on the two tickets. You and your spouse realize that you still have a lot of time and so venture out to get some dinner. When you get back to the symphony hall, you realize that you have lost the tickets. You go to the box office, but the original tickets are unmarked and hence cannot be traced back to a payment. Hence, the agent tells you that the only way you can get to see the symphony is to buy a second pair of tickets. The decision you need to make is – should you spend $100 to buy a second pair of tickets?

Meanwhile, in the parallel universe, a slightly different turn of events has unfolded. You go to the symphony hall with your spouse – just as in the first story – and pull out your wallet to retrieve the $100 for the tickets. But right after you do so, you see that you have two crisp $100 bills in your wallet – when you thought you had three! The decision you need to make – knowing that you have just lost $100 – is whether to spend $100 to buy a pair of tickets?

Now, if you're an economist, or a strict believer in the fungibility of money, or both, exactly the same story has unfolded in these two universes barring some minor (and irrelevant) differences. In both universes, you lost a piece of paper, you lost it presumably because of your own carelessness, and it was the same exact symphony and the same performance that you were about to consume with the same spouse. Yet, as Richard Thaler showed us in one of his landmark papers, people in the first universe are much more likely to refuse to buy a second pair of tickets than people in the second story. If you lost cash, it turns out you're willing to buy a ticket. If you lose tickets, you do not want to buy a second ticket. Why does that happen?

Mental accounting explains this story. What is mental accounting? It is the idea that people tend to label money with certain names. And the moment you label money differently, it gets spent differently. People behave like accountants. It sounds like a bit of a scary concept, but that is what people do. More formally, mental accounting can be defined as a series of cognitive processes that people use to track, organize, evaluate, and monitor their financial and economic transactions.

To illustrate the very basic idea of mental accounting, the following simple example will also serve as a crash course in accounting and bookkeeping. For expenses to be accounted, two things need to happen. First, they need to be noticed and entered into the accounting books (in the language of accounting, they need to be booked), and second, they need to be allocated to a particular category of expenses (in the language of accounting, they need to be posted). For example, if you decide to watch a symphony performance worth $50, a mental accountant might create an account in her head called "the symphony." That account will have a budget of $50. And the moment the person buys the ticket, that budget is gone. It's blown. So now if she loses the ticket, there is nothing left in that budget. On the other hand, if she loses cash, that's OK, because that loss comes from a separate account – from the general expenses account! So the point is very simple. People tend to divide their money into different categories, and, as a result they spend money differently depending on the category assigned to it. More generally, the mere act of labeling money could change the way it is spent.

A number of years ago, when I lived in Hong Kong, I met an interesting individual who had trained as an economist and worked for a bank. He had two young children (aged one and three at the time) and was financially very well off. During the late summer, though, Hong Kong was hit by a typhoon and his house needed repairs. He didn't have a large amount of liquidity – most of his assets were fairly illiquid; except one! He had a sum of money stashed away in a bank account that he and his wife had designated as their children's "college savings" fund. That money was earning no more than 3 percent; however, this person decided instead to borrow money against a line of credit at about 12 percent to fund the repairs. Why would he pay 12 percent rather than forego 3 percent? To paraphrase his words, it was because "he could simply not take away his children's education money because it was too sacred." The children were not going to need the money for at least thirteen or fourteen more years, but that was not the point; the point was that because the money was labeled it had lost its fungibility.

When I share the story of this individual in classes and seminars, people are quick to recognize the violation of fungibility, but are equally quick to acknowledge that they might have behaved in a similar manner themselves. One student told me that he had worked hard as a research assistant and earned $200, and the manner in which he spent that money was very different from when an uncle had given him a cash gift of $200.

Sue O'Curry Fogel, a professor at DePaul University in Chicago, interviewed a number of waiters and waitresses who earned their income in three forms – a monthly salary, daily tips, and an annual bonus.[3] The study found that these three sources of income were treated and spent very differently: for instance, salaries were typically used to "pay bills," tips were used to "eat out and go to the movies," and bonuses were used to "buy something nice." An important implication of this finding was that if a server's annual income went up by $500, the changes in consumption that would result would depend on which part of his income went up. If there were more tips, he would be eating out more; if the bonus was bigger, he would be making more department store purchases.

Indeed, many people I speak to relate to that last idea. If I did another parallel universe experiment in which your annual salary went up by $2,400 but in one universe you got that increase as a lump-sum bonus and in the other you got it as a monthly increase of $200, would your spending patterns be different in the two universes? I suspect they would be. You would be more likely to go on a weekend beach getaway in the first universe than in the second one!

Processes and Outcomes of Mental Accounting

There are three processes that form the basis of mental accounting. The first is the creation of the accounts itself: some mental accounts are consumption specific (like the "symphony account" we saw earlier); others comprise multiple categories of time, income sources, or spending categories. The second is the valuation of quantities that are posted to the account. Imagine you spend $50 on a symphony ticket. You would post to the symphony mental account not just -$50 but the value (think of it as emotional impact) of the -$50. Daniel Kahneman and Amos Tversky developed something called prospect theory, which tells us how we value monetary outcomes.[4] Specifically, prospect theory tells us that (a) we tend to refer to monetary outcomes in relation to other monetary outcomes as losses or gains, (b) both losses and gains show a diminishing sensitivity – the first dollar of gain (or loss) makes you happy (or sad), the second makes you happier (or sadder) but not by as much as the first dollar, and (c) losses hurt you more than gains make you feel happy. "Loss aversion" is definitely a key concept in prospect theory. You'll read more on the implications of prospect theory for pricing in chapter 13.

Once an account is created and the outcome is valued, both transactions need to be deposited (posted) to the same mental account. For instance, if I'm valuing the sadness associated with spending $50 and the happiness associated with consuming the concert, I need to put both those quantities into the "symphony" mental account. Furthermore, both these quantities need to be psychologically coupled – in other words, I need to be able to psychologically associate the value of -$50 with the value of the concert.

If I have a clear *symphony* mental account – think of that as a jar – and I've paid $50, I now have a -($50) still there in the jar. Let us imagine that on the day of the concert, there is a terrible snowstorm and it is probably safer (and much more comfortable) to stay at home and listen to music on my home sound system. But in my mind's eye, I can see that jar with a negative value attached to it. If I don't go and the ticket is non-refundable, there is nothing else I can do to make the value of that jar positive. Drazen Prelec of MIT and George Loewenstein of Carnegie Mellon University use terms from the manner in which we evaluate corporate accounts – where red is used to denote negative balances and black to denote zero or positive balances – to describe how we psychologically think of mental accounts.[5] In their research, they develop a brilliant mathematical model to capture the essence of the mental accounting process, but in simple English they point out that people hate to close accounts in the red and do whatever it takes to try and close them in the black. Think about it for a moment – as children we are taught to avoid waste and, with (especially hard-earned) money, that tendency to avoid waste is especially strong.[6] So – not going to the symphony will seem like a waste even when it makes sense not to go! This behavior is called the s*unk cost effect*; it drives us to consume things that we have already paid for because not doing so would seem like a waste.[7] In India, when I was growing up, I learned a phrase in Hindi that captures this thinking perfectly. The phrase was *"paisa-vasool,"* and loosely translated it meant "ensuring that you got your money's worth." As we'll see later, the sunk cost effect might be a very effective strategy for getting people to do things that they are disinclined to do. For instance, people might be more likely to go to the gym or get a flu shot when they have already paid for it, to avoid wasting that money.

That brings us to the concept of coupling. For the sunk cost effect to work, the mental accountant should psychologically be able to associate the amount paid with the specific consumption opportunity. As graduate students at the University of Chicago, John Gourville and I began some research into the question of how and when coupling might not occur.

Here is a simple example drawn from one of our articles.[8] Imagine that you love skiing, and you go to the mountains of Colorado and purchase a four-day ski pass. It costs you $160, but the ski pass comes in two different forms. In one universe, you get one card (marked $160) that you carry with you tagged to your jacket. The card gives you access to the mountains on all four days. In the second universe, you get four separate tickets (each marked $40), and every day you detach one and place it on your jacket tag.

Let's imagine that you have had three beautiful days of skiing, and on the last day there is warm rain. Everybody tells you it's no fun skiing and perhaps it's a better idea to simply head back home earlier and relax. Would you actually still go and ski? In other words, would the sunk cost effect of having paid $40 a day make you go to the mountain and ski even in sub-optimal conditions?

In the second universe, the format of the season ticket is such that there is an explicit coupling between each day's worth of skiing and the daily cost of $40. As a result, that $40 that you've prepaid is much more likely to burn a hole in your pocket and feel like a waste should you not ski. On the other hand, if you have a single card (as in the first universe), you can amortize – or allocate – benefits in any way you choose. For instance, you could easily convince yourself that "over the past three days, I've already had $160 worth of good skiing." The format of the pass creates one four-day mental account rather than four separate one-day accounts. What we would expect is that people would be much more likely to go skiing on a bad day in the second universe than in the first. And in fact, that's exactly what we found. We called this phenomenon transaction decoupling.

Decoupling happens whenever the format of the transaction is such that it is difficult to make a one-to-one linkage between costs and benefits. This happens in a wide variety of scenarios – in the purchase of bundles of products for one price, in the purchase of season tickets or access pricing, or when one uses credit cards and hence all expenses get lumped into one large account. In another of our studies, John and I were able to get data from a Shakespeare festival in Boulder, Colorado. Patrons could buy tickets in bulk (season tickets) or individually. We were also able to keep track of attendance. We found – consistent with the predictions of decoupling – that the no-show rates were higher for tickets that were purchased as part of a bundle than for tickets that were purchased individually.

There is another important factor that could cause the full psychological impact of the prepayment not to be felt – the passage of time. Let's go back to the ski tickets for a moment and focus only on one of the ski passes, the single four-day pass. Would it make a difference if you had purchased and paid for the pass just on the day you arrived at the mountain or six months ago? John and I developed a theory of what we called payment depreciation – in essence, we point out that just as the value of economic assets depreciates with time, so does the (negative) value of the sadness of making the payment.[9] The more appropriate term for the sadness of payment is the "pain of payment."[10] Early research in psychology into adaptation to stimuli showed that people adapt to aversive stimuli over time.[11] For instance, when people are asked to put their hands in a bucket of icy water it seems painful at first but over time seems less painful. We proposed that the pain of payment operates in similar ways – that as time passes, the pain of payment lessens and therefore has a smaller impact on the sunk cost effect.

In the context of the ski pass, our prediction would be simple. If you just purchased your tickets, you would be more likely to go skiing on the fourth day in warm rain because the pain of payment is still fresh. If you had purchased the pass months ago, the pain has probably dwindled and you might be kinder to yourself and decide to forego skiing in bad conditions.

John and I conducted several experiments to test this idea. We were also fortunate to get access to data from a health club that had just installed an electronic access system to the gym rooms – which meant that we had access to the attendance records of members.[12] This health club also had a number of payment plans that differed in the frequency of the payment but not in the total amount paid over the year. For instance, members in the annual plan paid once a year, while those in the monthly plan had an annual contract and paid the same amount – but in twelve equal instalments. Data from the health club suggested a "payment depreciation" story. Those who paid once in January were very active users of the gym in January and in February. By the time April and May rolled around, other things had started to get more important in their lives than exercising, and by September or October their attendance had dwindled to very low levels. The pain of the payment had declined to such low levels that the sunk cost effect was playing no further role. There was a return to the gym in late November, but we suspect that this was an effect of the renewal notices that went out at this time!

On the other hand, people who had paid monthly showed a much more smooth consumption pattern over time. Of greater interest, they were also more likely to renew their memberships as compared to people with an annual payment plan. When they received their renewal notices, they were consuming a lot more than people on the annual plan and hence they felt that the expense was worth it.

The Mechanics of Budgeting

A number of years ago, I was doing some research in Canada and India on different budgeting techniques that people use to manage their household expenses. I heard an interesting story from a friend of mine about how his grandmother used to budget their household expenses using the method "jar accounting." Viviana Zelizer, a sociologist at Princeton University, documents a similar phenomenon – among many others that demonstrate the fact that people routinely label their money and spend it differently as a result. Zelizer calls this method "tin can accounting."[13]

The idea behind this system of household accounting is simple. The parents think about all of the disposable income that they have to spend for the month and then budget that into separate categories. They then use actual physical jars (or tin cans) and label them with a category each. For instance, one jar may be labeled "Eating Out," another one "Entertainment," and a third one "Shopping." When a salary is earned, the parents actually bring home cash and put the appropriate amount in each jar. This makes decision making easy. The next time they are faced with a consumption opportunity, they simply look at the appropriate jar to see if they can afford the expense. If one of the kids asks to go out to the local burger joint with his friends, the response first includes questions such as "Have you finished your homework?" and "Will you make sure you're home by seven?" and then the simple instruction, "Look in the 'eating out' jar. If there isn't enough money, the answer is no."

So how do people mentally account? How do they create these different categories?[14] There are three specific ways in which you could categorize money. First, like Sue O'Curry Fogel's waiters and waitresses, one could mentally account as a function of how the money was earned. If I find money on the street, I'm going to spend it differently than if I had worked really hard to earn it – fun money versus laborious money. Fun money is spent on frivolous stuff. My salary is typically spent on paying my bills. Second, you could account for money by time period. You could budget by the week, or by the month, or sometimes even by the day. Third, you could budget as a function of different expense categories – as we saw with the jars and tin cans.

Chip Heath and Jack Soll, who were then both at the University of Chicago, did some research in 1996 that looked more closely at the processes and consequences of budgeting.[15] They presented a model in which booked expenses were posted to one of several accounts, each determined by a prospective budgeting exercise. For instance, I might sit down at the beginning of each month and draw up a budget in which I allocate a limit to one of four possible accounts. As with the jars, my spending decisions will then be driven by the amount of unused budget in each account. For this entire system to work, the following cognitive operations need to happen:

Step 1: Creating spending categories and allocating an amount to each
Step 2: Booking expenses and posting them to the appropriate account
Step 3: Maintaining a running total of expenses to date in each account, and hence of the unused funds in each account
Step 4: Determining which account a new consumption opportunity belongs to
Step 5: If other purchasing criteria are met, determining whether there are enough funds left to cover the expense.

By now, the reader will have realized that these are demanding tasks – chances are good that people will trip up somewhere. First, we know that people aren't very good at keeping track of expenses and staying on top of their budgetary calculations. In a 2001 paper, I proposed that people follow a simpler model that would produce the same outcomes as the Heath and Soll model, but using a different process.[16] In particular, my model still needed the creation of spending categories and the implicit booking and posting of expenses, but retrospectively and not on an ongoing basis. For example, I didn't believe that people kept a running tab and made accounts by the day. Instead, when confronted with an expense opportunity (say, a weekend beach getaway), they might ask themselves, "Have I spent a lot on expenses of this type in this period?" and if the answer is yes, they would likely decline the opportunity. In this view, booking is retrospective – I have to search through the cobwebs of my memory to retrieve similar expenses. Posting is also retrospective – it is only when making the purchase decision for the weekend getaway that I need to post the past expenses.

As you can imagine, this process creates the potential for two types of errors – booking errors and posting errors. A booking error in this context simply means that, in some cases, consumers are less likely to remember and incorporate past expenses in their decision making. This is likely to happen when the consumer uses payment mechanisms.

Payment Mechanisms Matter

To examine the influence of payment mechanisms, it is necessary to understand the evolution of money over time. At the beginning of civilization, people exchanged goods that they held in surplus for goods that they desired. Bartering, as it is called, was not an easy task because of the extended negotiations that arose about the value of the goods. The concept of money was an attempt to put into place a common measure of value to increase the efficiency of exchanges. Throughout its history, money has retained the task of providing a common measure of value, but it has taken many formats. In ancient times, cowrie shells, first valued as jewelry, were the most common medium of exchange. When humans discovered metal – first bronze, then more precious metals – money in the form of coins and ingots emerged, around 700 BCE. Much later, paper currency became widely used and continues to be used in almost every country today. In addition to the currency formats of coins and paper, modern money formats include checks, plastic cards such as credit and debit cards, electronic mechanisms such as direct debit and automatic pay, and, most recently, third-party payments such as C-mode. Classical economics groups all of these formats under an all-encompassing umbrella: money. No distinctions are made among the various formats, so the assumption is that of constant value across formats.

Researchers in the 1970s and 1980s conducted research to assess whether credit card stimuli can increase willingness to pay.[17] One study tested the effects of the credit card stimulus in a charity donation setting. In this laboratory experiment, participants were immersed in an unrelated experiment, where half of the subjects had a credit card stimulus present on a corner of the desk. Ten minutes into the experiment, a confederate entered the room claiming that the United Way was conducting a survey concerning the practicality of collecting donations on campus. The confederate then asked participants how much they would be willing to donate if they were approached on campus, recorded the response, and then left the room. Results indicate that participants exposed to a credit card stimulus were more willing to make a donation than those not exposed to a credit card stimulus.

In chapter 7 you will read about an experiment conducted by MIT professors Drazen Prelec and Duncan Simester, who had participants bid on sporting tickets and memorabilia with the understanding that they would pay either in cash or by credit card.[18] The results were clear – people bidded significantly higher amounts when they expected to pay by credit card. The question is – why does this happen?

I suspect it happens because credit card users make booking errors. My deep suspicion – and indeed my firm belief – is based on two separate studies I reported in that 2001 article.[19] In the first study, conducted in 1996, I stopped students who had just made a purchase at the University of Chicago bookstore and asked them to recall the exact amount they had spent (and also how they had paid). I then asked them to look at their receipt and let me know if their recollections were accurate. Of the purchasers who made cash payments, 66.7 percent accurately recalled the amount they had spent while the rest were within $3 of the amount on the receipt. Of the purchasers using credit cards, only 34.8 percent could recall the amount; the remaining 65.2 percent either reported an amount lower than the true amount or confessed that they had no idea. This was strike one against booking for credit card users.

In the second study, also done in Chicago in 1996, thirty single-income earners who had only one credit card were asked to do two things. First, they were asked to bring their (unopened) credit card bill to the lab. Second, they were asked to save and bring receipts from all significant transactions (greater than $20) during the same period. When they arrived at the lab, they were asked first to recall as many expenses as they could and then to open their statement and receipts and write down the actual amounts. On average, there were 7.7 credit card expenses, but participants could only recall an average of 4.6 (recall rate = 59.74 percent). There were 6.3 cash or check expenses, of which 5.6 were recalled (recall rate = 88.88 percent). This was strike two against booking for credit card users.

More generally, the pain of payment described earlier can be influenced by the manner in which we pay. Unlike in the simple economies of many years ago when cash was the predominant method of payment, consumers today have a vast array of payment options. While cash and checks are still prevalent in some parts of the world, plastic payment mechanisms (credit cards and debit cards) are very commonplace in most economies. In some countries, even these payment

mechanisms are becoming dated and are being replaced by more advanced mechanisms. For instance, in Hong Kong, a contactless and rechargeable smart card – the Octopus card – has allowed consumers to pay bus and train fares, buy snacks at vending machines and cafés, and pay parking fees and entry fees to sporting facilities. Google has an electronic wallet product; Apple has recently come up with its own mobile payment mechanism; and many other electronic and mobile payment systems have successfully been deployed in many parts of the world.[20] As technology presents increasingly convenient methods of making payments, it also results in payment mechanisms that are perceptually increasingly distant from conventional cash-and-carry transactions.

Consider payment by cash as the benchmark transaction. When we pay by cash, the payment is very salient in both physical form (i.e., it is easy to see that money is being spent) and in amount (i.e., since cash has to be counted and surrendered, the amount is memorable). When we move from cash to check payments, the salience of the physical form weakens somewhat, but the amount is reinforced (since it has to be written in words and numerals). With credit cards, the salience of both the physical form and the amount is weaker (i.e., cards do not have the physical properties of cash, and the degree of price reinforcement is limited). With electronic and mobile payments, the salience is even lower.

In addition to the salience of the form and amount, another factor can be used to distinguish between different payment formats. This relates to the relative timing of the monetary outflows and the purchase episodes.[21] For cash transactions, the monetary outflow happens at the same time as the purchase. This is also the case for purchases made with debit cards and ATM cards. For credit cards, the monetary outflow happens significantly after the purchase, while for value-storing smart cards, the monetary outflow happens before purchase.

Which of these differences might potentially explain differences in the pain of making payments by different payment mechanisms? In a survey, I found that the salience of form (and the salience of amount) of the payment mechanism best explained the perceived transparency of the payment, and hence the pain.[22] The relative timing of the monetary outflows and purchases did not seem to have any consistent relationship with the transparency. Table 4.1 shows the payment transparency associated with different payment mechanisms.

Good Housekeeping and Laundry

If you Google the keywords "how to do laundry," you will come across hundreds of articles offering you all sorts of advice on good laundry practices. One piece of advice commonly heard from moms and books on good housekeeping[23] is to separate your colored items from your white items and run them as separate loads. But how many people actually do that? Many have argued that separation is not really necessary, prompting Consumer Reports to do several tests.[24] The article reporting the test concluded that it "looks like there's no getting around it – you've got to separate your whites from your coloreds, unless you want your whites to pick up some of that color."

Many people admit that they would like to separate colored items from white items but do not have a large enough load to justify the expense of running two separate smaller loads. In other words, if cost were not an issue, people would do separate loads. But – does the tendency to separate also get influenced by the way in which you pay for your laundry? The study that I had the most fun doing was also reported in the same article on payment transparency, and it was done in the laundry room of a large apartment building. The management of the building had announced that the laundry machines were going to be retooled – they currently accepted four quarters as payment for each load of laundry, but after the retooling they would accept only prepaid

Table 4.1 The Transparency of Various Payment Mechanisms

Payment Mechanism (from most transparent to least)	Salience of Form	Salience of Amount	Relative Timing of Money Outflow and Purchase
Cash	Very High	High	Concurrent
Check	High	High	Payment after purchase
Credit Card	Medium	Medium	Payment significantly after purchase
Debit Card	Medium	Medium	Concurrent
Stored Value Card	Low	Low	Payment before purchase
Autopay (Direct debit from bank account)	Very Low	Very Low	Concurrent

laundry cards. A research assistant hung around in the laundry room ostensibly doing her own laundry. As she did so, she observed how many people separated their laundry. In the first half of the observation period – the time in which the machines accepted only quarters – 44 percent of people separated their clothes. However, in the second half of the period, when they paid the same amount but with a prepaid card, that number went up to 60 percent. More people separated their clothes when they paid with a prepaid card, probably because it did not seem as painful to pay with the card as it did with cash!

Currency Effects

Another spanner that can be thrown in the mental accounting works is the currency spanner. Presenting expenses in a foreign currency tends to make the metering process a bit more difficult. As the economy becomes increasingly globalized, it is more common to encounter different nominal values as a result of differing exchange rates. Economic literature has long noted that people focus on the nominal value of an amount of money rather than its real value when making economic decisions. Past research shows that this focus on the face value of money has a greater influence on consumer preferences than does actual purchasing power (even after accounting for interest and inflation).[25]

In research I conducted with Klaus Wertenbroch and Amitava Chattopadhyay of INSEAD, we proposed a currency numerosity effect on the valuation of money.[26] What does the numerosity effect really mean? It means that when actual size is held constant, people assess the size or value of something as bigger or more valuable as it is divided into more units.[27] People, then, rely more on the absolute number of units of a given object while giving less weight to the size of each unit. Klaus, Amitava, and I found effects consistent with the numerosity heuristic. In one particular study, we were interested in understanding whether consumers would prefer an expensive branded product to a cheaper private label. The consumer here is really asking the following simple question – is the better quality of the branded label really worth the extra price? Think about the same exact pair of products, but two scenarios. In one scenario, the difference in price is expressed in euros, and the difference is €1.33. In the second case, the difference is expressed in Indian rupees, and the difference is INR 78.25. The quality difference is the same in both, but the nominal difference in price appears much larger when expressed in Indian rupees. We predicted – and found – that people would be more likely to choose the private label when the currency was more numerous because the price of the extra quality did not seem as worth it!

So while we started this chapter with the adage of a dollar being just a dollar, I think it is now evident that a dollar is by no means just a dollar, and a penny saved is not necessarily a penny earned!

5 Time

In chapter 5
You will find answers to questions such as:

1 *How do people estimate how long an experience has lasted?*

2 *What can we learn from Harry Potter about how to help people accomplish tasks?*

3 *How can the perception of progress help better manage waiting times in queues?*

4 *How can we encourage people to take actions that will only have long-term consequences?*

Money plays a central role in economic decisions made by individuals. While the role of time is relatively underemphasized, it is nevertheless also important to understand time as a resource because it, too, is central to decision making at the last mile. In particular, an understanding of time allows us to better understand three specific areas in decision making. First, today's consumer will appreciate the literal truth in a metaphorical and philosophical aphorism by Ralph Waldo Emerson – "How much of human life is lost in waiting."[1] People have to wait in queues to check into their flights, to get flu shots, and to renew drivers' licenses; they need to wait while applications are being processed and products are being delivered; and they need to wait while programs are being downloaded and installed onto their mobile devices. Second, as managers of businesses and welfare organizations, we often want to get people to start working on tasks that might not seem very relevant to their present circumstances. For instance, we would like people to take flu shots, to start the process of retirement planning, or to switch to a healthier diet to prevent illnesses in old age – or, more generally, to work on projects or assignments that are not due immediately. Third, as we have discussed in chapter 2, people often make choices whose consequences can extend into the future. An understanding of the psychology of time might help us understand how to manage waiting times better, how to get people started on tasks, and how to help them make better intertemporal choices.

The Psychology of Time

Research suggests that people do not have a good sense of how to estimate objective durations of time. Think of a laboratory setting where people are made to wait in the absence of any gadgets that can tell the time, and are then asked to estimate how long they waited. It turns out that people are quite inaccurate in estimating how long they have waited. More generally, it appears that, unlike a "money meter," we don't have a duration counter in our brains that ticks at the same rate as a clock, and our estimates of duration are shaped by various pieces of information from the context. In their research on the memory for past experiences, Barbara Fredrickson and Daniel Kahneman[2] found that salient features of an affective experience (for instance, the highlights of the experience, the rate of change of the experience, and the end state) seem to influence memory of the experience more than the objective duration; they called this phenomenon "duration neglect."[3]

Clearly, right at the end of the experience, the salient features of the experience are immediately available as an input into judgment, while an "evaluation that incorporates duration must be constructed more laboriously."[4]

Another stream of research has focused almost exclusively on how consumers judge the duration of experiences.[5] There are two sets of insights from this research. First, our internal clock is affected by physiological factors like arousal and pulse rates. Second, duration judgment is often flexible and inaccurate, and influenced by multiple factors like emotions, mental engagement, novelty, and variety in activity, among others. Consequently, time seems to move faster when people are distracted from focusing on the waiting; hence the simple prescription, based on past research, to provide news boards, TV screens, and other means of distraction.

A few years ago, I collaborated with PhD students Hee-Kyung Ahn and Maggie Liu to develop a model of how people recall past experiences, and in particular how they estimate the duration of those experiences.[6] The basic setup of the model is best illustrated with a simple story. Imagine that last year Laurel and Hardy each went on an identical trip with family. Laurel took photographs of every family member he met and every event he participated in. Hardy did not take as many photographs. Several months later, when both men were asked to recall this otherwise unremarkable trip, they each went back to their digital photo album marked "family trip" and viewed their trip pictures as a slideshow. After viewing his 100 photographs, Laurel seemed to believe that he had had a longer and more eventful trip than Hardy, who had viewed his 20 photographs. Paradoxically, though, during the trip, Laurel might have felt as if time was passing by quickly since he had so many different activities that he and his family were engaged in. To put it somewhat differently, experiences that might seem short at the time because of distractions may actually seem very long in retrospect.

This story captures the basic intuition underlying our *memory marker* model. The following elements of the story are key variables in our model: (a) photographs that served as memory markers were taken by the two men during their trip; (b) the photographs were all stored in an album, which was tagged with the name of the experience; and (c) the number of photographs was used as a cue to judge duration. These correspond to the three stages of the memory marker model; the encoding of markers, filing them in appropriate memory bins, and retrieving them after a delay. Encoding refers to the process by which certain slices or moments of the experience are recorded for later retrieval, typically when the environment changes. Not all changes in our cognitive and sensory environment result in a marker. In the filing stage, the encoded memory markers are categorized and stacked in memory bins, a process consistent with a popular model from psychology – the bin model of memory.[7] This model conceptualizes memory as bins or storehouses of individual pieces of information about people, objects, and events. The output of information processing is transmitted to and stored in a relevant bin as a separate information representation, in the order in which it is generated. During the retrieving stage, the memory markers stored in memory bins are reviewed and used to make judgments. Given that a larger number of markers would result in greater time needed to review them, we expect that the number of memory markers will serve as a cue to infer the duration of the recalled experience. Note, however, that when an experience is rich in cognitive and sensory changes, time might seem to have flown by faster.[8] However, such an experience will result in a greater number of memory markers and, as a result, will be remembered as a long experience. This prediction of the memory marker model is consistent with the paradox noted by psychologist William James that "in general, a time filled with varied and interesting experiences seems short in passing, but long as we look back. On the other hand, a tract of time empty of experiences seems long in passing, but in retrospect short."[9]

This research, as well as similar research done by Wharton's Gal Zauberman and his colleagues,[10] points to the need for caution in using distraction as a queue-management strategy. While distraction might improve the perceptions of the wait while it is occurring, the strategy may backfire when the consumer is making choices about which service provider to visit on a subsequent purchase occasion. The ideal queue is one where the consumer does not feel frustrated during the wait, but where the distractions are not so vivid that they increase the remembered duration of the wait.

A second set of ideas that plays a role in the waiting environment is the manner in which people budget and mentally account for time.[11] A healthcare facility that offered ongoing therapy and rehabilitation services for its patients had succeeded in cutting down wait times at some of its clinics by about forty-five minutes to an hour. However, the management was surprised and disappointed to learn that these process improvements had no effect on patients' reported satisfaction with the experience. The explanation was simple – given the nature of

their treatments, most patients budgeted and had therefore psychologically adapted to be at the facility for a day or half-day. In the context of
this budget, the forty-five-minute time saving did not really matter!
Mental accounting research has also shown that consumers are risk-
averse in the domain of losses. Consequently, a wait becomes more palatable when they know how long they are going to wait with relative
certainty.

A third set of ideas relates to the manner in which people think about
future time durations. I collaborated with a very smart PhD student at
the University of Chicago, Yanping Tu. In our research, we proposed
that while time passes continuously, most people think about it cate-
gorically.[12] For instance, we organize our calendars by the week, and we
categorize projects as being due this week or next. Similarly, farmers
might categorize time by the harvesting season, fashion designers by
fashion cycles, and students by academic semesters. Categorization is
easy to do; it helps us organize information easily and with little effort.
And the moment we categorize things into different boxes or buckets,
then everything in a given box is treated the same as other things in that
box, and all the things in the other different boxes are considered to be
different from each other. This is exactly the same intuition that was
used to explain mental accounting in the last chapter.

Think of the following example: imagine two fictitious states within a
country, Yaha and Waha, as shown on the map in figure 5.1.[13] Let's imagine that you live in the city of Sheher, marked with a cross. You just read
about an outbreak of a viral disease in another city and think that you
should be concerned that the outbreak might spread to Sheher. Now,
let's imagine that the outbreak you read about has happened in a city
called Nagar (in Waha, marked with a triangle) or Gaon (in Yaha, marked
with a circle). The question that researchers Arul Mishra and Himanshu
Mishra asked was – in which case would you be more concerned?

Now as most readers will recognize, the distance between two
cities is perhaps a big predictor of the spread of an infection, assuming there are no unusual circumstances (for instance, that the rate of
movement of people between any two cities is not unusually high or
low). However, the Mishras found that people reported being more
concerned when the outbreak was in Gaon – in the same state as they
were – even when Gaon was farther away and despite knowing that
viruses do not respect state borders! The explanation for this phenomenon is simple. People use state membership to create categories (in this
case, Yaha versus Waha) and, subsequently, members within a category

Figure 5.1 Map of Waha and Yaha States

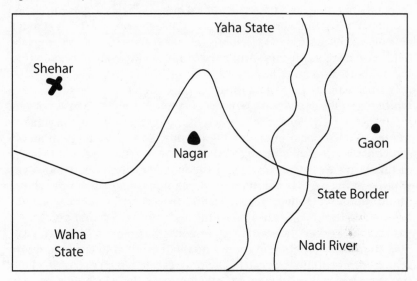

seem to be more similar to each other. If it can happen in another city in Yaha, it could happen here. But Waha seems more distant. Note that we could change these results if we could get people to categorize the space differently. For instance, if we highlighted the fact that both Shehar and Nagar were west of the Nadi River while Gaon was to the east, people might then use that as the basis of categorization.

Yanping and I believe that people think about future time in the same way. We sort events by membership in categories such as weeks, months, semesters, and harvesting seasons and treat them as a function of which category they belong to – now or later. If things belong to the "later" category, they are put on the back burner and left to simmer. Otherwise, they are right up front and are given full attention. Getting people to categorize the future deadline in the "now" category pushes the task to the forefront!

Implications for Waiting and Queuing

Queues are a ubiquitous consumer experience. We routinely queue up to take a bus to work, to use an ATM, to check into a flight, to send a parcel at the post office, to purchase groceries, or to speak to a telephone ticketing agent. There are queues for consumers to get a medical operation, and there are virtual queues that one gets into when one calls a customer service number and has to wait for the next available agent. Because of the ubiquity of queues, a rich literature in the field of *queuing theory* has sprung up to study efficiency in queuing using mathematical modeling.[14]

Queues have an important function – they determine the sequence in which – and the speed with which – customers arriving at a service location get served. As a result, much of the research in queuing theory has the explicit goal of maximizing the efficiency of the system on observable variables like throughput (number of people served per unit of time), average wait times, and the length of the queue. However, waiting in queues has a number of psychological and customer choice implications. Customers report feeling frustrated in queues, and the level of frustration often has very little to do with the actual duration of the wait. Moreover, the waiting experience often plays a significant role in customers' evaluation of service quality and their decision to return or to recommend the service. Behavioral researchers in marketing have therefore become interested in understanding the psychological costs experienced by consumers while waiting for service, and in offering prescriptions on how to reduce these costs.[15]

While a lot of the research on the psychology of waiting has focused on the retrospective evaluation of the service experience measured at the conclusion of the service, relatively less attention has been given to the experiences and decision making of consumers who are waiting in queues. As Meyer argued, consumers "are not mindless passengers in a human line," but can make decisions; also, their affective states are open to environmental influence.[16] In particular, consumers can decide to leave a queue to return to it later, or to completely give up on doing business with the service provider and go elsewhere. These decisions are driven by their perception of how long they have waited, and by social influences in the queue.

Waiting for products and services has an obvious downside – consumers get frustrated and impatient. Consequently, a large number of studies have documented the fact that increasing the waiting time decreases the level of satisfaction with the product or service, and negatively affects the overall experience. Researchers and practitioners in marketing have therefore embarked on the mission of trying to create systems that reduce wait times.

Economist Gary Becker first developed an economic approach to the valuation of time.[17] In his approach, consumers behave as if there is a real economic cost to waiting, and the magnitude of this cost is a function of the amount of time spent waiting. The "cost of time" is the weighted wage rate – the opportunity cost of wages that might have been earned had the consumer spent an hour working instead of waiting in a queue. In this traditional approach to studying waiting times, the actual length of the wait determines the cost (and therefore the negative consequences) of waiting. However, researchers in marketing have subsequently argued that it is not the actual duration of the time spent waiting but rather the perceived duration that influences the cost of waiting.[18] Past research on queuing has shown that consumers retrospectively overestimate the duration of waiting time, resulting in a reduction in service evaluation. Researchers have also attempted to uncover strategies for reducing the negative effects of the perception of time. For instance, Katz and his colleagues found that distractions during the waiting period (e.g., a news board or television) made the wait more palatable and improved service evaluation.[19]

Queues represent an ad hoc collection of people, typically with the same goal (of consuming the target product or service, or accomplishing a task). These people often talk with each other, use others as reference points in assessing how fast the queue has been moving, get annoyed with each other for slowing down the queue or jumping it, and sometimes also develop camaraderie through their shared suffering. In a sense, queues represent temporary social systems, and as such, a lot of the behaviors studied by cognitive and social psychologists can be found in queues. In particular, I outline three sets of behaviors that I have done a fair bit of research on: (a) the need to experience progress, (b) the tendency to make social comparisons, and (c) the desire for social justice.

The Importance of Making Progress

Imagine that you need to take a business trip from Denver to Toronto. There are no direct flights, so your travel agent gives you two options at the same price. One, you could fly to Chicago and connect to a flight to Toronto. Two, you could fly to Phoenix and then connect to a flight to Toronto. Further imagine that under both options, it would take the same time for the entire journey from start to end. It would then appear that most people should not differentiate between the two itineraries. However, my research done in collaboration with my colleague Mengze Shi shows that when they make a choice, most people strongly prefer the first itinerary.[20]

Our prediction is based on a theory that we refer to as *virtual progress*. While we have an elaborate model to explain this theory, the idea is pretty intuitive and is based on two simple principles. First, whenever people undertake journeys that transport them from one place to another over a period of time, the speed and direction of travel contribute to their sense of making progress toward their final destination – their goal. Travel directly toward their goal results in positive progress, travel away results in negative progress. The speed of travel relative to the average also matters. Traveling at speeds higher than average causes positive progress; speeds lower than average cause negative progress. Second, events that happen closer to the time of choice influence the choice more than events that are farther away.

Applying this to the business traveler in Denver, we see that the first itinerary starts off with a negative progress situation, and hence this routing will be seen as particularly unpalatable. In the second route, there is also negative progress but that happens at a later point in time and hence doesn't influence choice as much. Note that the actual progress – the distance covered divided by the time taken – is the same in both cases; however, one route *seems* to make more progress, and hence the term "virtual progress."

Our research on virtual progress suggests the following rules of thumb for designers of waiting environments (and for route planners) in order to maximize consumer choice and provide an optimum experience.

1. Queues (routes) without stops are typically better than queues (routes) that stall for a large period of time. Put differently, a queue system that has the consumer making steady progress is better than another where there are periods of rapid progress interspersed with periods of no progress at all.
2. Avoid any components of reverse progress (i.e., movement in directions opposite to the goal). In many queuing environments, the line snakes back and forth so that, during some parts, the consumer actually walks away from the end goal. Interviews with consumers in such queues confirmed our theorizing that these segments would feel counterproductive to the consumer.

3. Should reverse travel and/or stops be necessary, the later they are in the route the better. In our theorizing, impediments to progress early in the wait have a greater likelihood of deterring consumers from joining the queue or of making them renege early on.

This theory of virtual progress is not restricted to queues and travel planning. Think about two groups of people training to run a ten-kilometer cross-country race in a competition. They trained on two separate courses. In one course, there were posts planted along the route at every kilometer indicating the distance covered; in the second course these posts were planted every two kilometers. Interestingly, the athletes on the first course typically finished the distance sooner than athletes in the second race. That's because they received feedback on their progress more frequently and hence were motivated to try harder. In general, the more progress people think they have made, the more motivated they are to continue a task!

How do consumers estimate their rate of progress? In a straight queue, for example, consumers can visually scan the length of the line and locate themselves in the context of the whole line. Alternatively, consumers could be given feedback. In many government offices in Asia – and in theme parks (both places where long queues are common) – consumers typically see signs informing them of the expected wait from that point onwards. And in many online and telephone queues, it is common to hear a message informing callers about how many people are ahead of them.

Interestingly, we note that perceptions of progress are formed by data that may have nothing to do with actual progress. As an example, I gave a group of students thirty pages of text to proofread. Each page had either a short paragraph with fifteen lines of text, a medium paragraph with thirty lines of text, or a long paragraph with forty-five lines of text. Some students first had ten pages with short paragraphs, then ten with medium paragraphs, and finally ten with long paragraphs. A second set of students had the exact opposite sequence. All students flipped through the entire booklet before they started the task. When they were asked at the end of ten pages about how much of the task they thought they had completed, the typical response was – incorrectly – one-third. More interestingly, students in both groups reported experiencing the same progress even though it was evident that in the first group the actual amount completed was much less than one-third and in the second group it was much more than one-third. While their motivation to continue the task was about the same, those who had finished the long paragraphs should have been more motivated to continue.

All of this has interesting implications for how to structure long and complex tasks. Every so often we find ourselves doing tasks like writing a report, preparing a presentation, playing a limited overs cricket innings, learning a new computer program, or trying to lose weight. It is easy to be motivated in the beginning – after all, it is a new and exciting task; and toward the end – well, the end is in sight. It's the middle that often poses the problem. And that's when virtual progress can come in handy. By placing the small paragraphs, the easy tasks, and the frequent signposts in the middle, we can signal enough progress to keep us motivated and engaged throughout.

These findings provide additional prescriptions for queue management. In particular, I find that consumers are more likely to stay in long queues when they see visible signs of progress. Thus, queues in which people physically move (rather than sit), where the physical environment changes with time (e.g., in Disneyland, different parts of the queue are colored differently, have different photographs, or have different widths so that people have to walk faster as they get closer to their destination), and where people get feedback on how much progress they have made (e.g., in government offices in Hong Kong, signs posted along the queue inform people that "you are about 10 minutes away from the head of the queue") are more indicative of progress and hence more likely to retain consumers. The key again is to signal that progress is being made.

A corollary of the need for progress is the idea that consumers want not just to make progress in moving along in a queue but also to feel as if they are making progress in the actual task. Consider consumers at a consulate office issuing visas. The process of receiving a visa after the application has been made has three parts – the physical submission of travel documents, the payment of fees, and the stamping of the visa. In research with Min Zhao and Leonard Lee,[21] we compared two queuing disciplines that both involved the same total waiting time. In one discipline, the visa applicant waited for (say) sixty minutes before being called to a counter to get the entire visa receiving process done. In a second discipline, the three parts of the application process were separated, and each had a twenty- minute wait associated with it. We found that applicants found the palatability of the wait and overall experience in the second discipline to be significantly better. Why? In the second type of queue, consumers interacted with a service provider after twenty minutes, while in the first case, they did so only after sixty minutes. In the second queue, consumers were "in the system" sooner and hence were more committed to the task.

This idea of bringing people "into the system" sooner can manifest itself in many ways. In work I have done with a provider of specialty healthcare services, this principle has been used effectively to manage the anxiety of patients who have been referred to the facility. Patients traditionally had to wait for about thirty or forty days to get an appointment with a specialist, a period that is highly stressful and anxiety provoking. The facility made a simple change in procedure to make the wait more palatable. As soon as they received a new referral, a nurse from the facility would call the patient, collect some basic medical information, and offer to answer any questions. By making patients feel that they were now in the system, this procedural change resulted in a significant increase in satisfaction with the experience.

In a completely different domain, Sendhil Mullainathan and Eldar Shafir used the "bring consumers into the system sooner" principle to get more low-income consumers to open bank accounts.[22] Low-income unbanked consumers in a soup kitchen in the United States attended an education seminar on the benefits of opening a bank account. While seminar attendees reported a good comprehension of these benefits, only a small proportion (11 percent) went on to open an account. However, in a slight change of procedure, a bank representative was present at this seminar and collected the first of several required forms before the attendees left the seminar. These consumers now felt that they were "in the system" and were therefore more likely to follow through and complete the application process. Indeed, results showed that after this change in procedure, as many as 63 percent of the attendees opened accounts!

Social Comparisons

An extensive body of research in social psychology talks about a universal human tendency to learn about and improve oneself through comparison with others.[23] Social comparisons occur on an ongoing basis and have been described as spontaneous, effortless, and relatively automatic, but are especially likely in situations where there is uncertainty, novelty, evaluation, or change.

Consumers waiting in queues are good candidates for making social comparisons. The waiting situation is unusual – it is oriented toward meeting a personal goal and yet is social in that other individuals are also attempting to attain the same goal. It promotes evaluations, especially when consumers are contemplating reneging and even attempting to regulate their own affective state. And physical proximity to others can foster easy comparisons. One interesting consequence of this tendency to make social comparisons is the result that I found in research with Rongrong Zhou, that consumers are more willing to wait in line if there are a larger number of people behind them in the line.[24] This finding is puzzling from a rational standpoint – after all the only thing that should matter is the number of people ahead and the service rate, as these two data are suggestive of how long the consumer would need to continue waiting. However, in a generally unpleasant waiting environment, seeing people behind one is some comfort since "there are people worse off than me."

The term "counterfactual thinking" refers to a set of cognitions involving the simulation of alternatives to past or present factual events or circumstances. In queues, the arrival of a number of people behind the consumer can potentially lead to counterfactual thinking about the consequences of a possible delay. An example of such a counterfactual thought is, "If I had arrived fifteen minutes later, I would be a long way behind in the queue as compared to where I am now." This causes a sense of relief, positive emotion, and a greater commitment to waiting in the queue.

Implications for Getting Things Done

One of the most popular courses at the Rotman School of Management is an MBA elective called "Getting It Done." This course is not a marketing course – it is also not a finance, accounting, economics, operations, strategy, or organizational behavior course. It is simply a course that teaches students, well, how to get things done. Rotman students have to bid points to get into the more popular courses, and this course is the one that students spend most of their points on. The course also consistently receives the highest evaluations. I have always been intrigued by the success of this course, and I recall once asking its instructor, Brendan Calder, while we were standing in a queue at a coffee shop, why he thinks this course is as popular as it is. Brendan replied without a moment's hesitation, "Because life is a series of getting things done."

Brendan was – as always – right. Whether or not we like the philosophy underlying it, most of us will admit that we do think of life as a series of check marks on to-do lists. Books need to be written, bills need to be paid, home repairs need to be done, tickets need to be purchased for winter vacations, kids need to be picked up and dropped off – the list is endless. How do people cope and, in particular, how do they decide what tasks they should work on first?

Imagine that you have just been handed a task that is due two months from now. The assignment does require a fair bit of work, but – after all – it is not due this month. Plus, you have a number of other things to work on. Chances are high that you will put it on the proverbial back burner and leave it there to simmer while you devote attention to the more pressing matters at hand – the things that are due this week or this month!

Earlier in the chapter, we talked about the idea that people might divide future time into two categories: the "now" category and the "later" category. We also said that people treat all "now" events similarly and all "later" events similarly. In particular, in our research, Yanping Tu and I make a distinction between what is called an implemental mindset (a state of mind in which a person is more interested in finishing tasks and achieving closure) and a deliberative mindset (in which the individual is planning the task – thinking about what needs to be done and by whom).[25] We believe that events in the "now" category are all viewed with an implemental mindset. They are the events that people strive to put check marks against on their to-do lists!

How do events get into the "now" category? The first way is by actually being close in terms of time. Jobs that are due today, jobs that must be started now in order to make the deadline, are obviously in the "now" category. But a second way in which events could be categorized as now or later might have to do with how time periods are sliced up. People tend to use important landmarks to slice up time and create categories. In addition to the standard calendar slices of years, months, or weeks, we could slice up time in terms of birthdays, festivals, and days of personal relevance. My son is an avid reader of Harry Potter, and he told me about a short passage from *Harry Potter and the Goblet of Fire*.[26] Harry will be competing in the Triwizard Cup in search of eternal glory, and the competition is scheduled for February. It had remained on Harry's back burner for a while until right after Christmas – to quote from the book: "February twenty-fourth looked a lot closer from this side of Christmas."[27] Apparently, Harry Potter used Christmas as a slicing tool to categorize future time. Before Christmas, the Cup was in the future. But right after Christmas, it was in the "now" category, and he suddenly felt a greater sense of urgency in preparing for the Triwizard Cup, although the objective temporal distance did not change much overnight.

Across a series of several studies, Yanping and I studied people who had a fixed quantity of objective time to accomplish a task. For some of these people, the deadline was in the "now" category while for others it was in the "later" category. There were a number of ways in which we could change categorization. Consider a task that is due in twenty days: if it is handed out on the fifth of the month, the due date is this month, but if it is handed out on the twenty-fifth, it is next month. Or consider a task handed out on Monday that is due in six days, on Saturday. We created two versions of a calendar to influence categorization – in one version, each week was colored separately (so now the deadline was this week) while in a second version all weekdays were the same color and all weekends were a different color (so now it appeared to belong to a separate category). Across multiple studies, we found the same basic result – busy people were more likely to start work on a task when its deadline was perceived to be "now" than when it was perceived to be "later." Clearly, the manner in which we think about the future changes the way we work on things and perhaps even whether we get them done!

Countering the "It's Too Far to Bother" Problem

A simple reason why young people fail to engage in healthy behavior or to plan for retirement is that the potential negative outcomes of these actions are very far in the future. As a result, they are not very salient, and hence other action items where the consequences might occur more immediately take precedence. In some ways, people do not feel psychologically connected to their future selves, and as a result they do not make decisions for their future selves in the same way as they would for their present selves.[28]

There are two general ways in which one could increase the connectedness of the present self to the future self. The first route is through the manipulation of time itself. If the future self doesn't seem that far in the future, that alone might help to increase the feeling of connectedness. Could we – perhaps – use salient temporal landmarks to slice up time to convince people that they are now in the same time category as the future they are planning for? Doctors and wealth managers tend to implicitly use this idea through the use of milestones. For instance, students who graduate from advanced degree programs and start on their first job are reminded that their school days are over and then asked to think about planning for financial security. Likewise, doctors might remind their patients on their fiftieth birthday that they are now entering a different phase of life and encourage them to get check-ups for certain medical conditions. In essence, the research on time markers offers a simple prescription – when you want a span of time to seem long, introduce many markers in the interim; when you want it to seem short, eliminate markers!

A second approach is to increase empathy with the future self. Many people act as if they are emotionally disconnected from their future selves. In the words of Hal Hershfield and his collaborators,[29] "To those estranged from their future selves, saving is like a choice between spending money today or giving it to a stranger years from now. Presumably, the degree to which individuals feel connected to their future selves should make them appreciate that they are the future recipients and thus affect their willingness to save." These researchers – and others[30] – introduced a clever manipulation to increase the connectedness with the future self – an age-rendered image of oneself. An example of age rendering can be found on the web page of a financial services company that says "Preparing for Retirement Is Easy When It's Staring You in the Face."[31] The process is simple – visitors to the website can take a picture of themselves using the computer's camera and then submit it to be age rendered. The computer will then return an altered version of the picture to show what the users would look like at the time of their retirement.

Hershfield and his colleagues did something similar across four studies in which they used immersive virtual-reality hardware and interactive decision aids. Across their studies, they found that participants who interacted with future selves were more likely to choose later monetary rewards over immediate ones. Creating empathy with the future self through connectedness does result in greater patience and, perhaps, in choices that are more beneficial for the future self.

Of all the variables that we encounter in the study of choices, time is perhaps one of the most malleable. It is also one of the most central variables. Indeed, it can be successfully argued that all choices have implications that extend over time. In addition, while we are all familiar with the old adage of "striking when the iron is hot," there is room for more research that addresses questions such as:

- If I am going to send people reminders to contribute to their savings accounts every month, when during the month should I send those reminders?
- If I am trying to encourage people to get flu shots, when should I offer a flu clinic – during the weekend, when people have a lot of time, or on weekdays? While most people would plump for the weekend, I suspect that a weekday might be a better choice. Getting a flu shot is a "to do" item on a checklist, and most people are in an implemental mindset during the working week, not the weekend.
- If I were to get people to act on something, should I make the request in the morning or the afternoon? While they are at work, or during a break?

Clearly there are a number of other such time-related questions to which we don't have good answers yet, so if you have ideas – get out your notebooks, jot them down, and do the research! But better do it this week, not next.

6 A Theory of Decision Points

In chapter 6
You will find answers to questions such as:

1 *How does partitioning food change consumption patterns?*

2 *What is the effect of giving gamblers 100 tokens all in one bag, versus 10 bags of 10 tokens each?*

3 *Why are reminders so effective at changing behavior?*

4 *What happens if a buffet restaurant puts up a queuing guide along the periphery of the buffet table?*

5 *Who is the planner and who is the doer, and why do decision points give control to the planner?*

If you go to the concession stand at the movies and ask for a large helping of popcorn, you're going to get a bucket that contains ten to twelve cups of popcorn. That bucket is going to have the equivalent of about 1,200 calories. If you asked for buttered popcorn, you can safely add an extra 300 calories. Your dietician would tell you that it also contains perhaps three days' worth of saturated fats relative to what you should be consuming.

Interestingly, a lot of people who get popcorn of a very large size don't actually want to eat all of it. If you surveyed them at a different point in time or at a different place and asked them if they really wanted to eat ten cups of popcorn, they would say no. That said, a lot of them do eat all of the popcorn.

Here is a simple thought experiment. If the same quantity of popcorn now came in four separate bags, would you eat as much? The answer is – no. And the answer is no because of a psychological process that I and my collaborators Amar Cheema and Jing Xu call a Theory of Decision Points.

A lot of times when people decide to eat popcorn or potato chips or drink soda or eat chocolates, they tend to make what we call a meta-decision. They decide to eat popcorn, but they don't decide how much. They open the bag, and they start eating. And they don't look at the next kernel and say, "Well, should I eat this one? It's tasty." Likewise, they don't ask this question for every single kernel in the bag. They just keep going until the bag is all finished.

What happens when I have four bags? I start with the first bag; I eat until it's all gone, and now I have an active decision to make. And that decision is, should I open the next bag? And that's where the rational part of me kicks in, and I say, no, it's time to stop.

Do decision points always help? No, not always. They help for consumers whom we'll call *sophisticates* – this is a term introduced by researchers to describe consumers who recognize that they have a self-control problem and want to do something about it.[1] Decision points work very well for sophisticates because they allow the consumer to pause and think rather than simply to go with the flow. When you take a large resource – be it popcorn or soda or time or money – and you partition that into multiple units, you are creating a *decision point*.

Some of the toughest decisions in life are "*should* versus *want*" decisions. John should be saving money for the future, but the temptation of a hot cup of cappuccino creates a *want* that distracts him from his savings goal. Paula knows that she should be exercising at the gym, but she would rather spend the time with her friends at the movies. George knows that he should be eating healthy granola for breakfast, but his desire for an omelet gets the best of him. And while Ringo knows that he should only consume a small amount of his favorite potato chips, he suddenly finds himself fishing at the bottom of the bag and wonders where they have all gone.

These are just a few examples of the kind of decisions that have long challenged individuals and intrigued researchers. It is not that people don't know what they *should* be doing; they simply act impulsively when faced with a tempting consumption opportunity.

Researchers have proposed numerous theoretical accounts to explain such behavior. One such account is the Dual Processing Model, exemplified by the work of Richard Thaler and Hersh Shefrin.[2] The authors propose that each individual is actually an organization consisting of two entities, the planner and the doer. The planner has foresight, realizes the consequences of current decisions, and hence charts out an optimal path for the individual. The doer, on the other hand, lives in the moment and is myopic, and pushes the individual to pick the alternative that gives the greatest value in the present.

In Thaler and Shefrin's model, the planner controls the doer's desire through willpower. In general, the model suggests that when people are asked about their preferences, their *planner* comes forth and they respond with a *should* option. However, when they are faced with a tempting opportunity (like that bag of chips in Ringo's hands), the *doer* comes forth and pushes the individual toward the *want* option. The term "should option" applies not only to options that maximize an individual's future well-being but also to those that improve social well-being. For instance, one should not keep the air-conditioning running beyond what is necessary to stay comfortable, yet many people leave their units on all summer long. Likewise, one should conserve fuel and take public transit when available, but when the time comes, the comfort of a car is hard to give up.

A second theoretical account that has often been used to explain how individuals make *should* versus *want* choices is the Theory of Hyperbolic Discounting – a theory we have visited before.[3] At the heart of this theory is the idea that people pervasively de-value the future and tend to prefer a "smaller/sooner" reward (SS) over a "larger/later" one (LL). Note that the concept of SS and LL rewards is a handy metaphor for *should* versus *want* options. For instance, in the domain of eating, SS might represent a tempting chocolate cake while LL might represent better long-term health. That said, there is widespread agreement among academics and lay people alike that lives controlled exclusively by the planner – whereby people always make LL choices – might be exceptionally dull lives to lead. Consumption of indulgences in moderation is good for our well-being; the trick is to keep the consumption in moderation. The greater trick, therefore, is to design effective stopping rules for consumption.

Decision Points

In our research to date, we have focused our efforts on helping people who have self-control problems but who are aware of the problem and want to do something about it. Matt Rabin and Ted O'Donoghue have referred to such individuals as "sophisticates." Sophisticates are all around us – for example, people routinely say that they would like to lose weight or save more money but simply cannot because of forces they feel are sometimes out of their control. I propose that individuals could be encouraged to control their consumption behavior by providing them with "decision points."

Based on the Dual System Model of behavior discussed earlier, I believe that when individuals are in the process of consumption, they start off in a deliberative mode in which they actually think explicitly about the pros and cons of consumption. However, once they start consuming, they quickly shift into automatic mode, where continued consumption becomes mindless and habitual.[4] The provision of a *decision point* can enable the individual to snap back into a deliberative mode. For a sophisticate, this typically entails a "call to vigilance" and the realization that the consumption is something that he should do in a controlled manner. Such vigilance often results in the termination of the act of consumption. In the language of the theoretical accounts presented earlier, decision points allow the "planner" to take control of the individual's organization and transport the individual from the lapse zone to a detached view of the choices confronting him.

Several streams of research in cognitive and social psychology draw contrasts between *automatic* (implicit) and *controlled* (explicit or deliberative) processes of making decisions.[5] The former is typically assumed to occur outside the bounds of awareness, while the latter can be consciously modified. Our automatic system effortlessly processes salient cues, while our controlled (rule-based) system is conscious and effortful. Rules can control impulsive behavior (such as eating too much chocolate or spending too much) by inflicting guilt, remorse, or a loss of faith in oneself when rules are violated.

Amar Cheema and I conducted a series of experiments in various domains to test what we called the "partitioning effect."[6] In a number of different domains, we found that the partitioning of the resource into smaller sets reduces consumption. Reminiscent of the example of the large bucket of popcorn earlier, Amar and I came across a story from an Internet blogger who wrote about his consumption of Lay's potato chips.[7]

> Remember that commercial ... can't eat just one ...? YEAH, ONE BAG! Sitting at the computer munching and ... OMG. Where did all those chips go? Who can stop crunching and really close the bag? Clearly not me ... If you can eat 10 chips then put the bag away, I salute you. You are my hero.

When the popcorn-eating moviegoer (or the blogger) is fishing at the end of the bag and has no more popcorn or chips left, she has to make an active decision – "Should I open the next bag and continue consumption?" This triggers a cognitive process and kicks the individual back into a deliberative mode. And if this individual is a sophisticate, she will likely stop consuming. Partitioning works in curtailing consumption because it creates a larger number of decision points for the individual. Finishing each small bag of popcorn presents a decision point and therefore an opportunity for the individual to reassess the need to consume further.

In short, a decision point is any intervention that is designed to get individuals to "pause and think" about the consumption they are currently engaged in. There are a number of ways in which decision points can be created, but there are three broad methods:

1. inserting transaction costs (which works on the premise that requiring the individual to take a positive action makes them deliberate on the consumption decision);
2. providing reminders or information (which works on the premise that drawing attention to a neglected activity can provide the impetus to get it done with); and
3. creating interruptions to the consumption activity (which works on the premise that the interruption allows the individual to pause and think).

In many cases, these three basic methods can be combined to create powerful interventions or decision points. For instance, partitioning a quantity of a consumable resource (say food) into smaller portions uses all these mechanisms – the partition interrupts consumption, provides a reminder of how much has already been consumed, and imposes a small transaction cost.

Partitioning and Decision Points

One easy method of creating a decision point is to partition the quantity of resources to be consumed into smaller units, such that there is a very small transaction cost that needs to be incurred before consumption can continue. While the transaction cost itself need not be very high, it works because it creates an interruption and provides an opportunity for the sophisticate to move to a deliberative mode and make a decision to stop consuming.

In a series of experiments, Amar and I found support for the constraining effects of partitions. In one study, we compared users of international long-distance calling cards who had ordered a $50 card but received it in the form of either one $50 card or five $10 cards. Given that the buyers had randomly received one of these two options, we did not expect any differences in the calling patterns. However, we found significant differences in consumption patterns. First, we found that on average, people who had received a $50 card took 5.7 weeks to consume it fully, while those who had received five $10 cards stretched their usage over 10 weeks. Second, we noticed that the typical consumption pattern was such that people who had five cards tended to use each card over two weeks. When the card ran out during the second week, they had the choice of continuing their international call after redialing a sequence of numbers or terminating the call. Debrief interviews with some of the participants indicated that they were behaving in line with our Theory of Decision Points. One response summed up the idea perfectly: "I can keep talking with my family in India, but when I'm cut off I think about whether I really need to continue and often, the answer is – no."

In other studies, we found that people ate less chocolate (and cookies) when each piece was individually sealed in a box, gambled away a smaller number of game coupons when they were sealed in small quantities in an envelope, and even saved more money when their cash incomes were partitioned into separate sealed envelopes. In the domain of cookies, we found that people who had cookie boxes in which the cookies were partitioned by using wax paper cutouts consumed more slowly than people who got the same cookies in an unpartitioned box. In a similar vein, Brian Wansink and his colleagues[8] showed that inserting a red potato chip in a stack of yellow chips slowed down the consumption. In both cases, the partition served as a decision point.

The study on gambling was particularly interesting. We invited a number of people to participate in a study on gambling. As an aside, we did not have any problems recruiting participants for that study, especially since people knew they would get to gamble. When participants came to the laboratory, they were each given 100 gambling coupons that were printed on paper that was approximately the size of a 4-x-6-inch index card. Each coupon had a cash value of $0.50 (all dollar amounts are in Hong Kong dollars), which meant that every individual in our experiment was getting about $50 worth of assets which – they were told – they could exchange for cash at any point in time. So people could actually choose to simply leave the room, cash in their $50, and be done.

Of course, adding to the lure of the easy $50 was the simple fact that gambling was fun. A number of participants in our experiment told us that they knew they shouldn't gamble, but they had fun doing it and they wanted to impose some self-control on themselves. In the words of Ted O'Donoghue and Matt Rabin, these were sophisticates. Our idea was to see if partitioning these coupons into different sizes actually changed how much people gamble. Here is what happened. People were given coupons in one of two conditions (there was a third as described in our paper, but for now let's focus on two). In one condition, there were 100 coupons in an envelope sealed and given to participants. In a second condition, there were 10 coupons in an envelope, and ten of these envelopes were given to the participant. In every condition, each participant got 100 coupons. It's just that in one set of conditions, there were 100 coupons in one envelope. In the other, there were 10 coupons in ten envelopes. And we were interested in seeing how much people gambled in each of these two conditions.

The gambling exercise was fun. People had to roll a pair of dice and, with a probability of 10/36 (slightly below one-third), they won 5 coupons for every coupon they had gambled. There were only two rules – but two important rules – of the gambling game. Rule number one was that participants could not gamble away their winnings, so they could only gamble up to 100 coupons. In fact, the envelopes they had been given were placed in one tray in front of them and any winnings were placed in a second, separate tray. Rule number two was that they had to gamble one coupon at a time.

What happened? When all the coupons were placed in one envelope, a number of participants (33 percent) chose not to gamble at all. But the ones who gambled tended to gamble a lot – an average of 64 coupons per participant who opened the envelope. One participant gambled all the 100 coupons he was initially given.

What happened when participants received ten envelopes, each with 10 coupons? Now almost everyone gambled – only 13 percent decided not to gamble at all and cashed in their entire 100 coupons. How much did they gamble? Some people gambled a handful, some gambled 20 coupons, some 30, some 40. And in fact, 40 was the highest number that was gambled. Among those who gambled, the average was 19 coupons.

Most of the amounts gambled represent multiples of 10, which essentially means that participants opened an envelope, spent all the coupons, and then stopped. Or they opened two and stopped or three and stopped. And one person opened four.

These results suggest the following – when you take a particular quantity of a resource and partition it into smaller chunks, two things happen. First, the average consumption declines. Second, more people are willing to try consumption. The coupons were like popcorn in bags that are of different sizes. When people opened one envelope, the psychological tax on their usage had been paid and now the coupons appeared to be free. There was not much thinking that went on in terms of how many to consume. People consumed a lot. When people had coupons spread across a number of envelopes, the need to move on to the next envelope served as a decision point that forced them to stop. Importantly, in this study most of our participants had expressed a desire to exert self-control on their gambling behavior. In a follow-up study, also in the domain of gambling, we showed that partitioning had no effect on people who did not think that they needed to curb their gambling behavior. In other words, we had a nudge that worked only for people who would have wanted the nudge, but not for others!

Transaction Costs and Decision Points

While partitioning is a good intervention to create decision points for fixed, tangible quantities of resources, the general idea of using small transaction costs to interrupt consumption can be used more broadly. In one (informal) study, I examined the consumption of food at buffet meals served at corporate events. Food is typically served on a long table for participants to walk up and help themselves, and in such a setting most diners complain that they eat too much.

Over a series of such buffet lunches that each lasted an hour, I kept track of the total quantity of food consumed by category (salads, meat, and dessert) as well as the percentage of people making a repeat visit to the buffet table (54 percent). Then, in a simple transaction-cost intervention, I put a queuing stand with ropes parallel to the buffet table. The rope served to guide the queue of diners along the table; but more importantly, it made it difficult for people to make a quick dash for an extra helping of meat or dessert. We found that the additional transaction cost did the trick: now only 23 percent of people made a repeat visit, and the quantity of meat consumption went down significantly, by about 18 percent.

In a completely different domain, we studied the consumption of air conditioning and found that many households switch on the air conditioning and simply leave it on for extended periods of time, whether they are at home or not – a colossal waste of electricity. Interviews suggest that people are well aware that they need to conserve energy, but they just never get around to switching off the air conditioning. In our research, we studied households that had installed timers to make their unit automatically switch off every four hours. When this happened, the decision to continue using the unit became an active, deliberate decision, rather than a passive one. Early results showed that the provision of these decision points reduces consumption.

A final example of the use of small transaction costs on consumption comes from the research of Todd Rogers, Heather Schofield, and Sendhil Mullainathan.[9] In a cafeteria at Harvard University, they found that a large number of patrons used disposable cups rather than reusable cups. They altered the layout of the cafeteria so that the disposable cups were placed a small distance away and occupied a smaller area and found that the number of patrons taking the disposable cups was reduced significantly (by 65 percent).

In a third condition, the researchers kept the original arrangement of cups but included a sign asking patrons to "Reduce waste by taking a reusable cup." Again, they found that the number of patrons taking disposable cups decreased (by 75 percent). In the language of our theory, these researchers created decision points by adding a small transaction cost, as well as by providing information (or a reminder) via a sign. Interestingly, they also asked people what they expected the effects of these interventions to be, and found significant under-prediction. As such, it appears that the provision of decision points has a much bigger effect on consumption behavior than people's intuitive responses might suggest.

Reminders and Decision Points

There are a number of ways in which reminders can serve as decision points. First, reminders can serve to activate the idea that the consumer has the option of making a choice rather than going with the default. In earlier chapters, we looked at examples from the world of organ dona-tion (actively prompting people about whether they wanted to donate organs in the state of Illinois increased the likelihood of organ dona-tion) and flu shots (actively asking people about their intention to get a flu shot increased the likelihood that they would get one) in which the act of asking an explicit question creates a decision point. Many people who fully intend to donate organs or get flu shots never get around to doing it because it always remains on the back burner. However, being asked to make an active choice now pushes it to the forefront.

The same is true for many other things in life. Many of us intend to pay our bills on time, donate to charity, take our cholesterol medica-tions on time, contribute to our retirement funds, visit our relatives, and take time for ourselves. Yet, many of these things do not happen because they are on the back burner. Providing a reminder – and in particular a reminder that makes it easy to complete the desired action quickly – pushes the decision to the forefront. Other decision-point in-terventions might include the creation of a ritual or a timetable for con-sumption such that there is an easy mnemonic for when the activity is to be undertaken. I recall that I once had a medical condition in which I needed to take medications three times a day. My doctor told me to take the medication with my breakfast, lunch, and dinner. On one particular day, I somehow could not take my lunchtime dose and so I left a frantic message with my doctor's office. My doctor called me to say that it was perfectly fine to take the medication at any other time – however, telling me to take one dose with each of my regular meals created a decision point, a time pattern of consumption, which made it more likely that I would actually take three doses. Of course, there are some medications that need to be taken with food, and it's always a good idea to do exactly what your doctor tells you to do, but I found this to be a clever example of the general idea of creating a decision point.

Providing reminders can have surprisingly large effects on decision making. In a series of separate studies, Dean Karlan and his colleagues partnered with local banks in three separate countries – Bolivia, Peru, and the Philippines – with the goal of assessing the effect of reminders on savings rates.[10] Across their studies, participants in savings programs offered by these banks received reminders to make contributions to their plans. The reminders were in the form of either mailings or mobile text messages and varied in terms of how specific they were. Karlan and his colleagues found that a generic reminder to save increased savings rates by 6 percent, while a more specific reminder that also reminded people of their savings goal increased savings by as much as 16 percent.

Envelopes and Savings Behavior

Amar Cheema and I also did a study in India with construction laborers who earned (and spent) wages in cash.[11] These families had very little access to formal banking. Of the Rs. 670 they earned each week, a financial planner had determined that they should be able to save Rs. 40. Despite agreeing with the budgets that this planner had set for them, participants in our study found it hard to save. The simple intervention that we used was an envelope – a plain white envelope. All we did was to physically put Rs. 40 in the envelope each week, seal it, and task our participants with attempting to keep that envelope unopened. For some participants, we also added pictures of their children on the envelope. We predicted that participants whose earmarked money was labeled with their children's pictures would save more (i.e., would be less likely to spend earmarked money) than participants whose earmarked money was not labeled with pictures. Our results confirmed our expectations. Creating a small transaction cost to accessing the money helped, but the pictures of the children on the envelope also helped to create a reminder of the savings goal and further increased savings rates.

In Closing

Much research in the area of the behavioral sciences has suggested that people continue to consume in excess of what they should. In many cases, this is not because they are unaware of the detrimental effects of consumption but because their willpower is not sufficient to conquer temptations. In the language of past theories, their *doer* takes over from their *planner*, and they fall into a lapse zone.

The Theory of Decision Points suggests that external interventions can help individuals curb excessive consumption by providing them with an opportunity to pause and think about consumption. In the case of individuals who are seeking to control consumption, these decision points typically snap them from an automatic mode to a deliberative mode – or return control of the individual to the planner.

The preceding four chapters have explored academic research in the areas central to decision making at the last mile and generated some relevant insights for practitioners. The next two chapters adopt a slightly different tack and take some time to understand the methods of the behavioral scientist. I get into a moderate level of detail because I believe that this will improve readers' ability not only to understand and interpret the results of research but also to design better interventions and develop trials to test them.

PART TWO

The Methods of the Behavioral Scientist

7 Experiments and Trials

In chapter 7
You will find answers to questions such as:

1 *Why are behavioral experiments or randomized trials pretty much the same as chemistry experiments?*

2 *What is the pennies-a-day pricing phenomenon? What is it mediated and moderated by?*

3 *What are laboratory experiments and field experiments? Is any one of them better than the other?*

4 *How can I experimentally prove that people using credit cards spend more than people spending cash or checks?*

5 *Why is it difficult to get a taxi when it is a rainy day, or when there is a convention in town?*

One of the most vivid memories I have from my days in high school was the time I spent in laboratories. It didn't matter whether it was a physics lab, a chemistry lab, or a biology lab – the lab sessions were always the most eagerly anticipated. The classes were good, too, but in the lab you got the chance to put theory into practice. You could see the pendulum swing to exactly the same height that it was released from, you could see differing degrees of refraction as a function of the index of the glass you were using, and you could see through a process of titration that an acid and an alkali mixed together in the right amounts produced a salt solution. This was all very fascinating to see because, though we had read about it in our textbooks, it was fascinating to be able to test everything for ourselves and to confirm that the theories were indeed true. I also have to thank my lab teachers in the high school I went to because, in addition to merely confirming age-old theories, they allowed and encouraged us – within the bounds of safety – to experiment and to collect data that would let us answer questions that we had.

The word "experiment" somehow conjures up images of people in lab coats at a work desk littered with beakers of chemicals and Bunsen burners. These people are making scientific discoveries and carefully testing scientific ideas. There is, though, a different sense in which the word "experiment" is used in businesses and other kinds of organizations. When a CEO of a company says that they are trying to experiment, it has nothing to do with conducting scientific tests. Rather, the CEO is saying that the company is trying to do something new, something radically different from what it had done in the past.

Conducting experiments (or trials, as they are sometimes called) is a large part of becoming a behavioral scientist. The experiments that behavioral scientists conduct are, in principle, no different from the experiments conducted by a chemist. For example, suppose a chemist is trying to evaluate the ability of a strong acid to corrode a precious metal, such as gold. The scientist first puts a chip of gold in a beaker of hydrochloric acid. The gold stays undissolved. Next, the scientist puts an identical chip of gold in a beaker of nitric acid. The gold is again undissolved. Third, the scientist creates a mixture of these two acids (the mixture is called *aqua regia*) in a beaker, and puts another identical chip of gold in it. Now the gold dissolves.

Let's think about this specific experiment in some level of detail. Notice that there were three separate parts to the experiment. We usually call these the three *conditions* in an experiment. For completeness, let us also imagine a fourth condition – one in which there was no acid but instead the same quantity of water. In each case, a chip of gold was being put into an identical quantity of a liquid in an identical beaker by the identical scientist using an identical process. The only things that varied across the conditions were the chemical composition of the liquid that was in the beaker. In the language of experiments, the scientist was controlling everything except one variable – the chemical composition of the liquid. The scientist wanted to test whether this variable (the "cause") would make the gold dissolve (the "effect"). The experiment shows that the effect does not happen when the liquid is either hydrochloric acid or nitric acid but does happen when both acids are present. These two acids interact with each other in some way so as to cause the gold to dissolve.

We could think of this experiment using a simple 2 × 2 matrix as shown in figure 7.1. We have two acids that can either be absent or present. When both are absent, we have only water, and the gold remains. When we have only one acid, the gold remains. When we have both acids mixed in the right proportion, we have an interaction effect and the gold dissolves!

I go to such lengths to describe experiments with using corrosive acids to dissolve gold not because I think either gold or acids are relevant to human behavior but because the experiment serves as a handy metaphor to illustrate the kinds of situations that a behavioral scientist might encounter. In this chapter, I write about the basics of experiments. If you're reading this book, you're interested in the behavioral sciences and you will find the material in this chapter useful at two levels. First, when you read articles and books in this area, you'll be able to look at the findings presented in those papers in a more nuanced way than before. At the end of this chapter, you'll know about the basics of experimental design and the different kinds of experiments, and you'll be able to better interpret the results that you read about. Second, some of you might end up doing your own experiments and testing your own behavioral ideas and nudges. The hope is that this chapter will get you started thinking about how to design your own program of research.

Behavioral Experiments

Let's think back to an example from chapter 2. Imagine you want to study the effect of the manner of asking a question about flu shots on people's willingness to get the shot. In drawing an analogy with the

Figure 7.1 An Experiment with Four Conditions

		Hydrochloric Acid	
		No	Yes
Nitric Acid	No	Water in beaker Gold remains	Hydrochloric acid in beaker Gold remains
	Yes	Nitric acid in beaker Gold remains	Both hydrochloric acid and nitric acid in beaker Gold dissolves!

dissolving gold experiment, think of the manner of asking questions as the type of acid and the fact that gold dissolves as the decision to get the flu shot. Holding the timing and content of the information constant, we can create multiple groups, each of which sees a different version of the question, and we simply observe the likelihood of getting the shot in each group.

This brings us to an important difference between experiments in the pure sciences and the behavioral sciences. Many theories in the pure sciences, especially ones that most people tend to be familiar with, are *deterministic* – you can make predictions with a fair degree of certainty. For instance, if you drop a ball from a height while standing on planet Earth the ball will fall toward the planet's surface. Or, one could safely conclude that a chip of gold will dissolve in *aqua regia* as long as the appropriate procedures are followed. I acknowledge that there is an element of uncertainty in much of the pure sciences. For instance, a passage in mathematician George Gamow's book *One Two Three … Infinity* warns us that there is a non-zero probability that all the air molecules in a given room might decide to congregate in one corner of the room leaving the human occupants in the other parts of the room to gasp and choke for air.[1] But as Gamow goes on to say, while this is a possibility it is so unlikely that we can safely ignore it as a real possibility.

Behavioral theories, on the other hand, are *stochastic*. That's a fancy way of saying that behavioral theories can make predictions about the likelihood that a particular outcome will happen over a sufficiently large group of people, but they cannot make any such claims with certainty. Consider the flu shot example. The claim could state that "Enhanced active choice (the version in which the costs and benefits of the bad and good option respectively are highlighted) *increases the likelihood* that people will choose the good option." This is not the same as a second claim – "A person presented with an enhanced active choice will choose the good option" – a claim that *cannot* be made in the behavioral sciences. This is because, compared to molecules of air or a ball on planet Earth, there is significantly greater variability in human behavior. What works for one person might not work for another. Or, the strength of the nudge required for one person may be significantly greater than the strength required for another. Let's say we show each of 100 people a different version of the question and test to see what percentage of people say yes to getting a flu shot. Our prediction is stochastic in nature – that the percentage of people saying yes in the enhanced active choice option is greater. Perhaps the strongest finding in the behavioral sciences is loss aversion – the idea that losses hurt you more than gains make you happy.[2] Even that prediction, though, is tested using a stochastic approach.

Let's step back a bit and think about the nuts and bolts of experiments as they apply to behavioral science. An experiment is basically a tool that researchers can use to establish whether or not there's a causal relationship between one particular variable and an outcome that they care about. If you have an idea for research, it could simply be expressed by a statement like, "I want to test whether the method of posing questions changes the likelihood of getting a flu shot." Or, thinking back to Tanjim Hossain's research in chapter 2, "I want to test whether the manner of framing bonuses changes productivity." A more generic template for the research question is, "I want to test whether [a cause] changes [the effect]."

At the most basic level, experiments compare two (or more) groups – the control group and the treatment group. The researcher will deliberately "manipulate" (create variations of) the presence of the "cause" between these two groups. In the treatment group, all participants will experience the "cause" variable. In the control group, the "cause" variable will not be present, and then the researcher will compare both groups' responses on the "effect" variable. Researchers can start off with this very simple structure and create more elaborate experiments, as I'll examine later.

It's also important to think about why experiments are done in the first place. There are five reasons for doing experiments. The first is to document behavioral phenomena. Major phenomena, like decision biases or strategies used for making decisions, are typically documented by doing a series of experiments over time that converge toward the same conclusion. Second, experiments are often run to develop a theory to explain the phenomena that have been documented. Why does the format of the question change compliance? Why does the framing of a bonus change productivity?

Third, we often do experiments to study the size of different phenomena. For instance, how large is the effect caused by framing a bonus as a loss instead of a gain? A fourth reason for running experiments is to reconcile and test across theories that make conflicting predictions. And finally, we often do experiments to test for the efficacy of what we call, in behavioral economics, nudges or behavior-changing interventions.

Pennies a Day: Building a Program of Experiments

One phenomenon that John Gourville – whom I mentioned earlier – has spent a fair bit of time documenting and understanding is the "pennies-a-day" effect (hereafter, PAD effect).[3] As consumers, we are often bombarded with messages asking us to part with our money. A marketer might want you to part with $700 for a new espresso machine or a charity might want to ask you for $350 to support its on-the-ground efforts at combating hunger. If the life of the espresso machine is two years, the marketer could frame the purchase price as "less than a dollar a day," which might start to look very attractive. You've already read at length about the PAD effect. But how might you design experiments to test it?

First you need to identify the cause and the effect. As a researcher, you want to show that if you frame a price using PAD (cause), people are more likely to part with their money. So you could design a simple experiment with two groups (or "conditions" as they are called in the parlance). In both conditions, you offer people the same exact product or the same exact opportunity to donate. If you're going to present people with advertising, you would keep the content of the advertising and the message identical. You would also keep identical the conditions under which the advertising was seen. The only difference across the conditions would be the manner in which you express the price – in the control condition, you would tell people that the price is $350; in the treatment condition, you would tell them that the price is just under $1 a day over one year (see figure 7.2). You would invite a number of people to participate in your study and randomly assign them to one of these two conditions. They would see the advertising and read the information about the product, and would then be asked to make a decision about whether or not they would like to make the purchase. Your prediction would be that a greater proportion would say yes to purchasing when the price is PAD (of course, you would need to test for the difference in these proportions using appropriate statistical techniques, but I'll keep it simple here and refer the interested readers to more advanced books on the analysis of experimental data).[4] If that is indeed what your data show, you have designed an experiment that successfully tests your prediction.

Of course, it would be foolhardy at this stage to proclaim to the world that you have uncovered a new phenomenon. It would be important to show that this phenomenon is robust and holds true under a number of conditions. For instance, let's imagine that in the first experiment you use a product-purchasing scenario. You might now want to redo the experiment using a different product category, or using charitable donations. Likewise, in the first experiment you presented people with a purchase opportunity and asked them a binary ("Yes, I will purchase" versus "No, I decline") question. You might now want to ask them to indicate their purchase likelihood on a seven-place scale. Finally, your first experiment might have used a hypothetical purchase scenario, and in a follow-up study, you might use a real purchasing situation. If you continue getting the same pattern of results across different product categories, offering different kinds of scales people can use to respond, and presenting both hypothetical and real purchasing scenarios, you have a robust phenomenon.

The next question you would need to address is – Why does this happen? What is the underlying psychology that explains this pattern of data? John Gourville suggested that, when a price is framed as a pennies-a-day price, it triggers a comparison process. When I am asked

Figure 7.2 Cause and Effect

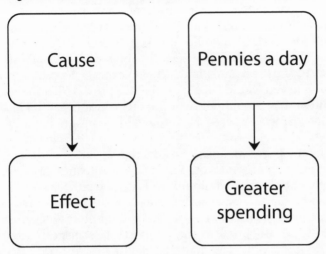

to make a charitable donation of only a dollar a day, I start retrieving other ways of spending a dollar, and I can retrieve many! Coffee, parking charges, stamps, vending machine snacks – many examples come to mind – and I use this cue to categorize the donation opportunity along with many other things that I routinely spend on. This increases the perception of affordability. If I paraphrased this argument in one sentence, it would read something like, "A PAD price makes things feel more affordable, and hence people are more likely to spend." The "affordability" is an intermediate state between the cause and the effect, and hence it is called a *mediator* (figure 7.3).

In order to test for this mediator, the experimenter would need to measure the perception of affordability using a suitable scale. The details of the statistical analysis needed to test for mediating effects are beyond the scope of this discussion, but interested readers are referred to David Kenny's website.[5]

To go one step further in thinking through the theory and the experiments – recall that this effect happens only when the PAD frame results in a dollar amount that can be compared easily to other expenses that the consumer might make on a daily basis. But, let's say that I am now looking at a product that costs $2,500, and its equivalent PAD price is about $7 a day. Applying the same process as before, I try to retrieve instances of things I spend $7 per day on, on a daily basis, – and I draw

Figure 7.3 A Mediator

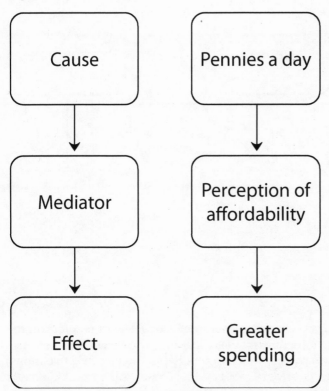

a blank! I do occasionally buy lunch, but that is the only instance that comes to mind. The strategy of framing price on a per-day basis might backfire because now the consumer cannot recall anything else he does that routinely costs $7 a day. In other words, PAD pricing will result in greater spending, but the effect depends on the level of the expense. Specifically, it works only for small daily amounts and not when the daily amount is large. In the language of experimental design, this third variable is called a *moderator* variable (figure 7.4). The relationship between cause and effect is changed as a function of the moderator. The moderator in this specific example eliminates the effect. But it could also strengthen or weaken the effect in question.

How could one design an experiment to test for this moderator? Recall that the first set of experiments – ones that found support for the

Figure 7.4 A Moderator

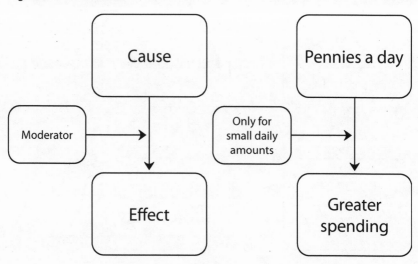

basic phenomenon – had two conditions, a control (a regular, aggre-gated price) and a treatment (a PAD price). Suppose we do an experi-ment in which we repeat these two conditions and then add two more; a second aggregate price ($2,500) and a second PAD price ($7 a day). The experiment now has four conditions, and it looks a bit like a 2 × 2 matrix. On one dimension of the matrix, we have two levels of price framing (aggregate and PAD) and on the other dimension, two levels of the amount ($350 and $2,500) – and the four (2 × 2) resulting conditions employ all possible combinations of these two dimensions. This type of experimental design is called a fully crossed design (figure 7.5).

What do we expect to find when we conduct the experiment? We expect to find a difference between the two price framing conditions when the amount is $350, but not when it is $2,500. It's a lot like saying that hydrocholoric acid will dissolve gold in the presence of nitric acid but not without. In other words, what we could predict here is an inter-action effect!

Notice that we have very quickly moved on from a simple experi-ment in which we compared two conditions to mediators, moderators, fully crossed designs, and interaction effects.

Figure 7.5 A Before-and-After Design

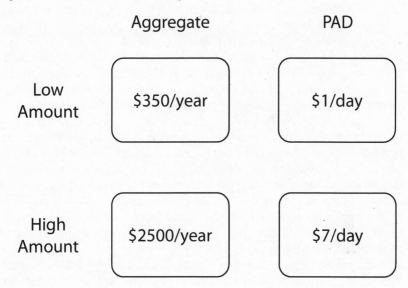

Additional Ideas and Key Concepts

You often encounter the word "manipulation" when you read anything in the behavioral sciences. What is a manipulation? No, it doesn't refer to the fact that the experimenter is a scheming, Machiavellian person. Rather, it is any aspect of a process or a task that the experimenter changes across experimental groups. In a behavioral lab, the entire set of experiences that a participant goes through can be manipulated. This includes the way in which the information is presented, the font in which a text is written, the comfort of the seat that the participant sits in, the size of the room, or even the color or temperature or different elements of the background. Any element of the experience that an experimental participant goes through that is changed by the experimenter across groups is called a manipulation.

There are a couple of other terms to keep in mind when thinking about experiments. The first is "background variables." A background variable is any set of variables that is held constant and is not manipulated. Often, the location at which data have been collected, the nationality or ethnicity of the participants, their gender, or their education level all represent background variables that are a given in the context of an experiment. The behavioral scientist has to make sure that they interpret the experiments in the context of the background of that experimental setting. In particular, care must be taken not to generalize too much from a given set of background variables and push the results of the experiment into other conditions of background variables. When key experimental results can be replicated across different sets of background variables, the researcher has greater confidence in the results.

"Randomization" refers to the act of allocating participants to different conditions randomly. Randomization is critically important because it minimizes what are called selection bias and allocation bias. Think about doing a study of consumers who use credit cards versus cash or checks when they make purchases. If you simply observe the purchases made in a store by people who spend using credit cards versus those who use cash or checks, you might conclude that people who use credit cards spend more than people who use cash or checks. However, it could be the case that people who expect to spend more decide to use credit cards in the first place. If so, the true "cause" is the level of spending and the true "effect" is the choice of payment method. Without random assignment of people to the two conditions, it is possible that one might come up with a faulty conclusion.

Likewise, experimenters or research assistants who actually collect the data are typically blinded to the cause of the experiment, to minimize the chance of any allocation biases – the chance that they will allocate participants to certain conditions (or interpret data in a certain manner) that they think would push the results in one direction or another.

Experimental Designs

It's important not only to have a general understanding of what an experiment is but also to think about the different kinds of experimental designs that are available. Recall the laundry experiment that I described in chapter 4. This experiment showed that when people pay for their laundry by using a prepaid card (as opposed to cash), they are more likely to separate their white loads from their colored loads.[6] That experiment observed people doing laundry over a forty-day window. In the first half of the window, the machines accepted quarters. The machines were then retooled, and in the second half of the window, they started accepting prepaid cards.

This is what we call *a before-and-after design*. Something has happened in the environment, in this case, the way the laundromat is managed, that has changed the way in which people do their laundry, or, in an experimental sense, the focal task. This change has occurred outside of the experimenter's control and hence this sort of experiment is called a natural experiment.

Does this experiment conclusively prove that, if you change the payment method from coins to cards, people will change their laundry behavior, and that the change in the laundry behavior is attributable only to the change in payment mechanism? Keep in mind that the "cause" is the movement away from coins to a prepaid card. The "effect" is the separation of laundry into the white and colored loads. Let's imagine a hypothetical situation where, for some reason, people in the middle of this time window have suddenly started reading *Good Housekeeping* magazine and have realized that separating is the right thing to do. This change in knowledge alone might explain the new pattern of results. In order to rule out that possibility, the experiment needs to include a second set of conditions – a control condition in an identical laundromat where there is no change in payment method (figure 7.6).

In the control condition, you would have the same forty-day window, pretty much the same location, and with the same kinds of people doing their laundry. But in the control, rather than switching from coins to a prepaid card, you would continue using coins throughout the entire forty-day window. And what you ideally want to show is that the changes that you saw in the top panel are not attributable simply to the passage of time.

You'll also come across many references to *within-participants* experimental designs versus *between-participants* experimental designs. The example of the laundromat essentially tracked people over a forty-day window, but it was the same group of people – people who lived in that apartment building – who kept visiting the laundromat. Essentially, the same people were exposed to two treatments, the cash condition and the prepaid card condition. That is called a within-participants design. In contrast, people taking part in Gourville's experiments on PAD pricing either saw an aggregate price or a PAD price. In other words, there were two different groups of people each of whom saw only one kind of pricing in their experiment. That is called a between-participants experiment. Obviously, both between-participants and within-participants experiments have their own merits.

Figure 7.6 Before-and-After with Control

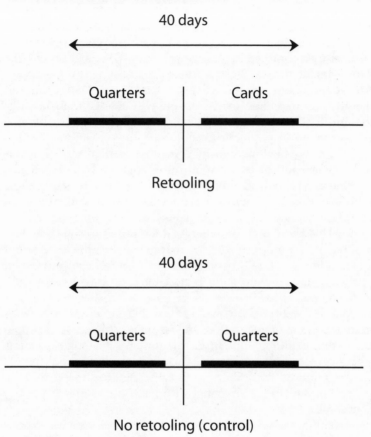

Illustrative Experiments: How You Pay Changes How You Spend

In 2001, Drazen Prelec and Duncan Simester, both professors of marketing at the Massachusetts Institute of Technology (MIT), conducted a couple of experiments to address a very simple – yet very important – question: Does the use of a credit card increase spending? They wanted to show that the willingness to pay increases when people pay using a credit card rather than cash.[7] In a laboratory experiment, participants (sixty-four MBA students) made choices that had real consequences.

The experiment used two conditions – either the credit card condition or the cash condition.

The procedure was very simple. Participants were given a chance to purchase a ticket for a sporting event in an auction setting. They were asked to write down the reservation prices – the prices they would like to bid – for three items. The first item was a pair of tickets for the Boston Celtics and Miami game, the second item was a pair of tickets for the Red Sox-Toronto game, and the third item was a consolation prize that had one Celtics banner and one Red Sox banner. The rule that was used to determine the winner was as follows – the auction was a second-price sealed bid auction, in which the item is given to the person who wrote down the highest value, but at a price equal to the second-highest stated value. In the credit card condition, participants were told that the payment would be made by credit card, and they were asked to write down their credit card details, the card type, and the expiration date, much as they would need to do if they ordered any product or service using a credit card. In the cash condition, participants were told that they would actually pay by cash. They had access to an ATM, and therefore liquidity was not an issue.

So what did this experiment show? Using a simple two-condition design, Prelec and Simester were able to show that purchasing a product with a credit card rather than cash increased the amount of money that people were willing to pay. The premium that people were willing to pay was about 113 percent for the Celtics tickets, 76 percent for the Red Sox tickets, and 59 percent for the banners, although the last difference was statistically not a significant difference.

In that same year, I published a paper that looked at the same general area of research but posed a slightly different question: Do people who routinely pay using credit cards differ in the way they make purchase evaluations from people who routinely use checks?[8] In one experiment discussed in this paper, the hypothesis that I was looking to test was that consumers who had paid for past purchases by credit card would be more likely to purchase an additional discretionary product than consumers who had paid for the same purchases by check, all other things being held constant.

The experiment used three factors each of which had two levels. The first was payment mechanism (either credit card or check). The second factor was feedback – some participants were given a running total of their cumulative expenses to date as they made payments while others were not. And finally, the third factor was a credit limit ($3,000 or

$8,000). This 2 × 2 × 2 fully crossed experiment resulted in a total of eight conditions, and participants were randomly assigned to one of them. All participants were asked to imagine that they had a job that paid $3,000 a month. They had bank accounts as well as a credit card with a given limit. Next, every participant was shown thirty index cards with expenses that they would incur in a typical month. Note that this experiment was conducted in 1998 – if I had to do this again, I would use a computer program to increase the realism of the task. That said, the idea of this procedure was simply to recreate, in a laboratory setting, the mechanics of payment that an individual would go through in a given month over the space of thirty days.

As participants saw each index card, they actually made simulated "payments," either by writing checks or by signing credit card receipts. At the end of this entire process – about an hour later – participants answered several questions, including the one that measured the "effect." They were given some information on a box CD set by a favorite artist with a specific price and a number of attributes. And they were asked to indicate, on a 10-point scale, how likely they were to make this purchase given all the other expenses they had incurred in the month.

The data were analyzed by a technique called ANOVA, which compares the average across all of the conditions that we talked about. And we found that purchase intentions varied as a function of payment mechanism (people paying by credit card were more likely to buy), credit limit (people with greater limits were more likely to buy), as well as feedback (people who received feedback were less likely to buy). However, these findings should be interpreted by interactions (of the hydrochloric acid–nitric acid type). I want to focus for a minute on the first interaction – a payment mechanism influenced by feedback interaction. The data showed that feedback reduced purchase intention – but only in the credit card conditions and not the check conditions. Another interaction effect showed that greater credit limits increased purchase intention, but only for people who actually used credit cards.

Our conclusion was simple. Paying for a series of expenses by credit card rather than by check increased the purchase intention for an additional discretionary product. However, these differences weakened as we provided people with feedback, and as we reduced the credit limit.

A Typology of Experiments

Thus far the chapter has described a number of different kinds of experiments: experiments in the laboratory and in the field (laundromats); fully crossed designs; simple before-and-after designs; experiments with students as participants and experiments with adults and people in the marketplace as participants. But how should the different kinds of experiments be organized?

I want to organize the different flavors of experiments into three sets. The first set is the laboratory experiments. In the laboratory examples, people made either hypothetical choices (my 2 × 2 × 2 experiment) or real choices that had real consequences (Prelec and Simester's bidding experiment). The second set of experiments was what are called natural experiments, or experiments using archived data – such as the laundromat study. But sometimes the natural experiment happens without our even knowing that an experiment has happened. For example, Colin Camerer and his colleagues were trying to understand the driving behavior of taxi-cab drivers in New York.[9] They were simply trying to answer the question, "Does drivers' behavior change as a function of whether they have a high wage rate day (e.g., when it rains or there is a convention in town resulting in a greater demand for taxis), or a low wage rate day?" Colin and his colleagues looked at archived data from trip sheets (handwritten records of trips made by each driver), at weather reports, and at a record of conventions to determine if it was a "good wage" or a "bad wage" day. They found a surprising result – on high wage rate days, drivers work for a shorter period of time. They do so because – as the authors hypothesize – they have set a daily target for earnings. On good days, they reach the target earlier and, voila … they go home!

Or think about the euro in the 1990s. In the 1990s, when most countries in the European Union decided to substitute the euro for their home currencies, some countries had currencies with a high number of units in the local currency relative to the euro.[10] An example is the Italian lira. An interesting focus for study could be the way in which the same people who were used to spending numerous liras behaved when spending a smaller number of euros, using a before-and-after experimental design.

There are two kinds of experiments that nature conspires to create for us. There are some in which there is an archive of data that already exists somewhere that you as the researcher need to tap into. Or there are experiments in which the work conspires to create conditions for the researcher who then might need to go and ask people questions or observe behavior to document the effect of that intervention on people's behavior.

Finally, there are two types of experiments that we call field experiments, and they differ in scale. In both field experiments and randomized controlled trials, the researcher actively goes out into a real-world setting and comes up with an intervention or a manipulation. Think about the research I wrote about in chapter 4 on decision points.[11] We helped people save more money by putting a portion of their cash salary in envelopes. That was a field experiment. On a larger scale, you could think of studies with thousands of respondents. A study by Marianne Bertrand and her colleagues had as many as 15,000 to 16,000 respondents.[12] They worked with a company that sends out mailings for loan products, and they manipulated a total of ten features (each at two or three levels) of the mailing in order to see the effect on take-up or acceptance of those loan products. As you can imagine there were a very large number of conditions.

If you put all of these together, you see a spectrum that goes from the very top, with simple laboratory experiments in which people make hypothetical choices, to the very bottom, with fairly complex randomized controlled trials in which lots of things are being manipulated and data collection is done in a real-world setting (figure 7.7).

What you get at the top of this spectrum is control. In the laboratory, you can make sure that all of your background variables are controlled. What you get at the bottom is realism. You make sure that what you are studying in this experiment is real, because at the end of the day, you're documenting real effects on real people making real decisions.

What do we learn more from – laboratory studies or field studies? The answer depends on what you are looking to test. If your goal is to test nudges or interventions in a realistic study, or to see how big an effect a particular nudge will have, being close to the bottom of the spectrum might be more appropriate. But in situations where the goal is to test theory and uncover the underlying psychology, the top of the spectrum might be a more fruitful place to be. Most programs of research are trying to do both, and hence you are likely to see a package of different flavors of experiments!

Figure 7.7 A Typology of Experiments

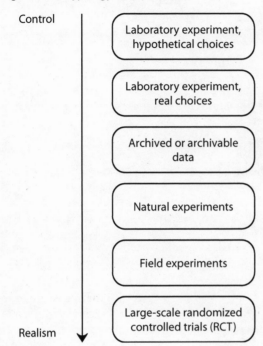

8 Understanding Preferences and Judgments

In chapter 8
You will find answers to questions such as:

1   *What is intuition and how can it be represented?*

2   *What is your judgment machine and why it is better than you at making predictions?*

3   *How can you make your own judgment machine at home?*

4   *How can intuition be educated and improved?*

5   *Why do people make better choices in wine, objects of art, and quilts when they are given a consumption vocabulary?*

Chapter 3 described the cognitive approach to making choices. In particular, it noted that in order to compute their preferences, individuals first need to have complete data for all options on all attributes. Ideally, the data must be quantifiable. Further, each attribute should be given a score that represents its importance. Once all of these data are available, the computation of preferences follows a fairly mechanical process, which can be described as follows:

- For every option: Go to each attribute and multiply the score by the importance weight.
- Then add up the resulting numbers across each attribute. The resulting score represents an index of your preference or value for the product.
- Repeat the process for every option and choose the option with the highest score.

In the language of chapter 3, this process represents the WADD (weighted additive decision) rule of decision making. In the case of a risky choice – a choice between many gambles, the procedure is pretty much the same as the one just described except that the importance weight is replaced by the probability that each particular outcome will occur. Mathematically speaking, if we have an option A with three attributes whose respective importance weights are w_1, w_2, and w_3, and whose scores on those attributes are A_1, A_2, and A_3, the preference score of that option can be written out as:

$$\text{Score (A)} = w_1 * A_1 + w_2 * A_2 + w_3 * A_3$$

This mathematical formula could also be used to represent the judgment that we make about options or individuals. In simple English, this equation essentially says that the individual is taking some form of weighted average of the score on each of the three attributes to arrive at the judgment. It's entirely possible that people aren't actually doing exactly what the equation says; I don't think they are actually jotting down numbers (on a piece of paper or even mentally) and doing the multiplication and then the addition. Instead, all we can say is that they are doing something cognitively that can be represented by this equation. In other words, they behave as if the equation were true. Psychologist Paul Hoffman coined the term "paramorphic model" in 1960 to describe these "as if" models.[1]

At the risk of digressing, I would also like to point out here that some readers might be able to see that the equation looks superficially like something they may have come across in classes on statistics – the *regression* equation. Regression is a tool that allows the researcher to infer the weights associated with different attributes (in the language of regression analysis, the weights are called "coefficients"). Put differently, if I asked an individual to place a value on – or make a judgment about – a very large number of options that had different levels of the three attributes (A_1, A_2, and A_3), we should be able to use regression analysis to infer the values of the respective "w"s.

In many situations, we need to make judgments as well as choices. For instance, we are often asked how much we would be willing to pay for a service. Or we are asked what we thought of the quality of the service we received after a hotel stay. These are both examples of judgments expressed on different scales. Willingness to pay is expressed on a dollar scale while service quality might be expressed on a seven-point scale.

Judgments are made using some of the same processes that we use to make choices. In an economic sense, one could think about the utility or value that one gets from a product as a judgment. From a cognitive standpoint, one could think about judgments as being the first stage in the WADD approach to making choices. In addition, people are constantly making judgments about people they meet, products they sample, and situations they encounter. It would probably be fair to say that we have many more opportunities to make judgments than to make choices.

Judgments about Unobservables

In many situations in life, we need to make judgments – or predictions – about properties of objects or people that are not observable at the time of making the judgment. There are two specific cases in which such judgments need to be made. First, we often need to judge an object or a person on a feature that is inherently impossible to observe and measure. For instance, a loan officer has to assess the credit-worthiness of a loan applicant, a PhD admissions committee at the University of Toronto may need to judge the intellectual ability of a graduate applicant, a judge in a court might need to determine the sincerity of a person standing trial for a misdemeanor, and a real estate agent might need to determine the "curb appeal" of a house. These four variables

– credit worthiness, intellectual horsepower, sincerity, and curb appeal – are ill-defined variables. They are also variables that can be represented by a combination of ability and intention, and each can manifest itself in many ways. Second, we might need to make judgments about the future behavior of an object or person based on the data at hand. Think about investing in the stock market, for example. Let's imagine you have two mutual funds to choose between. You need to decide which one to choose on the basis of your prediction of the prices that those funds are going to yield in the next few years. Or let's say you're hiring a new employee. You need to make a judgment about the quality of the performance this person is going to give you over the next three years on the basis of evidence that you can see in front of you now. But unless that performance actually happens, all you are left with is simply your judgment.

How do people make these judgments? One of the earliest models used to capture these forms of judgments comes to us from a branch of psychology known as Social Judgment Theory. As the name suggests, the theory was developed to help us understand how individuals make decisions in a social setting. In its central paradigm, judgments are assumed to result from the integration of different "cues" or sources of perceptual information from the environment. This paradigm leads us to the lens model, which was first developed and proposed by psychologist Egon Brunswik[2] and is illustrated by figure 8.1.

Before diving deeper into the model and its implications, I need to establish some terminology. In a representation of the lens model, I will use the term "truth" to identify the variable the person is trying to make a prediction or a judgment about. Remember that the truth is not observable, either because of the nature of the variable (e.g., creditworthiness or intellectual ability) or because it will only be knowable sometime in the future (e.g., the market value of a mutual fund). However, there are many pieces of information in the environment that could be used to make an inference about the truth. In the lens model figure, these pieces of information are called "cues." For instance, a PhD admissions officer might use your scores on some standardized tests like GRE or GMAT and your undergraduate grades as cues in making a judgment about your intellectual ability. Likewise, an investor might look at the past performance of the mutual fund, trends in macroeconomic indicators, and indices of investor sentiment as cues in making a judgment about the future market price of a mutual fund.

Figure 8.1 The Lens Model of Judgments

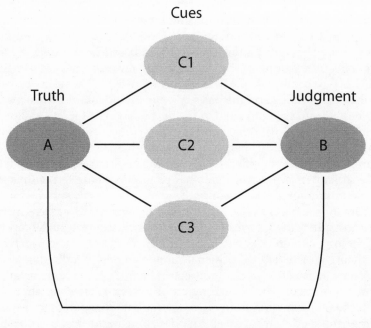

Finally, how good is the judgment? While we will never know the quality of the judgment for any one particular judgment, we could perhaps come up with a measure of how good a judgment is overall. In order to do this, we use a simple concept from statistics called correlation. A correlation refers to a statistical variable that captures the relationship between two strings of data. A correlation of +1 suggests that there is a perfect relationship between the two sets of data such that one set can perfectly predict the other set. A correlation of -1 again suggests that one set of data can perfectly predict the second set, but in the opposite direction. A correlation of 0 implies that there is no way of predicting the performance of either string of data by looking at the other one.

Now that we have a sense of what a correlation is, let's go back to the situation where an individual is making a judgment about the truth based on a number of cues. For now, let's focus on the subset of cases where the judgment is predictive in nature. For instance, an investor is looking to predict the market value of a fund in a couple of years, and a human resources manager is looking to predict the performance of a job applicant after two years. Suppose that these judgments were made on some sort of a numerical scale, much like those test scores referred to earlier. We make a record of all these (numerical) judgments and file them away for two years. After two years have passed, we can now observe the truth – we can actually see the market price of the mutual fund and have access to the performance evaluation of the employees. Therefore, we now have two sets of numbers – the judgments and the truth. Going back to our tool from the previous pages – correlation – we can now compute the correlation between the judgment and the truth. If the correlation is close to 0, our judge isn't very good – her judgments do not allow us to make any predictions about the truth. If the correlation is closer to 1, we have a good judge. We will therefore refer to the correlation between the judgment and the truth as the *performance* of the judge.

Or take a situation in which a human resources (HR) manager needs to make judgments about the performance of new recruits over the next three years (figure 8.2). These new recruits have recently been hired from the University of Toronto (or another fine university). The manager has done a lot of research to show that there are three cues that predict the performance of the employee. The first cue is the employee's IQ score. The second cue is the kind of work experience that he has had in the past, both in terms of quality and quantity. And finally, the third cue is his performance as a student and his educational qualifications. For now, assume that there is a common scale on which one could measure each of these three items.

A Judgment Machine

Focus first on a situation where the truth is not yet known. Our hypothetical HR manager goes through dozens – say 200 – of files containing data on these three cues about each recruit. She then uses her years of experience to make a judgment for each. Focusing on the right-hand side of the lens model for a minute, let's imagine that you could run a regression that looked at this HR manager's judgment as a function of the three cues across these 200 employees. Imagine that you had a "judgment machine" that would mimic the HR manager's judgment process. This is really an experiment where you are running this

Figure 8.2 The Lens Model Applied to the Recruiting Judgment

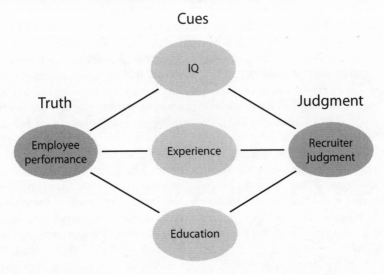

machine 200 times to see what judgment it produces. The resulting regression equation might look something like this:

$$\text{Judgment} = A + b_1 * \text{Cue}_1 + b_2 * \text{Cue}_2 + b_3 * \text{Cue}_3$$

What is this? This is a model of the HR manager's judgment. It is indeed the judgment machine that you imagined in the last paragraph.[3] If tomorrow the manager is sick and hence unable to come to work, you could use this model to predict what the manager would have judged about this particular applicant.

The question is – why would you do this? What value does this bring to the quality of the decision making? A number of studies were done in the 1970s and 1980s that looked at the idea of using a model of the judge – a judgment machine – to see if, in fact, it did better or worse than the judge herself.[4] The basic procedure of these studies was as follows:

Step 1: A panel of experts was asked to make a judgment about some truth on the basis of a number of cues on which data were provided.

Step 2: A "judgment machine" regression equation was created for each judge using the approach described above.

Step 3: The judgment machine was used to generate a prediction of what judgment the expert would have come up with. This is referred to as the Machine-Generated Judgment. Note that at this stage there are two different judgments for each expert for each prediction made: (1) The actual judgment, and (2) the machine-generated judgment.

Step 4: The performances of both the expert and the judgment machine were determined, typically by computing the correlation between the expert's judgment and the truth (when it became available), and the machine-generated judgment and the truth, respectively.

What did this research find? Interestingly, the common theme emerging from several studies was that a judgment machine produced more accurate predictions than a judge. For instance, Caltech economist Colin Camerer[5] reviewed six separate studies and came to the conclusion that using a judgment machine should improve judgments under most realistic judgment situations. In a 1971 study, Lewis Goldberg[6] asked twenty-nine experts to use scores from a standard psychological test to judge which of a sample of 861 patients were primarily psychotic or neurotic. Goldberg presented the experts with scores on eleven variables from the psychological test. He then used a portion of the data to develop a "judgment machine" for each expert and then tested the machine on the rest of the data. In one particular set of tests, the judgment machines were more accurate than 79 percent of the experts.

In another classic study from 1971, one of the legends in the field of judgment and decision making, the late Robyn Dawes, studied PhD admissions decisions by a committee of faculty experts. Dawes found that the decisions made by the judgment machine matched the decisions of the committee. Further, for those applicants who were eventually admitted and accepted to join the PhD program, Dawes found that the performance of the judgment machine in predicting their scholastic achievements was twice as good as the performance of the experts.

As another example, researchers used the domain of marketing to test for the usefulness of judgment machines.[7] Thirteen experienced marketing managers were tasked with forecasting the number of advertising pages *Time* magazine would sell annually over a large window of time. These managers each made forty-two forecasts on the basis of data for a subset of the period. The results showed that (a) of the thirteen managers, the number of errors made by the machine was smaller than the number made by the expert in eleven cases, the number of errors made by the machine and the expert was the same for one case, and the number of errors made by one manager was smaller than that of the machine in one case; and (b) using the judgment machine reduced the number of errors, on average, by 6.4 percent.

I could go on and on describing additional results. There are some studies in which the expert has performed better than the judgment machine, but in the vast majority of cases the judgment machines outperform the experts.

I need to pause here and clarify a very important point. Experts are not being beaten by a machine that has more data or other supernatural capabilities. We are not talking about Deep Blue, the chess-playing computer that famously defeated chess grandmaster Garry Kasparov in 1996 and 1997.[8] Deep Blue had a lot of stored data and complex algorithms that its human opponents clearly did not have access to. In the research just described, the term "judgment machine" refers to a simple regression model of the very same expert it is matched against. In fact, each one of you could easily create a judgment machine for any judgments you routinely make. If you are a clinician, you could create a judgment machine for your clinical judgments; if you are a weather forecaster (or a regular investor), you might again be able to create a judgment machine that can mimic your own judgments. The trick is to know exactly what cues you are using, and to religiously record your judgments and the value of the cues you based those judgments on. The rest is as easy as firing up a spreadsheet on your laptop computer and running a regression.

Is Your Judgment Machine *Really* Better Than You?

When I first read these findings as a PhD student at the University of Chicago, I had one of those a-ha moments – a "This is why I came back to graduate school" moment!

So, the finding naturally raises two questions:

1. Why does this happen – why is a regression model of us better than us?
2. If this is true (and there seems to be a lot of evidence to suggest that it is), what can we do armed with this knowledge?

There is a simple reason for why this happens. Experts are great at knowing what information is relevant (in our language, they are great at identifying cues). Experts are also fantastic at identifying how these cues should be combined and what weighting to use. However, these judgment models are often paramorphic – that is, people don't actually sit down with a paper and pencil and calculate the scores. This is precisely where experts are fallible, because they are mathematically inconsistent. Experts get tired and are easily distracted. Give an expert even a relatively straightforward mathematical task – but one that involves a lot of numbers – and you'll see that he is inconsistent at combining the numbers accurately. This is where the judgment machine helps. Since the judgment machine uses regression, sophisticated readers will be quick to point out that it removes the "error terms" in the judgment. More generally, the judgment machine is consistent – just as a metronome routinely returns the exact same number of beats per second once it has been set, the judgment machine returns the same answer every time it is fed with the same data. This cannot be said for humans, even experts.

Does this mean that we can simply replace experts with their equivalent judgment machines? Could we replace stock analysts, doctors, admission committee members, HR managers, and weather forecasters with regression models? While this seems like an intriguing possibility, only a very naïve student of judgment would propose this as a universal truth. Why? Because the judgment machine is merely a model of the expert. If you have no expert, you have no model. It may be fine to use the machine in the short run, but in the long run there may be several reasons why an expert is essential. First, the environment might change so that additional cues become relevant. Only an expert will know which additional cues to incorporate, or which cues might now not be relevant any more. Second, even if the cues do not change, the relative importance of each might change and this, too, can only be captured by the expert's judgment policy.

Nevertheless, judgment machines have much to offer. Think of a rare form of expertise – perhaps a small number of clinicians in a specialty area of medicine. These specialists tend to be clustered in a small number of locations rather than being spread far and wide across the globe, and hence access can be an issue for patients who are not within geographic range. However, suppose that we were able to create a judgment machine that could mimic the diagnosis of the expert on the basis of a few symptoms (cues). A healthcare worker in a remote area might now be able to use a judgment machine to predict what the specialist would have diagnosed and make triaging decisions based on the outcome. Note that I am not suggesting *replacing* the specialist with the judgment machine, merely using it to make judgments about the urgency of the case and whether emergency treatment is warranted. Expert systems like these could be tremendously helpful in many domains.

Intuition

If we think about expert judgments – whether they are made by managers, physicians, scientists, or financial analysts – one of their defining hallmarks is that they are often made relatively quickly and are the product of much experience and practice. We often refer to such judgments as intuitions. We read earlier about Kahneman's distinction between two systems of processing, where system 1 is intuitive and system 2 is deliberative. What exactly is intuition? Consider the following definition of intuition from Ken Hammond.

"The ordinary meaning of intuition signifies the opposite – a cognitive process that somehow produces an answer, solution, or idea without the use of a conscious, logically defensible step-by-step process."[9]

In this definition, Hammond emphasizes that intuition is a cognitive process, but that it may not be possible for the expert to provide a step-by-step explanation of how he arrived at the judgment. In a similar vein, Robin Hogarth (whom I had the great good fortune to study with as a graduate student at the University of Chicago) wrote a fascinating book called *Educating Intuition* in which he said that "the essence of intuition or intuitive responses is that they are reached with little apparent effort, and typically without conscious awareness. They involve little or no conscious deliberation."[10] Again, this describes the judgment process of experts very well. The reason the experts can make these judgments with little effort is that they have – over the course of their many years of experience – learnt fairly complex patterns of interrelationships between cues and the truth. In the language used in this chapter, they have developed a relatively reliable model of how the cues interact to predict the truth.

In essence, therefore, the judgment machine described earlier is a model of our intuition. Why would you actually look at your own judgments and use regression to model them? There are at least three reasons why this can be beneficial. The first is, it gives you insight into your own decision-making policy and your own judgment policy. It's almost like opening up your head and figuring out how you make choices and judgments. In particular, creating a model of your own intuition can be useful if you find yourself saying, "Well, gee, I know I want to choose [a particular product] or I know I really like [this product], but I'm not quite sure why." Looking at the weights of the different attributes will let you understand what you consider important and what you don't. And perhaps once you have insight into your own judgment and choice, you can then start making changes and corrections to your judgment policy. For instance, perhaps you thought you were weighing price to a great degree in your judgments, but your judgment machine tells you that you were not. So, simply looking at your own equation gives you (a) more insight and (b) avenues for improving the quality of your decision making.

Second, you can actually use a model like this to track changes in your own decision-making policy over time. You could run regressions like this every six months. You could then see if the importance of certain attributes has gone up or gone down. And again, you could perhaps consider more carefully whether, in fact, those attributes should have become more important – or not.

Third, you can use the example of other people whom you consider to be good judges as a benchmark to evaluate your own decision making. Let's imagine you're a doctor. And let's imagine that there is a physician whose judgment you trust. This physician always makes the right diagnosis. And you wonder how she does it. You could try and convince that physician to run a judgment machine of her own clinical diagnoses. At the end of that process, you would end up with an equation. You could then potentially compare your own judgment policy with the policy of this expert and identify the differences between how you and the trusted physician weight the different symptoms.

You could actually make this process a bit more elaborate. Let us imagine that you have two or three experts: one is an expert in domain A, a second is an expert in domain B, and a third is an expert in domain C. Let's say Doctor A is great at making judgments about children's illnesses, Doctor B at diagnosing neurological problems, and Doctor C at diagnosing cardiac problems. You could then create different models for each of them that allow you to draw on Doctor A's expertise in one domain, Doctor B's in a second, and Doctor C's in a third. And you could create much more nuanced models of the intuition that you have of these different positions.

I'd like to step back into the world of intuition (versus deliberation). How should people make good rational choices? In earlier chapters, I discussed a model of decision making called the WADD – the weighted additive decision model. In this model, the utility of a given option or a given product is a function of the combined utility that is delivered by each of its attributes. In particular, if you can decompose a product into multiple attributes and you can assess the importance of each of those attributes to your decision, then the utility is the sum of w, which is the weighting that you place on a given attribute, multiplied by the utility of that attribute, added across all of the attributes. If you really think about that systematic form of decision making, it requires a lot of effort. How does a consumer, for example, choose between two products? How does a policymaker decide which of two policy options he or she should choose?

Here's what they need to do. They need to decompose that policy or that product into as many relevant attributes as they think are important. Then they need to come up with an importance weighting for each of those attributes. Finally, they need to evaluate each attribute on a scale, multiply the weight by the value of the attribute, add up the total to give them the utility or value of every given option, and then pick the option that actually provides the highest value. This is a very complex process. Most of us don't engage in that process for every single decision that we make. Instead, we follow something called intuition or gut feel, or even visceral reactions. Recall that Robin Hogarth proposed that intuitive choices or judgments are reached with little apparent conscious thought. Sometimes we make intuitive judgments in the snap of a finger. We go to a store, and we know what we're going to purchase just by looking at products. Or we look at policy options and we know what the right thing is.

The first thing that is important to keep in mind is that intuition is not necessarily emotion. When you have a good intuition, it doesn't mean that you're just acting on an emotional response. Rather, it means that you have somehow developed a fast approach, a sophisticated yet quick approach, to making choices and making judgments. Where does that sophistication come from?

Typically it comes from expertise. Think about another expert – a weather forecaster called Mr. Sun. Mr. Sun has spent ten or fifteen years of his life seeing different elements of weather (e.g., wind direction and speed, cloud types and nature, atmospheric pressure etc.), understanding their correlational patterns, and relating these patterns to final outcomes (e.g., rain, drizzle, or snow). Mr. Sun does not have a mathematical equation in his head. But every time he sees a certain cluster of weather elements happening at the same time, he can identify the most likely outcome of that pattern. That is intuition. Like any expert, Mr. Sun has somehow assessed the correlation among different variables and has come up with a quick response to that particular set of stimuli.

Training Intuition

Likewise, consumers could have an intuitive set of preferences that they use in making choices. For instance, I know what sort of colors I like. I know what sort of fragrances I like. And I know what sort of visual appearance I want. So when I go to a store and pick up a product like a quilt or a work of art, I don't necessarily spend the time deconstructing that product into its attributes, because I know what I like when I see it. And that, again, is intuition. So, in sum, you can think of intuition as being something that arises from expertise, from a vast experience of dealing with similar tasks in the past. And the process that is used to arrive at that intuitive judgment is something called pattern matching.[11]

What is pattern matching? It is a process in which people look at their historic database – metaphorically speaking – of similar choices that they've made, make a comparison of each with the current situation, retrieve a past situation that looks a lot like the present one, and apply what they did there to the present situation. Pattern matching can be a very quick process and a seemingly effortless process, but that doesn't mean that it is a mindless process.[12] It simply means that the individual is using a lot of rich history in order to make that quick, intuitive decision. When does good learning happen based on experiences in the past? Good learning happens when you get feedback, when that feedback is quick, and when the feedback is unambiguous.

Think of Mr. Sun. Say he makes a prediction that it's going to rain. Within a day, he knows whether it has rained or not. There's no ambiguity to the feedback and it is quick. As a result, weather forecasters not only get quick and unambiguous feedback, they get lots of it, because they make these judgments every single day. Research shows that in fact weather forecasters are fairly well-calibrated.[13] Being well-calibrated means that they have a good intuition about how much they know. In fact, when they say that they're confident, they are generally fairly confident that that outcome is going to happen. When they say they're not confident, then in fact they are truly not confident. But they have a good handle on how much they know.

So, in a nutshell, the trick to developing good intuition is twofold. On the one hand, you should seek to get unambiguous, quick, and voluminous feedback on judgments and predictions that you make. And second, you could develop your own judgment machine and use it as a dashboard to understand, monitor, and improve your intuitive judgments over time.

Consumption Vocabularies

From the topics of mathematical models, judgments, and intuition, I want to drift a bit into an area of research that I have long admired. I'll start the discussion with a simple question: What is common to wine, quilts, and classical music? Obviously, on the surface, they seem like three completely unrelated product categories. But they do have something in common.

If you ask the majority of people who consume one of these three things what they like, they probably will be able to tell you their preference with a fair degree of confidence. Most people can tell you that they like a given wine versus another one, that they like a given piece of music, that they love the pattern on a quilt. But if you ask them why they like what they like, most people do not have a good answer. This sounds a lot like Hammond's definition of an intuitive judgment described earlier!

Now why does this happen? Perhaps people don't know why they like what they like. However, this seems odd given how strongly they like it. If we think about it a bit more deeply, it is easy to realize that a lot of these categories involve sensory inputs. Developing a preference means that the user needs to process sensory information from many different sources and combine them meaningfully. For example, I have a glass of wine in my hand – and my preference is driven by the taste of the wine, the smell, the fact that it feels good in my hands, and the fact that the experience is a good one.

If you ask me why I like this particular glass of wine, I'm probably going to say something along the lines of "because it tastes good." Someone with more expertise in wines than I have might have been able to say that his preference for this glass of wine is a function of the complexity, the bouquet, the aroma, the acidity, and the tannins – all of that lovely stuff that you read about in *Wine Spectator* magazine.

If I only knew what all of those things meant, and if I were able to identify each of those terms with a specific feature of this glass of wine, a few things could happen. First, I would be better able to describe my preferences to you. Second, I might be able to learn more about my own preferences by trying wines that are constant on every single dimension except one. Third, over time, I might start actually making better choices. This is the basis of research by Patricia West and her colleagues on what they call consumption vocabulary.[14] Here's the idea. In a lot of different domains, people know what they like, but they don't know why they like it. And simply providing them with the language to express their preferences helps them not only express them but also develop those preferences further.

Let's look at the example of quilts, a stimulus that was used in some of the studies that West and her colleagues conducted. You can actually deconstruct the liking for a quilt along a number of different dimensions – the border patterns, the sashing, the blocks, the alignment, or the arrangement. These are all the attributes of quilts that you and I would probably not think about but that the expert quilter knows well.

Now imagine a simple experiment. Suppose you have five or ten such attributes and you create a large number of quilts by looking at different combinations of these attributes. Suppose that you come up with 150 different patterns of quilts. Then you do an experiment that looks a lot like a randomized controlled trial but using a *within-participants* design. You then ask each participant to evaluate each of those 150 quilts on a liking scale. Using the participants' liking for each of these quilts and the evaluation of each of those quilts on different attributes (which you can obtain from experts), you could come up with a regression for every particular individual that allows you to model liking as a function of various attributes. This is exactly the equivalent of the "judgment machine" but in the domain of consumer preferences. You have just allowed these individuals to figure out why they like certain quilts and not others. You could similarly decompose people's liking for all kinds of consumption experiences – music, food, clothing, movies, and objects of art – and provide them with a consumption vocabulary.

Results showed that giving people a consumption vocabulary produced the three effects described earlier. First, participants who had received the vocabulary were much better at expressing their preferences. Second, people who had received the vocabulary could understand their preferences better and learn more about them. They were able to come up with their own experiments. They were – for instance – able to compare two products that were identical on all attributes save one to see what the effect of that attribute was. And they therefore understood their preferences better in relation to each attribute. And finally, over time, people who had learned the consumption vocabulary actually made better choices. Their preferences were much more stable. They now had a hook to anchor their preferences on, and hence were able to come up with much more fine-tuned preferences for those quilts.

Much of this chapter has examined the difference between an analytical process and an intuitive or a gut-feeling process in making judgments. By providing people with a consumption vocabulary, we can take a process that is largely intuitive and convert it into an analytical process. By giving people the right vocabulary, we can give them the right criteria to use in assessing their own preferences for products such as the lovely glass of wine that's sitting on my desk. Cheers!

PART THREE

At the Last Mile:
Engineering Behavior Change

9 Choice Repair

In chapter 9
You will find answers to questions such as:

1 *What is choice repair?*

2 *What is de-biasing and how is it different from re-biasing?*

3 *What is the relative superiority of choice architecture over crutches as a choice repair approach?*

In the past twenty years or so that I've been researching in the area of the behavioral sciences, I've come to realize that human behavior is – at its very best – boundedly rational.[1] At its worst, the story is not very pretty at all. The more important question is – how do we help people who clearly have a deficiency in making optimal decisions to make better choices? What do the processes of choice repair look like? In this chapter, I start developing a broad framework on an important last mile challenge – how do we help people make better decisions?

Before digging in any deeper, let me take a minute to clarify terminology and the sense in which I am going to use some words. First, I am going to use the term "choice repair" to talk about anything that is done to help people make better choices. This "anything" could be a product, a program, changes in context, information, or a decision aid, and it could be done by the person who wants to change her behavior or by an external agent. As long as there is an active intention to help improve choices, I will call that activity choice repair. Second, I will keep using the term "intervention." In my book (in both the literal and metaphorical sense), an intervention is a specific tool that is employed to help choice repair. Earlier in the paragraph, I gave the examples of a product, a program, a change in context, information, or a decision aid – and each of these is an excellent example of an intervention.

I would like to draw a simple analogy between a cognitive deficiency and a physical deficiency. A few years ago, my son – who was then a competitive sportsperson – did what many sportspeople do once in a while. He broke his ankle and had to undergo surgery to repair the broken bone. I can imagine that the whole process was not only extremely painful but also extremely inconvenient. Thinking back to my son's broken leg and the rehabilitation programs he had to go through to return to full fitness, it was evident that there were two sets of things that needed to be done. The first involved making sure that he was in a safe environment. A worker from the assisted living department visited our home and made several suggestions about how we could change the context and the environment in which my son lived and engaged in his activities. The goal behind the worker's suggestion was simple – the fact that my son had a temporary handicap meant that he was likely to stumble and fall in environments that were not safe, and the worker wanted to minimize that risk.

The second set of activities that we needed to do to get him up to full fitness included providing him with a mobility device and having him work with a physiotherapist to strengthen the area that had been operated on. I collectively refer to this set of activities as the provision of crutches – devices that help mobility and repair and strengthen the original source of the problem.

I would like to use the metaphor of a physical injury for a cognitive handicap as well. Let us think about the basic paradigm that was built up in the first few chapters. The first claim made was that there is often a discrepancy between what people would like to do and what they actually end up doing and that there is an intention-action gap. The second claim is an implied one – that the goal is well chosen and is constructed with the best of intentions. However, the actions fall short because of some form of cognitive handicap. The handicap could be wide ranging in terms of its origins; perhaps it is an issue of choice complexity and option overload; perhaps there is a framing problem; perhaps the context is conspiring to create perceptual problems for the decision maker; or perhaps cognitive inertia is calling the shots and the choice remains a passive choice and is not dealt with because there is no decision point. No matter what the issue, it is fair to say that there is some sort of cognitive handicap that prevents the closing of the action-intention gap.

If we apply the same line of thinking that was employed for handling a broken ankle to cognitive deficiencies, we'll again see that there are two kinds of ways in which we can help people make better decisions. The first approach involves careful scanning and redesigning of the context in which the decisions are made so that the environment at best steers people toward what they really want to do and at worst doesn't let them stumble and fall. I will refer to this as the choice architecture approach, or the nudging approach. The second approach involves the strengthening of the apparatus that has failed to perform in the first place. This would entail the crutch approach, which simply means giving people the tools to make better choices. These tools could include decision aids, better information and feedback, and access to expertise through advice and consultation. It might also include education – literacy programs that teach people to make better choices in a number of different domains.

Which is the better approach – the choice architecture approach or the crutch approach? I have heard this debate played out in many different forums. For example, in the area of financial well-being, the debate takes on a more specific form – is nudging or financial literacy the better option to promote financial well-being?[2] Proponents of the nudging approach point to empirical evidence suggesting that financial literacy programs actually don't really improve financial outcomes.[3] They also point to evidence showing that people who don't save as much as they would like to are aware of what they need to do but simply don't get around to doing it.[4] Proponents of the literacy approach make the point that while education is empowering, nudging is demeaning. Likewise, they argue that education equips people for lifelong success.[5] There are similar debates in the worlds of healthy eating, weight management, and procrastination management.

Both sides are correct. Let's look at financial well-being or physical activity and exercise. The road to success in both of these domains typically starts with an important action – opening a retirement savings account or joining a health club. These are activities that individuals can be nudged into. There might be a number of other actions they could be nudged into taking; for instance, a default deposit program or a default exercise regimen might get them started toward their ultimate goal. But there will soon come a point where nudging might not help much. Once a person has a retirement account with a few dollars in it, he needs to know where to invest and how. Likewise, a heath enthusiast needs to understand what exercise regimen is best suited to her physiology and how it should evolve over time. Literacy becomes important; crutches become important. In addition, it is important to keep people engaged and motivated in the activity over time. The last chapter revisits the topic of motivation and explores the concept of gamification as one tool to keep people engaged and motivated.

There are three camps of people – one that supports nudging, another that supports a crutch approach, and a third that supports a motivation strategy – and each camp believes that its approach is the best. In reality, I see the three approaches as complementary. Think of well-being as a three-legged stool with nudging, decision crutches, and motivation as the three legs. If you pull out any one leg, the stool comes crashing down.

Getting Started with Choice Repair

Now, before getting into the topic of choice repair, there are a few things to keep in mind. In particular, there are five ideas that I want to focus on. The first is *know your tools*. These tools include an understanding of the psychology of decision making and relevant practical insights from the translation activity we talked about earlier.

Second: before you start designing your intervention, *make sure you know exactly what behavior you want to change*. While this sounds simple, let me assure you that it can be tricky. Sometimes we can define behavior change at a very broad level. For example, I might say that I want people to eat more healthy food or I want savings rates to go up.

But if you think about it, each of these outcomes has a number of specific actions that need to happen to achieve that outcome. For example, how do I get people to save more money? I need them to actually open a retirement account. I need them to make sure that they're monitoring that retirement account, and that they're reviewing and constantly making changes as a function of changes in the environment as well as their own income. For example, do I want people who currently have a bank account to save more? Or do I want more people to open bank accounts? These are two very different outcomes. But they might both result in the same grand outcome, which is an increase in savings rates. If I want people to reduce their electricity consumption, I could either have them upgrade to energy-efficient appliances or simply run their appliances less often or for shorter times.

Third: *clean up your pipes*. What does that mean? Think about the following simple example. Let us imagine that I run a call center for a financial literacy agency that people can call for advice on how to save money. I notice that there are a lot of dropped calls. The calls are dropped because people call in, wait for a period of time, and when their calls don't get answered, they hang up.

Thinking back to the chapter on the psychology of time, there are a number of interesting behavioral strategies I could use to keep those people in the queue. For example, I could play music, or I could give them information about how many people are ahead of them in the call, or I could give them some other distraction task to keep them engaged in the process.

However, if I have a faulty process for answering the calls, these interventions are not going to play a big role. For example, suppose I have no triaging system where a caller calls in, reports the kind of information they need, and then gets directed to one of five different agents. If that doesn't happen, the initial wait times are going to be very long. So what I really need to do is to make sure that my processes for delivering the service are as good as they can be before I try to nudge people into doing what I want them to do. Having a clean pipe allows the behavioral intervention to work as well as possible. Having a clogged pipe reduces the effectiveness of the behavioral intervention. So, before employing any behavioral intervention, be sure that your processes are as good as they can possibly be.

Fourth: keep in mind that *eventually you will need to experiment*. Once you come up with an intervention – be it a crutch or a nudge – you need to be able to assign some people to a control condition and other people to the treatment condition, and then test for the effectiveness of the nudge. So you need to make sure that you have all the processes in place that will allow you to come up with that particular experiment. And fifth: ask yourself *which is the best option for your particular situation* – nudging or a decision crutch? Are there other alternatives? Might an economic incentive be better than a nudging incentive?

As I mentioned earlier, we should not think about the four strategies of behavioral changes as competing against each other. We need to think about using them in conjunction with one another to make sure we end up with the kinds of outcomes we want. Outcomes such as increasing financial well-being have multiple components. Perhaps some of those components are best dealt with by an economic intervention. Perhaps others are best dealt with by using persuasion. And yet others are best dealt with by using a nudging strategy. It is important for us to think through which is the best fit for each component before designing a nudging strategy.

A "bias" is any systematic deviation from a response or decision that you would expect a decision maker to make. Keep in mind that the deviation needs to be systematic. It always has to be in one direction and not random. If the deviation is random, it is noise. If is systematic, it is a bias. Think about a simple bias called overconfidence, a condition in which people believe they know more than they actually do.[6] I will discuss overconfidence in more detail in chapter 11, but for now it is important to note that it is a bias because people do tend to believe that they know more than they do. It's not that some people believe they know more and others believe they know less. That would be noise. The finding that most people believe they know more than they do is a bias. Now, how do you correct for biases, and what are the different ways in which we can think about those corrections?

Corrections can be made by either de-biasing or re-biasing.[7] Both de-biasing and re-biasing are strategies for making a bias go away, but they do so in different ways. Perhaps the best way to illustrate the difference between the two is with a simple visual metaphor. Think about some of those old Western movies in which a fight breaks out in a pub and the bad guy is thrown out of the door. If you close your eyes and recreate such a scene in your head, you'll see the door swinging open, the bad guy being thrown out, and the door swinging shut on its own. The door has a simple spring mechanism. Every time you push it open (which requires some force), the spring compresses and creates a force that pushes the door back into its shut position. These doors are found not only in Western saloons but in more mundane locations such as airports, offices, barns, and stores. But what if there is a defect in the spring – what if the spring is worn and does not exert a force which closes the door when it is in the open position? How would I fix that problem?

There are two things I could do. First, in the language of the social sciences, the fact that the door stays open when pushed is a bias which I need to correct. The first thing I could do is to bring in a handyman to remove the mechanism, clean it up, replace the spring if necessary, re-install it, and make sure that the door now closes. That is a de-biasing mechanism. I have identified the cause of the bias, and I have fixed the cause so that the bias no longer happens.

Alternatively, I could introduce a locking mechanism, a latch that clicks into place when the door is in the shut position. Every time I open the door, I now simply push it back to the closed position and the latch clicks into place to keep the door shut. Let's think closely about what I've done here – the bias still remains, because the underlying cause of the bias, the faulty spring, is still in place. But I have imposed a second mechanism on top of the first to cancel out the effects of the defect. That's called re-biasing.

Let's look at some simple examples of each. I briefly touched on the overconfidence bias. How do we make sure that people are not over-confident? It turns out that there are two common strategies for reducing overconfidence. One strategy is getting people to write down two or three reasons why their judgment or prediction might be wrong.[8] Simply getting people to think about the "what if" scenarios reduces overconfidence. Why? The faulty spring in the cognitive apparatus that causes overconfidence is this – when people make judgments about their ability to accomplish a task, they spontaneously bring to mind scenarios of success, when they were able to get things done. In contrast, they typically fail to think about environmental factors that might impede their progress. By explicitly instructing people to envisage the possibility of failure, you can repair the faulty spring and de-bias that particular judgment.

Now, let's look at a second example, a self-control failure. I have spoken a lot about the fact that people want to save more for the future but have difficulty doing so. I mentioned a simple program called Save More Tomorrow – the idea that you commit to save for the future by promising to set aside a portion of your next salary increase.[9] That program works. People who participate in the Save More Tomorrow program actually do save more. However, it is not clear that they have become any better at either exerting self-control or becoming more of an expert on retirement savings. What the program does is use the principles of loss aversion and the default effect to nudge people into saving more. The program hasn't repaired the cognitive apparatus, per se; it has simply added a latch to change outcomes. That is a classic re-biasing example.

Table 9.1 below provides a description of several common biases that have been documented by behavioral researchers, their underlying cause, some corrective strategies, and a comment on whether the corrective approach is a de-biasing approach or a re-biasing approach.[10]

There are three kinds of de-biasing strategies. The first kind is motivational. If you motivate people to come up with the right answer, they will. How do we motivate people? You could give them financial incentives. Or you could respond to their sense of being socially correct – exert peer pressure by having them make public commitments. Once there is some external stimulus that gets people to be more motivated to be accurate, they are more likely to process information more effectively and to draw more information into their decision.

The second kind of strategy that can be used to reduce biases is cognitive – getting people to think differently, or training people, or generating templates to use that provide them with the right kind of data, or forcing them to think through model-based approaches for making decisions. The strategy identified above for correcting for overconfidence is an example.

The third kind of strategy is technological. This type includes the use of decision supports or aids or online databases to provide people with the data they need to make the best choices.

While the distinction is not completely cut and dried, I like to think of choice architecture strategies as re-biasing approaches and decision crutch strategies as de-biasing approaches. The next two chapters will do a deep dive into both sets of approaches.

Table 9.1 De-biasing versus Re-biasing

The Bias	The Cause	Corrective Strategies	De-biasing or Re-biasing
Overconfidence People believe that their knowledge and abilities exceed their actual knowledge and abilities.	Selective focus on evidence supporting the chosen answer; spontaneous scenarios of success	Generating for-and-against arguments for the chosen answer and identifying ways in which things could go wrong	De-biasing
The duration heuristic bias People believe that services that last longer are more valuable than those that last a shorter time.	An implicit belief that time is a carrier of value, and that more value accrues as more time passes	Asking participants to evaluate the efficiency of the service provider[11]	De-biasing
Placebo effect People believe that the greater the perceived price of a product, the greater its apparent efficacy.	A belief that higher-priced products are made from higher-quality inputs	Drawing attention to price-efficacy beliefs and having participants question those beliefs[12]	De-biasing
Anchoring effect A salient number in the environment results in an estimate being numerically very close to the anchor	Increase of anchor-consistent knowledge.	Asking respondents to consider the opposite response[13]	De-biasing
Conjunction fallacy People believe that the likelihood of a conjoined event (e.g. "Federer will lose the first set but will win the match") is greater than the likelihood of a component event ("Federer will win the match").	Low ability to reason about probability	Translating probabilities into frequency formats[14]	De-biasing
Negative wage elasticity Cab drivers work less on high-wage days when in fact they should be working harder to cash in.	Narrow bracketing of decision and loss aversion – they meet daily quotas sooner	Increasing experience and educating people about intertemporal allocation of income and leisure[15]	De-biasing

The Bias	The Cause	Corrective Strategies	De-biasing or Re-biasing
Overspending with credit card People who routinely use credit cards (vs. checks) to make payments report higher willingness to purchase indulgences.	Weak memory of past payment and its aversive impact	Payment mechanism facilitating past payments rehearsal and immediacy payment depletion[16]	De-biasing
Sunk cost effect for time The sunk cost effect, which is a robust phenomenon for money, is not easily detected in the domain of time.	Mental linkage of cost and benefit and the pervasive need to account; difficulty of evaluating the cost of time hampers accounting	Presenting costs as time[17]	Re-biasing
Low holistic judgment consistency When judges are presented with the same set of cues over time, their judgment based on the cues differs.	Inconsistency of individual judgments across situations as a result of shallow cognitive processing	Providing people with linear statistics models[18]	Re-biasing
Preference reversal resulting from separate vs. joint evaluation When people choose between pairs of options, the option that gets chosen in a binary choice setting might not be the better one when people are asked to make satisfaction judgments.	Attribute evaluability – some attributes are easier to evaluate when there are two options side by side, and these attributes matter more for choice than for satisfaction	Changing the attribute importance manipulation[19]	Re-biasing
Low rates of organ donation Organ donations are low in many countries.	Lack of awareness and motivation	Changing the default on organ donation	Re-biasing
Low retirement savings The average savings rate is lower than what people would like it to be.	Self-control failure	Changing the status quo and making use of precommitment	Re-biasing

10 Choice Architecture: A Process Approach

In chapter 10
You will find answers to questions such as:

1 *What are the different types of nudging approaches and how can they be categorized?*

2 *What are some examples of these approaches?*

3 *What are the four questions to ask as you start designing nudging interventions?*

4 *What is a decision audit? How is it done?*

5 *What is the process for designing a nudge?*

The past few chapters have looked at a variety of behavioral insights and outlined some of the methods of the behavioral scientist. They have also described several examples of nudges. The nudge is perhaps one of the most effective tools for making the last mile more navigable for organizations and their stakeholders alike. Where do the ideas for nudges come from? Is there a process for identifying potential nudges? What criteria should we use to choose among the many possible types of nudges?

From slight changes in text to new product innovations, nudges vary widely in terms of their implementation and characteristics.[1] Regardless of the method or medium used for implementation, there are four dimensions along which these nudges could be categorized

1. Boosting Self-Control versus Activating a Desired Behavior
2. Externally Imposed versus Self-Imposed
3. Mindful versus Mindless
4. Encouraging versus Discouraging

The first dimension looks at whether a nudge is designed to *boost self-control* and help individuals follow through with a decision that they had hoped to act on but failed to do so in the past (e.g., contributing to a retirement plan). With certain behaviors, such as saving money or exercising, there is a discrepancy between what people would like to do and what people end up doing. Nudges that help boost self-control will correct this discrepancy. In other domains such as littering, individuals might not always actively consider what the right behavior should be. In this case, nudges are designed to activate a desired behavior or norm and influence a decision that an individual is indifferent or inattentive to. These behaviors are not top-of-mind for the majority of people; hence people are unlikely to impose nudges on themselves that influence these behaviors. Therefore, nudges that seek to activate latent or non-existent behavioral standards in people rely on exposing them to conditions in which those standards become more salient.

The second dimension considers whether a nudge will be voluntarily adopted. Self-imposed nudges are voluntarily adopted by people who wish to enact a behavioral standard that they feel is important. Such nudges may include using products, such as the well-known Save More Tomorrow™ program,[2] or practices such as voluntarily asking for a reduction on one's credit limit. Another example of a self-imposed nudge is a product called the Clocky.[3] This is an alarm clock that has the ability to run away and hide itself in a corner of the bedroom when the user attempts to hit the snooze button. Externally imposed nudges do not require people to voluntarily seek them out. Rather they passively shape behavior because of the way they present available options without constraining them.

The third dimension considers whether a nudge will guide the individual to take a more cognitive, deliberate approach to decision making and remove some of the effects of the often unconscious behavioral influences present in the context; or whether it will guide them toward a more automatic, implicit approach that utilizes well-established behavioral influences or heuristics. Mindful nudges guide individuals toward a more controlled state and help people achieve a behavioral standard they aspire to but have trouble meeting. Such nudges influence the intention to eat healthier, stop smoking, exercise, and save more. Mostly, these nudges help people make better intertemporal choices so that their behavior in the present better reflects their wishes for the future. Mindless nudges include the use of emotion, framing, or anchoring to sway the decisions that people make.

The fourth dimension considers whether a nudge encourages or discourages behavior. Encouraging nudges facilitate the implementation or continuation of a particular target behavior. Discouraging nudges on the other hand, hinder or prevent behavior that is believed to be undesirable, or behavior that hinders the achievement of the target behavior.

These four dimensions combined result in twelve different types of nudges. The framework in table 10.1 below displays a taxonomy that has been developed based on the dimensions discussed above and lists specific examples for each type of nudge. More comprehensive programs might have multiple "nudges" embedded in them, and hence it is possible that these programs fall across multiple categories.

Nudging: Some Case Studies

This section describes a few representative cases to illustrate how nudges have been used to help individuals make better decisions. A table is included at the end of each case to locate the nudging intervention in the context of the taxonomy just described.

Table 10.1 A Taxonomy of Nudges

		MINDFUL		MINDLESS	
		ENCOURAGE	DISCOURAGE	ENCOURAGE	DISCOURAGE
ACTIVATING A DESIRED BEHAVIOR	EXTERNALLY IMPOSED	Simplifying tax rules to make tax filing easier	Placing signs to remind people not to litter	Advertising that most people are recycling to increase recycling efforts	Using fake speed bumps to discourage speeding
BOOSTING SELF-CONTROL	EXTERNALLY IMPOSED	Simplifying application processes for college grants to encourage higher-level education	Installing car dashboards that track mileage to reduce gas usage	Automatically enrolling for prescription refills to encourage taking medication	Placing unhealthy foods in harder-to-reach places
	SELF-IMPOSED	Maintaining an exercise routine by agreeing to pay a small penalty if a gym session is missed	Avoiding drunk driving by hiring a limo service beforehand	Joining a peer savings group to encourage saving money	Channeling money into a separate account to reduce the likelihood of its being spent

Case 1: Using Descriptive Social Norms to Increase Voter Participation

The need to improve voter turnout is a common issue in many countries. A common strategy used by voting campaigns is to emphasize low voter turnout in the hopes that it will motivate citizens to vote and make a difference. Emphasizing the opposite – that voting is a common social practice – could be a more effective strategy (see table 10.2).

The experiments conducted by Alan Gerber and Todd Rogers compared the effects of both strategies on voter intention during the 2005 New Jersey and 2006 California elections. A phone campaign was developed using two sets of telephone scripts – one emphasizing that voter turnout was expected to be low (low-turnout script), and another

Table 10.2 Case 1

		Mindful		Mindless	
		Encourage	Discourage	Encourage	Discourage
Activating A Desired Behavior	Externally Imposed			X	
Boosting Self-Control	Externally Imposed				
	Self-Imposed				

emphasizing that voter turnout was expected to be high (high-turnout script). After listening to the script, respondents were asked how likely they were to vote in the upcoming election.

The results showed that the high-turnout script increased the likelihood of receiving a "100 percent likely to vote" response by 7 percent. In addition, researchers found that the high-turnout script was most effective with respondents who were occasional and infrequent voters.[4]

Case 2: A Nudge to the Garbage Bin

Littering is a problem for many cities. While many people know the harmful effects of littering, they still continue to litter. In Copenhagen for example, it is estimated that one in three individuals will occasionally litter. To resolve this problem, a research team from Roskilde University tested a nudge to help pedestrians avoid littering (see table 10.3).

The team placed green footprints that led to various garbage bins in the city and handed out caramels to nearby pedestrians. After handing out the caramels, they observed how many pedestrians would follow the footprints to the garbage bin and dispose of the caramel wrapper. The results showed that there was a 46 percent decrease in caramel wrappers littering the streets when the green footprints were in use.[5]

Case 3: Gym-Pact: Using Motivational Fees as a Commitment Device for Exercising

Exercising is a common New Year's resolution many people make but fail to follow through with during the year. One reason, according to

Table 10.3 Case 2

		Mindful		Mindless	
		Encourage	Discourage	Encourage	Discourage
Activating A Desired Behavior	Externally Imposed			X	
Boosting Self-Control	Externally Imposed				
	Self-Imposed				

Yifan Zhang, co-founder of Gym-Pact, has to do with gym membership. Gym memberships are usually paid at the beginning of the year. Once that hurdle has been taken, for the individual the money is spent (sunk), and missing a gym session does not hurt any more than it would to attend. Yifan Zhang and Geoff Oberhofer developed Gym-Pact to counteract this problem by using what they call "motivational fees." Participants set a target number of gym visits each week and need to pay a penalty fee when they miss a gym session.

In Gym-Pact's initial trial phases, Zhang and Oberhofer purchased memberships on behalf of the participants. Participants did not pay for their membership but committed to exercising four times a week. If they failed to follow through, the participants would need to pay $25. If participants left the program, they would need to pay $75.[6]

Gym-Pact has become a full-fledged business, and while the business model has been adapted slightly it still uses the concept of motivational fees. Specifically, participants still pay a penalty for missing their commitments, but the penalties are now distributed back to the participants who managed to follow through, as a small reward. The program is quite successful and, in its first five months, participants have followed through with their commitments 90 percent of the time (see table 10.4).[7]

Gym-Pact has been featured in the press and has expanded its business to help individuals track workouts not only at the gym but also at home and outdoors.[8]

Case 4: Self-Help with Peer Pressure as a Savings Commitment Device

A group of researchers studied the effects of peer pressure in self-help groups on savings behavior and found that it was effective in helping

Table 10.4 Case 3

| | | Mindful | | Mindless | |
		Encourage	Discourage	Encourage	Discourage
Activating A Desired Behavior	Externally Imposed				
Boosting Self-Control	Externally Imposed				
	Self-Imposed	X			

individuals save money. The experiments were conducted in Chile with low-income micro-entrepreneurs who earned an average of 84,188 pesos (U.S. $175) per month. Sixty-eight percent of participants did not have a savings account prior to the study and were required to sign up for an account based on the savings group they were assigned to:

1. Savings group 1 – a basic savings account with an interest rate of 0.3 percent.
2. Savings group 2 – a basic savings account with an interest rate of 0.3 percent. The participants were also part of a self-help peer group, where they could voluntarily announce their savings goals and monitor their progress on a weekly basis.
3. Savings group 3 – a high-interest account with a rate of 5 percent (the best available rate in Chile).

The study found that participants who were a part of the self-help peer group (savings group 2) deposited money 3.5 times more often than other participants, and their average savings balance was almost double that of those who held a basic savings account. The high interest rate had very little effect on most participants.

To further understand why self-help peer groups work, a second study was conducted a year later. The participants were divided into two groups. One group received text messages that notified participants of their progress and the progress of other participants. They were assigned a savings buddy with whom they would meet on a regular basis and who would hold them accountable for meeting their savings goals. The other group only received text messages that notified participants of their progress and the progress of other participants.

Table 10.5 Case 4

		Mindful		Mindless	
		Encourage	Discourage	Encourage	Discourage
Activating A Desired Behavior	Externally Imposed				
Boosting Self-Control	Externally Imposed				
	Self-Imposed	X		X	

The results of the second experiment (see table 10.5) found that having a savings buddy made very little difference and that receiving text messages indicating their progress and the progress of their peers was just as effective. As noted by the researchers, having peer groups was an effective commitment device to achieving savings goals, but meeting in person was not necessary.[9]

Case 5: The Waterpebble: A Water Conservation Device

The Waterpebble is an inexpensive device designed to help individuals conserve water when showering. The device memorizes the length of the first shower and uses it as a benchmark for subsequent showers. Rather than displaying the amount of water being used, the Waterpebble automatically reduces the shower length and uses a series of traffic light signals to suggest when it is time to get out of the shower.

Instead of requiring individuals to monitor their water usage and adjust their consumption accordingly, the Waterpebble removes much of the effort needed to reduce water consumption and makes the process effortless (see table 10.6). It is also possible that over time, individuals will get into the habit of taking shorter showers.[10]

The Process of Designing Nudging Interventions

As a choice architect in any given domain, you need to ask yourself the following simple question: What are the various behaviors and activities that need to happen for any ultimate goal to be achieved? Answering this question requires you to identify every single stage that the individual needs to go through and link them together like a flowchart. For

Table 10.6 Case 5

		Mindful		Mindless	
		Encourage	Discourage	Encourage	Discourage
Activating A Desired Behavior	Externally Imposed				
Boosting Self-Control	Externally Imposed				
	Self-Imposed				X

instance, for an individual to get a flu shot, she should first recognize the need, then identify when and where she can get the shot, then actually find time in her calendar to schedule a visit to the clinic, and finally go with any necessary paperwork. I like to think of this process as a series of pipes through which individuals need to flow from one stage to another stage. As with the plumbing in your house, these pipes sometimes get clogged. In a plumbing context, the clogging happens because of accumulated debris; in a behavioral context, the clogging happens due to behavioral phenomena like inertia, the status-quo bias, or the lack of attention to and awareness of the importance of moving ahead. And just as a plumber will use a brush to clear away the clogs and restore the flow, the choice architect needs to bring out an arsenal of behavioral brushes to clean up the bottlenecks that prevent the desirable outcomes from occurring.

The first step in the process of designing an effective nudging strategy is to audit the decision-making process of the end user. This requires analysis of the context and the task (e.g., How do people make decisions? What are the typical circumstances in which they do that?) followed by identification of the key heuristics and influences that may affect the decision outcome. Figure 10.1 identifies a process approach to the design of a nudge.

Step 1: Map the Context

Auditing the decision-making process will identify factors that prevent individuals from following through with their intentions. These factors (bottlenecks) represent areas where a nudging strategy might yield quick dividends.

Figure 10.1 A Process Approach to Designing a Nudge

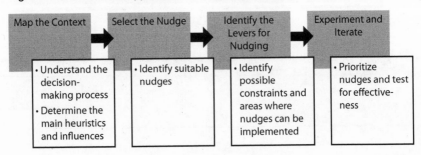

Appendix 2 in this book presents a worksheet listing a set of questions that should be answered when performing an audit. The questions address four different aspects of the decision-making process:

1. **The properties of the decision** including understanding the incentives and motivations associated with the decision, and how much attention the decision receives. It also includes identifying the choices presented to the individual, especially the default option.
2. **Information sources** and how information related to the decision is gathered and presented.
3. **Features of the individual's mindset** and whether emotions influence the outcome of the decision.
4. **Environmental and social factors** such as peer pressure and lengthy application processes. These factors can also influence the outcome.

After the decision has been audited, a map of the decision-making process should be made. This decision map outlines the critical actions involved with following through with a decision. Figure 10.2 shows a decision map for contributing to a retirement savings plan.

Typically, the outcome that a practitioner is aiming to influence is the culmination of a number of smaller decisions and actions. One of the biggest challenges (especially in domains like health or wealth management, where the outcomes are distant and seemingly irrelevant to a young person), is to trigger recognition of the importance of health and wealth management.[11] The desire to achieve an outcome (e.g., savings for a family home, children's education expenses) could be the

Figure 10.2: A Decision Map for Retirement Savings

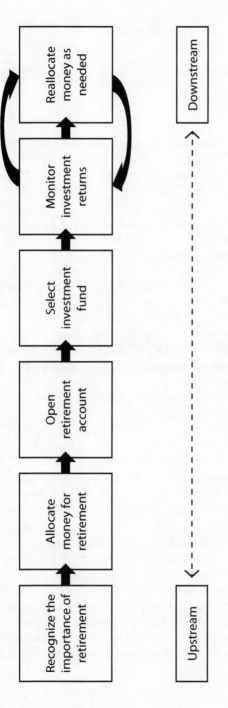

result of a life event (e.g., marriage, birth of a child) that motivates an individual to complete the needed actions (e.g., open an account, purchase a fund). These life events are good moments to nudge people to action.

Step 2: Select Nudges

Bottlenecks in the process are good starting places to implement a nudge. For example, determining a contribution amount requires two evaluations: determining how much money is available for retirement savings, and determining how much is needed for retirement. Understanding how much money is needed for retirement can be a bottleneck because individuals may not have the appropriate calculation tools. Another bottleneck is related to emotion – individuals may not feel they have enough money to contribute to retirement and do not bother to investigate their options. An additional bottleneck that exists further down the line occurs when selecting an investment fund. Too many investment funds are available as options and the individual does not have the capability to analyze all options.

In thinking through a solution to the bottlenecks that an individual might face, it is recommended that the choice architect think through these four questions that map onto the factors in our taxonomy:

1. Is the individual aware of what he needs to do but unable to accomplish it, or does a desired behavior/action need to be activated?
2. Is he motivated enough to impose a nudge on himself?
3. Is the action more likely to be taken with increased cognition, or is the individual currently hampered by cognitive overload?
4. Is the desired action not being accomplished because of a competing action or because of inertia? Consequently, should we aim to discourage the competing action or encourage the target action?

Figure 10.3 shows the decision map for retirement savings that was sketched earlier with several potential bottlenecks also sketched in. Note that these bottlenecks could be caused by one or more of the many behavioral insights discussed throughout this book.

Perhaps the biggest bottleneck in solving the retirement savings problem is need recognition – the fact that people seem to believe that retirement is still some time away and that it is too early to start thinking about it. Other bottlenecks might include cognitive difficulties,

Figure 10.3: Identifying Bottlenecks in the Decision Map

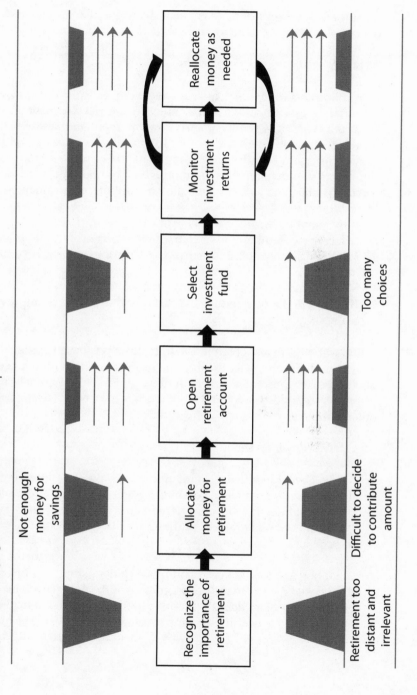

inability to get things done (e.g., open the relevant accounts), or being overwhelmed by too many options.

Step 3: Identify a Lever for Nudging

Identifying constraints such as cost and resource availability, as well as potential levers for nudging will quicken the development process. What is a lever? It is simply a behavioral intervention that can be used to address the bottleneck and reverse its effects. As discussed in chapter 8, the lever could be either de-biasing in nature or re-biasing in nature. While this step depends heavily on the type of nudges identified, it is useful to determine whether the following options are available:

1. Implementing an automatic enrolment process.
2. Offering a default option or changing the current default option.
3. Modifying or changing the current choices that are available to the individual.
4. Simplifying the decision-making process.
5. Using technology to reduce the cost (per individual) or improve scalability.

In addition, the responses to the four questions posed in step 3 will allow the choice architect to align the problem areas with the taxonomy (and cases) presented earlier in this chapter. This alignment might provide specific ideas about how bottlenecks have been "cleared up" in other situations.

Step 4: Design and Iterate

You may have identified several nudges as possible interventions. While it is always possible to combine nudges, it is useful to prioritize. One factor that needs to be considered is the operational costs associated with implementation. In addition to the operational costs, one should consider:

1. What bottlenecks the nudges address. Nudges should be prioritized based on where the bottlenecks lie in the decision-making process. Choose nudges that resolve bottlenecks that are further upstream in the decision-making process.

2. Relative reach. Self-imposed nudges such as pre-commitment may not reach as many people as defaults or automatic enrolment. Although it may be in his best interest, an individual may not want to make an upfront commitment.
3. Capacity for customizing. Interventions like automatic enrolment have a high adoption rate but require everyone to accept the same terms and benefits.[12] An automatic enrolment program, for example, may require an individual to contribute $200 a month to a predetermined retirement savings plan. A significant portion of the target audience may not benefit from such a program, perhaps because the contribution amount is too high or because the investment fund does not match their risk appetite. What may be preferable is to allow everyone to determine their own contribution amount and select from a small assortment of investment funds. Determining whether segments of the target audience have different behavioral preferences will provide answers to this issue.
4. The long-term effectiveness of the nudge and whether the intervention could lead to the development of new, more beneficial habits.

As discussed in an earlier chapter, it is important for the choice architect to test and document the effectiveness of nudging strategies. Richard Thaler provides two mantras for testing nudging strategies: (a) if [one wants to] encourage some activity, make it easy (and/or make it fun), and (b) [one can't do] evidence-based policy without evidence.[13] To these two mantras, I offer a third mantra – document the results and share them widely. This will allow for the creation of a database of what works and under what conditions.

It is recommended that the testing of nudges incorporate both a process evaluation and an outcome evaluation. An *outcome* evaluation merely confirms that the nudge has produced the desired outcome. For instance, an outcome evaluation of the "Planning Aid to Increase Savings Participation" would simply demonstrate that people who were randomly assigned to have access to the nudge participated at a greater rate than people who did not. A *process* evaluation seeks support for the underlying mechanism. For instance, people who were nudged should report a greater ease in comprehending materials and a shorter time in completing the necessary forms.

I would like to leave the reader with some food for thought. A number of people who read the work of behavioral stalwarts like Thaler,

Kahneman, Ariely, or members of the Behavioural Insights Team in the United Kingdom (to name a few) ask me how these researchers come up with brilliant interventions. Is it that they are steeped in the study of psychology that makes them experts who can intuitively pull ideas out of the bag? Or are they simply very clever people? While I do not deny that both of these are true, I also offer two additional observations. First, the process of mapping and identifying bottlenecks and then using levers to clear them up that is articulated in this chapter is – in essence – a good paramorphic model of what many successful behavioral researchers do. Second, many readers fall prey to the availability bias because of the nature of the scientific publication process. More particularly, most readers have access to the success stories but not to the failures. Over years of developing and testing interventions, our success rate improves, but it is still never quite 100 percent.

One key reason why it isn't 100 percent is the simple – yet powerful – fact that, when it comes to making choices, everything matters! When you're in a store, absolutely everything around you could influence what you buy: the display, the price presentation, the background color, the presence of crowds, the ambient temperature, smells ... the list goes on. What's more, these factors could also interact with each other. For instance, price presentation could make a difference but only for products in a certain category. Therefore, many decision scientists make predictions that work well in some contexts but not in others. If we wanted to develop a comprehensive theory of decision making, we would need to theorize about and test a very large number of factors, and an even larger number of interactions between these factors. Given the inherent stochasticity of human behavior, such an undertaking seems not only enormously difficult but, realistically, impossible. After all, even hard sciences such as physics have failed to articulate a theory of everything.[14]

The reality, then, is that theory can take us so far in our quest for nudging interventions and no farther. Theory can show us the way, but without testing the interventions using the principles of experimental designs described earlier, we risk failure because of something in the background context that trips up the effectiveness of our intervention.

11 Decision Crutches

In chapter 11
You will find answers to questions such as:

1 *Why does people's long-distance calling drop temporarily after they receive a phone bill?*

2 *How do businesses like Weight Watchers, Fitbit, and Toyota capitalize on the basic need of people to act on feedback?*

3 *If two experts gave you advice on a judgment, how should you combine their advice?*

4 *What is a model-based decision-support system and what is a case-based system? Which one is better?*

5 *How can a model be combined with managerial intuition for the best results?*

After going through the choice architecture approach to helping people make better choices, I turn in this chapter to the use of decision crutches to aid decision making at the last mile. In particular, the chapter elaborates on five different forms of decision crutches.

Crutch 1: Feedback. Giving people feedback about their past choices and outcomes improves decision making.

Crutch 2: Advice. Providing the right kind of advice can improve decision making.

Crutch 3: Past Cases and Examples. Providing people with situations that are similar to the present situation and the resulting outcomes can improve decision making.

Crutch 4: A Model. Providing people with a structured model can help them make better choices.

Crutch 5: Consumption Vocabulary. Providing people with a consumption vocabulary allows them to better understand and test their preferences.

Feedback

The simplest crutch you can provide to people is data or feedback. Think for a moment about a host of behaviors that most people have trouble with: curbing spending, healthy eating, procrastination, and energy conservation are some examples. All of these domains are classic examples of distributed decisions. What is a distributed decision? In the words of the late Harvard psychologist Richard Herrnstein and MIT's Drazen Prelec, a distributed choice is "an aggregate of many smaller decisions distributed over a period of time."[1] In other words, any one shopping trip does not make you bankrupt, any one instance of eating a chocolate cake does not damage your health, any one unproductive day does not cause severe backlogs at work, and any one instance of leaving the lights on does not deplete the world's energy reserves significantly. However, a long sequence of making such choices will indeed cause negative outcomes.

One corollary of the way in which distributed decisions are defined is that each single decision – each choice – is not significantly effortful, and also not significantly memorable after the fact. There are obviously some exceptions to this corollary; for instance, smokers can often look back at their first cigarette as a significant decision, and a spender might recall a particularly busy day at the shopping center where he went on

a shopping binge. But, these particularly memorable instances notwithstanding, it is hard for the human brain to keep a ledger of past
instances. When reaching into our wallets to retrieve a credit card to
make a quick purchase or leaving home without checking to see if un-
necessary lights and appliances have been switched off, we are typically not burdened by the memory of past instances. In the language
of research into heuristics and biases, past instances are typically not
available to us. What if we could make them available?

In chapter 4, I described an experiment I did many years ago, when
I invited a number of participants into the laboratory and recreated the
mechanics of making payments by checks and credit cards. Participants
in my study made a number of payments – ostensibly over the duration of a month – either by credit card or by writing checks. At the end
of this "month," everyone was presented with a purchase opportunity
for an indulgence; a product they didn't need but would like to have.
People who used credit cards were more likely to want to make that
purchase.

There's a twist to the story, though. In a second set of conditions
in that same experiment, I provided my participants with feedback –
specifically, at the beginning of each day of the "month" – telling them
what their cumulative spending for the month up to that day had been.
This intervention had two effects. First, the difference between participants' use of credit cards versus checks disappeared – now their willingness to purchase an indulgence did not depend on which payment
method they had used in the past. Second, their willingness to purchase the indulgence declined overall. Clearly, the feedback mattered
significantly. Since most of the past payments were relatively pallid
and non-memorable, the provision of the feedback allowed participants to accurately calibrate their past expenses and make a more informed purchasing decision.

A second example of providing feedback comes from an informal
experiment that I and some students did in the city of Toronto in 2004–
2005. We were interested in seeing how we could encourage people to
recycle more and hence to reduce how much garbage they generated.
Garbage is a classic example of a non-memorable distributed decision.
Every week householders left their garbage bags on the curbside, and
the municipality arranged to have trucks come by to pick up the garbage. We actually gave people feedback on the amount of garbage they
had produced in a given period of time. Households received a statement – much like a credit card statement – showing our estimate of how

much garbage they had generated. We found that making people more aware of the quantity of garbage they had generated caused them to produce less garbage and engage in more recycling. A third example comes from research I did with Vivian Lam, a former research associate in Hong Kong.[2] This study was done in the 1990s when long-distance calling from one's home phone was still fairly expensive. We collected long-distance telephone calling records of a number of individuals in Colorado over a period of time. We had information on when these people made calls, what each call cost them, when they received their monthly bills, and when they paid their bills. We found that there was a strong and significant dip in long-distance calling activity shortly after the consumers received their bills, and that this effect happened even when most of the calling activity had occurred early in the month. Clearly, feedback about consumers' long-distance calling resulted in a dip in consumption.

In addition to numerous other examples of academic research showing that feedback can help decision making, there are a number of examples of businesses that rely on the need for feedback. In the domain of weight management, Weight Watchers relies extensively on the principle of feedback by creating a system in which users keep track of their caloric intake and are then fed back the information that they can slice and dice to help them make better eating choices.[3] To encourage people to remain physically active, FitBit asks users to wear a device that monitors their activity and provides them with feedback on their physical movement that they can benchmark against other days or other patterns of activity.[4] Likewise, in order to help their users sleep well, SleepBot – a smartphone app – provides them with detailed feedback on sleeping patterns.[5] And the dashboard of hybrid vehicles like the Prius provides drivers with feedback on many aspects of their vehicle's current performance so that they can take suitable actions to improve their vehicle's functioning and reduce fuel consumption.[6]

Feedback not only helps people make better consumption decisions; it can also help improve decision making by addressing other decision biases. Consider, for example, one of the more documented biases in the field of the behavioral sciences – overconfidence,[7] a bias discussed earlier in chapter 9. The overconfidence bias refers to the idea that people think they know more than they actually know. One powerful way in which to correct for the overconfidence bias is to provide rapid and unambiguous feedback.[8] In one example, geologists at the petroleum company Shell made forecasts about the likelihood that oil might be struck at certain locations. They were overconfident, resulting in a lot of wasted effort, time, and money in looking for oil. In response, Shell developed a training program in which geologists were given past cases, asked to make a prediction, and then given immediate feedback on what had actually happened in that case. Elsewhere in this book, it was noted that weather forecasters get a large volume of quick and unambiguous feedback. As a result, it is perhaps not surprising to learn that weather forecasters show very little to no overconfidence!

Advice Taking

We've all gone to local fairs and amusement parks where a popular attraction is the "jellybeans in the jar" guessing contest. The idea is simple – there are a number of jellybeans in a glass jar and your job is to guess the number. The person whose guess is closest to the correct answer wins (and in many cases wins the jellybeans and the jar!).

How does one estimate the number of jellybeans in a jar? Perhaps one of you knows how many jellybeans fit in an average jar, so you could make an estimate of the proportion of the jar that is filled and then come up with an estimate. Alternatively, you could estimate two quantities – how many jellybeans would occupy the floor of the jar if they were packed into one layer, and the number of layers – and then multiply the two to form an estimate. Or, you could simply ask a friend – or friends!

Let's imagine we know that there are forty jellybeans in a jar. Now let's imagine that you ask two people how many jellybeans there are, and let's say that those two people give you an estimate each. How would you aggregate their two estimates in order to arrive at a judgment of your own?

What I like about the "jellybeans in a jar" game is that it is a metaphor for many kinds of judgments that we make about things that are going to happen in the future. When you hire a new employee, you're making a judgment about how well he or she is going to perform for you. When you buy a stock, you're making a judgment about what its price is going to be five years from now. We routinely undertake many, many judgment tasks of this type. And asking other people or experts for advice in making these judgments is often a very good strategy to use.

So let's go back to the jars. One of the people – the experts – you asked for advice estimates the number to be fifty, the other sixty. What do I do with these estimates? There are two sorts of things you could do. First, you could decide which of the two people is the more reliable expert and go with that person's estimate. Or you could combine the two estimates by simply averaging the two numbers. Which is the better strategy?

Given that we know that the correct answer is forty, we also know that both experts over-predicted. One of the experts was off by ten jellybeans; the other was off by twenty. But let's say you took the average of the two estimates. The average is fifty-five, and the average error, therefore, is fifteen. It's better than one expert, but not as good as the other one. The second possibility is that one of the experts over-predicts while the other one under-predicts. So let's say, for example, one expert tells you that there are fifty jellybeans in the jar; the second estimates twenty-eight. Now the average is thirty-nine, and the average error is one.

In summary, if you ask people for estimates, one of two things could happen. First, both of people might over- or under-predict, in which case your average is better than one expert, but not as good as the other one. Or, one under-predicts and one over-predicts. If that happens, the average is always going to be better than either of the two judges independently.

What is that telling us? That's telling us that in many real-world cases, averaging the opinion of two judges is often better than taking the advice of any one judge on her own.[9] It is definitely better than trying to figure out which of these two experts is the more reliable and going with that person's estimate. In particular, if you could engineer differences between the two experts such that it is likely that one over-predicts and the other under-predicts, then averaging is guaranteed to be a better strategy than going with any one estimate.

Much of the work in this area has been done by two professors at Duke University, Jack Soll and Rick Larrick.[10] Jack and Rick essentially argue that, while we can prove mathematically that averaging is a dominant strategy, most of us don't believe it is. Most of us believe that averaging results in an average judgment. This is simply not true. Averaging actually results in a superior judgment.

Let's view this problem slightly differently. Let's imagine you need advice on a situation. You have a problem to solve for which you need to make an estimate. You have done your homework, but you want a second opinion. You've got two experts you could go to, Mr. A, or Ms. B. Mr. A has the same background as you and the same training as you. Ms. B has a different background. Who would you go to? Many people would tell you they would go to Mr. A, who has the same background as they do. But, as it happens, Ms. B might be a better bet. Why? Because you and your judge would bring different information to the table, and the average of your two judgments is more likely to be accurate.

Here is a second scenario. Let's think about the same situation again. You need an estimate and you could to go to Ms. X or Mr. Y. Ms. X has seen the same reports that you have seen. Mr. Y has had access to a different set of reports. Whom do you get advice from? Again, people will tell you that they think they should go to Ms. X. After all, they speak the same language and have seen the same reports. But again, Mr. Y is perhaps a better choice because he brings more data and more information to the judgment that you're going to make.

A number of years ago, Daniel Kahneman and Dan Lovallo wrote an interesting paper that they called the Inside versus the Outside Views of problems or predictions in organizations.[11] Imagine that, like these researchers, you have been studying startup ventures in order to learn what has made some of them successful. You asked the entrepreneurs questions such as, "What do you think is the likelihood that your company will be successful (where success is defined in a precise way) five years from now?" Let's say the entrepreneur said 50 percent. You then pointed out that the average success rate in this industry is only 10 percent. The entrepreneur might have replied, "Yes, but a number of those firms made mistakes that we would never make." The difference between the two estimates of 50 percent and 10 percent is the difference between an inside view and an outside view.

The outside view collects a different set of information and takes a different perspective from the inside view. The inside view looks at the insider's capabilities. The outside view looks at the environment and context and asks, "What in the environment could go wrong?" The point that Kahneman and Lovallo were making was that combining the inside view with the outside view gives you a much better overall perspective because it gives you access to a broader range of information.

The well-known proverb "Two heads are better than one" happens to be true. Many heads are better than two. The best way of winning a contest where you have a jar and you have to guess how many jellybeans are in it is to ask as many people as you can for their estimates. Simply average them, and that's likely to be more accurate than any single person's judgment.

So, what is all of this telling us? It gives us four interesting perspectives on how to think through getting advice. Tip number one: Seek advice from people who are different from you. They could have a different disciplinary background and different training. They could come from a different part of the world; or they might have had different experiences, or have access to different data. Tip number two: Weight your estimate at the same level as the expert's advice. Most of us tend to take a second opinion, and we like it if it confirms what we want, but we discard it if it doesn't. This is a wrong strategy. Make sure you give the judge's advice as much weight as you give your own opinion.

Tip number three: Get advice from as many judges as you can. If the average of two is better than a single judgment, the average of three, four, five, or more opinions is even more reliable. Tip number four: If you don't have access to advice, if you do not have anybody you can turn to, use yourself as a second person. What do I mean by that? Think about making the same estimate again under a different set of circumstances. For example, if you made the original judgment at work while you were busy in the middle of a meeting, try and think about the same problem in a different context, when you're relaxed and sitting at home. Simply by thinking through the same problem differently, you might come to a different judgment. Then take the average, and that is likely to be better than either of the two individual judgments.

Decision-Support Systems: Case-Based and Model-Based

A decision-support system (DSS) simply refers to the use of any computer-based data delivery system that can help people make a better decision. There are two kinds of DSSs. The first one is a model-based decision-support system. The second one is a case-based or data-based decision-support system. Professor Stephen Hoch – then at the University of Chicago – and Professor David Schkade – at the University of California and San Diego – wrote an important article on these two different types of DSSs and their relative efficacy.[12] But, what exactly are model-based and case-based DSSs?

Let's take a model-based decision-support system first. Recall from our discussion of the lens model in chapter 7 that there are many situations in which a judge or an expert is trying to make a prediction about a variable called the "truth." Working along the same lines, let's imagine that you are a loan officer who works for a bank. You receive a large number of loan applications from small businesses, and now you have to make a judgment about the creditworthiness of a given applicant with a view to deciding whether or not to approve a loan. Let us further imagine that there are four criteria/attributes that will be used to make this judgment – the debt ratio of the company, the cash flow, the company's revenue trend, and its location. A model representing this judgment might look like this:

Creditworthiness = $\alpha + w_1$ * Debt Ratio + w_2 * Cash Flow + w_3 * Revenue Trend + w_4 * Location

You could actually get estimates for w_1, w_2, w_3, and w_4 from a number of different sources. For example, you could have a group of managers or experts discuss and collectively determine these numbers. Alternatively, you could use information about these attributes (or cues, as we called them in chapter 7) from previous applications, monitor the success of these companies, and then use a regression analysis to come up with the true values for w_1, w_2, w_3, and w_4 that best describe that success. Finally, you could simply run a judgment machine yourself along the lines of the one in chapter 7.

So now, if you had a computer system that used this equation, all you would need to do is to plug in the values of the four attributes, and it would then give you the credit rating score as an output. And you could then make the loan decision based on that score. That – in essence – is a simple model-based decision-support system.

Now let us think about a case-based DSS. In a case-based DSS, when you get an application, you ask the system to find a previous application that looks similar to the application you have just received. The system will use some simple mathematical algorithms to identify a number of past cases for which you already have credit-rating information. The system might pull out, for example, four companies, A, B, C, and D. You could then use one of these four as the reference case for the new applicant, first looking at the applicant's creditworthiness score and making any subjective adjustments based on the perceived differences between the two companies. The psychological process that we follow to make these kinds of judgments is called anchoring and adjustment. The DSS gives you a past case to anchor on. Let's say you decided that the new applicant is most similar to Company B, which had a score of forty-five. You would then anchor on the forty-five and make adjustments. You might say, for instance, that B had a score of forty-five but was located on the East Coast. Midwestern companies, of which the new applicant is one, tend to be a bit lower on creditworthiness, so perhaps you should lower that to forty.

In a series of experiments, Hoch and Schkade actually compared these two different kinds of systems. They had managers come in and make judgments in two different domains. They employed a fully crossed 2 (Case Based DSS: No or Yes) × 2 (Model Based DSS: No or Yes) design resulting in four conditions. Managers had access to no decision-support system, to one of the two types of decision-support system, or to both forms of DSS.

What did they find? They found that when environments are stable – when no major changes are happening, no new products are being launched, and there are no dramatic income shocks – model-based decision-support systems actually outperform case-based systems. In other words, managers who use model-based systems end up making more accurate judgments or predictions than managers who use case-based systems. However, when the environment is noisy – for example, when there is a recession or a new product has been launched or a new regulation has been imposed so that the old model might not be true anymore – a case-based system is actually a little bit better than a model-based system. Interestingly, however, no matter what the environment is, using both is better than using just one of them.

Another key issue in using decision support systems has to do with the manner in which you integrate the output of the DSS with your own judgments. Most of us have to make choices at work or in our lives. Should we use our intuition, our judgment, and our expertise to make a choice or a judgment, or should we rely on a model?

Why does a model outperform an expert? There are three simple reasons. First, models are consistent. They are, after all, mathematical equations. They can compute well, they can compute consistently, they don't get bored. And so anytime you give the model a particular set of data, it will always return to you the same prediction. Second, models are never biased. Models don't care about framing, they interpret information down to its very basics, and they are not influenced by organizational politics. They are also completely unemotional and have no personal attachment or affiliation to any of the options. Third, models never get tired. The attention that a model gives to a problem is going to be the same whether it has already solved a hundred such problems or if it's doing it for the very first time. With experts, all three of these considerations are issues. We are, like it or not, influenced by the context. We are influenced by tiredness. And we're emotional. That said, experts have a place in the world.

There are four reasons why experts make better decisions or better judgments than models. First, a model only knows what the expert tells it. It is the expert who decides which cues are relevant. It is the expert who decides how to value those cues. If you don't have an expert, you're not going to have a model in the first place. Second, when you think about attributes, there are some attributes (such as price) that are easy to evaluate. However, there are some that are not. So let's say you're hiring and are looking for someone who is creative. Creativity is not an easy-to-measure attribute, especially for machines and models. Experts are good at evaluating attributes that are difficult to evaluate. Models don't know how to do it.

Third, experts can change strategy as a function of time, of what is changing in the context. If there's a recession, the expert knows what to overweight and what to underweight. If there's a new product being launched by a competitor, the expert knows how to adjust the importance weights of the attributes. Models don't know how to do that. And finally, experts have access to more cues, more pieces of information, than models ever do.

Clearly both experts and models offer some advantages, so – which one should we choose? This question was the focus of an interesting research paper written by Bob Blattberg and Stephen Hoch.[13] These authors compared the quality of the outcomes for a model versus an expert in six different domains. In every domain, either a manager or a model was given the same set of data and made predictions on either fashion sales from a catalog, or coupon redemption rates. Going back to chapter 7, the respective performances of the manager and the model were determined by the correlation between their prediction and the truth – the actual sales and the actual coupon redemption rates as they happened.

In each of the six domains, the researchers computed the performance of the manager and the model, and weighted averages of the two predictions. They found that the performance of the average of the model and the manager is better than that of the model alone or the manager alone.

Now this is a story we've seen before. We said the same thing with experts. If you take two experts and you average their prediction, it's better than the prediction of any one expert. Think of the manager and the model as two different experts. They are diverse and they bring different skills. One brings consistency; the other brings an ability to look at cues differently. So when you average them, you end up with an engine that is superior to either one by itself.

So, when you wonder whether to use a decision support system or rely on your own judgment, ask yourself not "Which one should I pick?" but "How should I combine them?" And the easiest prescription based on the research you just saw, is fifty–fifty. Make a judgment independently of what the model says, let the model make its judgment, look at the outputs, take the average, and you will do better than you would using either independently.

The fifth crutch is something that was talked about extensively in chapter 8. Giving people a consumption vocabulary improves their ability to develop a framework for making a decision. Objects of art, bottles of wine, fine quilts, and classical music are all hard for people to evaluate because they don't know enough about the most relevant attributes of those things. And so providing people with the vocabulary to evaluate and give weight to each of those attributes will improve the quality of their decision making.

12 Disclosures

Dis.clo.sure: the act of making new or secret information known.

(Oxford English Dictionary, 2014)

In chapter 12
You will find answers to questions such as:

1 *Why does the disclosure of a great deal of information sometimes lead to poorer choices?*

2 *How can the disclosure of a conflict of interest by an agent reduce the welfare of the agent's clients?*

3 *What is the "What-the-hell effect" and how could it put a constraint on the effectiveness of public disclosure?*

4 *What makes a disclosure effective?*

5 *What is smart disclosure and how can it be achieved?*

A key last mile challenge is to think through the implications of providing consumers and stakeholders with product-related information. One of the most common interventions – disclosure – is used by policymakers, governments, and marketers all over the world to ensure consumer protection. All of us have probably seen the (sometimes copious) information that accompanies purchases such as prescription medicines, condominium units, credit cards, financial products, and medical or insurance services. Warnings such as "This bag is not a toy" or "Do not walk on the roof of a moving train" are also a form of disclosure.

The term "disclosure" is typically used to describe interventions that require firms to make information publicly available that could allow their clients/customers to make better decisions.

In recent years, the use of disclosures has increased rapidly.[1]

There are three forms of disclosures that are commonly used. The first form is a *disclosure of features* related to the purchase of products and services. These features might include information on multiple attributes, potential risks associated with using the product, potential costs of using it, and the possibility of changes to any of these pieces of information. Disclosures accompanying your credit card statement provide a list of interest rates and possible fees that may apply, as well as clauses that indicate that changes in these fees are possible. Likewise, disclosures that accompany prescription medications give a summary of possible side effects and complications.

The second form of disclosure is the *conflict of interest disclosure* in situations where an agent (say, an adviser) makes a recommendation to his principal (say, a client). A conflict of interest occurs when there is a discrepancy between an outcome that maximizes value to the client and an outcome that maximizes value to the agent.[2] Let's imagine that you have hired me as an adviser and have asked me to recommend the most appropriate MBA program to apply to. Of two possible options, let's further imagine that one of the programs – Program X – offers me a cash reward for every student I direct to the program. I will now have two separate incentives – one that maximizes my personal interest and pushes me to recommend X, and another that maximizes your interests and could result in either an X or a Y recommendation. Situations like these abound. For instance, scientists might receive funding from a company to conduct research on the efficacy of a new product, healthcare workers might receive tangible or intangible gifts from pharmaceutical companies, and financial advisers might receive a cash incentive from fund providers for recommending their products. In a conflict of interest disclosure, the scientist, healthcare worker, and financial adviser would need to reveal the funding, gifts, or incentives to their clients before the clients make a choice or reach a conclusion based on the information and advice offered to them.

The third form of disclosure is called *public disclosure*.[3] While public disclosure can take many forms, I specifically refer to one form – the act of implicitly or explicitly making public a list of entities that fail to comply with any requirement with the belief that the disclosure creates an incentive to eventually comply and results in a change in behavior. For instance, the Department of Labour and Advanced Education, an agency in the Canadian province of Nova Scotia, is accountable for delivering regulatory management for the health and safety of workers in Nova Scotia.[4] The department releases – on a quarterly basis – a list of "convictions." This list includes the name of the organization that has failed to abide by the law and names the specific offense and also the resulting penalties imposed. The Canadian province of Alberta has a similar program in the domain of workplace safety,[5] while the Toxics Release Inventory in the United States similarly discloses corporations that violate industrial toxins safety standards.[6] This form of public disclosure is often referred to as a "naming and shaming" approach to behavior change and compliance management.

These three forms of disclosure have different objectives, and hence I will cover them separately. However, note that at the last mile they all rely on the same assumptions. First, they assume that the disclosed information is read and comprehended by the user. Second, they assume that the information will be incorporated in subsequent choices. Third, they implicitly assume that the more comprehensive the information, the better off the recipient of the information will be. And finally, they assume that the user of the information values the same things that the policymaker values – transparency, abundance of information, and the incentive to be seen in a positive light at all times. Based on our journey of the last mile thus far, we now know that all of these assumptions are questionable!

Disclosure of Product Features

Implicit in the increased use of disclosure worldwide is *the assumption that increased disclosure improves consumer welfare.* Increased disclosure implies that consumers have more access to information and hence are more likely to make a well-reasoned decision. There are two further implicit assumptions that underlie the chain of logic – the first is that consumers have the ability to process this additional information; the second is that they have the motivation to make an accurate decision. These are both questionable assumptions.[7]

I often get asked a question about the goals of disclosure programs that relates to the distinction between Kahneman's System 1 and System 2 processing. The question can be loosely paraphrased as follows – "System 2 processing results in 'better' decision making in which consumers seek and use all the information that is necessary to make a fully informed choice. Is the goal of consumer protection policy, therefore, to encourage all consumers to use System 2 processing?"

I would argue that this is not the case. The *goals of consumer protection* are not to influence consumer decision making in any way whatsoever, but rather to *ensure that consumers have access to the most appropriate information* while making choices.[8] Therefore, the choice of an appropriate decision strategy should be entirely left to the consumer. However, consumer protection requires that consumers have access to all the information they might need to make the decision, that the information be clear and unambiguous, and that it be available in a form that the consumer can process efficiently. There are three specific ways in which there might be a failure in providing the relevant information.[9] The distinction between these forms can be illustrated with a scenario in which a consumer makes an online purchase from a website that will ship the purchased goods from an overseas location.

The first type of failure is an *outright failure* to disclose information. Imagine that the consumer clicks through and makes the purchase using her credit card. After her credit card has been approved and her order has been confirmed, she sees a message saying that all shipments to Canada will be subject to an additional $5 surcharge. This fee had not been disclosed during the entire purchase process and hence this example shows an outright failure to disclose an important piece of data that would likely have influenced the decision to purchase. A second failure relates to *delayed or distant disclosure*. Imagine that the consumer clicks through and is about to make a purchase using her credit card. In the final screen, she learns that she will need to pay a $5 surcharge for shipping to Canada. At this stage, she is psychologically committed to purchasing the product, and hence this information does not affect her to the same degree as it would if it had been presented on the main product page. Alternatively, the disclosure could have been made in an earlier screen (but different from the one in which pricing information is provided).

A third form of failure is called *shrouding or obfuscation*. The firm may disclose the surcharge on the same screen as the other purchase information, but the disclosure is "shrouded" in that it is not easy to read and interpret.[10] Shrouding or obfuscation could be done in a number of different ways – (a) using small or otherwise difficult-to-read fonts that make it likely the customer will overlook the disclosed information; (b) breaking down the surcharge into smaller bits that require computation on the part of the consumer; or (c) using complicated and confusing language about when the surcharge might become relevant.

Researchers studying disclosure effectiveness have come to the simple conclusion that merely mandating disclosure does not guarantee effectiveness.[11] In the domain of financial disclosure, some research shows that government efforts to increase disclosure have been unsuccessful in the case of mutual fund disclosures, as information is generally poorly formatted, uses complex language, provides an overload of information, and makes *poor use of graphic design*.[12] These researchers also found that simplifying the disclosures did not significantly impact outcomes but made it easier for consumers to process the information. In the domain of mortgages, researchers studied the relationship between consumers' extent of search and the annual percentage rate (APR) of their primary mortgages.[13] They found that increased search paid off for refinancers but not for other consumers. These researchers also raise another important issue: increased disclosure confuses many consumers who do not understand the intricate details of financial disclosures, so it only tends to benefit those with previous experience and financial knowledge. Of course, the policy objective of disclosures should be to benefit and protect novice consumers more than experts. Nevertheless, considerations from the last mile suggest that complexity in disclosures could have an opposite effect to the intended one. What is the solution to problems associated with the complexity of disclosed information?

The answer is – simplicity! In a 1977 study in the domain of consumer credit, a standard (typically very complex) contract was compared with a simplified and easier to comprehend contract.[14] The data demonstrated that simplification resulted in a modest benefit to high-income consumers by improving their comprehension to the tune of 10 to 15 percent. However, the data also showed that the overall understanding of low-income consumers improved by as much as 50 to 60 percent. These results seem to suggest that focusing on the simplicity and comprehensibility of disclosures (rather than merely focusing on the quantity of disclosure) better aligns the outcomes to the underlying policy objectives. Obviously, there are caveats – sometimes there are risks associated with oversimplifying nuanced financial concepts. However, rigorous laboratory testing of alternative disclosure formats would allow the policymaker to identify the best compromise between oversimplification and overcomplication.

Another variable that can determine the effectiveness of disclosure is the formatting of the disclosed information. In order to ensure successful disclosure, consumer contracts should strike a healthy balance between information load, comprehensibility of format, and familiarity with concepts and ideas. We know that reading through copious amounts of text can be cognitively demanding, and hence the appropriate use of visuals and charts might increase the likelihood that the disclosed information is actually understood and used. Financial decisions – and perhaps many healthcare decisions – are primarily made as a function of the tradeoff between risk and reward. The perception of risk could be modified by the specific manner in which information is presented. Consider the following findings:

Formatting through framing, use of graphics, and use of numerical information can influence recipients' perception of risk by focusing on certain aspects of disclosure.[15] For instance, disclosing facts in terms of percentages is perceived as less problematic than disclosure in terms of frequency. Graphs are often an effective way of describing mathematical operations and presenting information in a concise manner.[16] In short, careful consideration should be given to formatting as a tool in communicating information appropriately and effectively to consumers.

The font size and color used to make disclosures also has an effect on consumer decision making. A study on current MasterCard application forms showed that while the appropriate content was disclosed on credit card application forms, the print was too small to be easily read, the language required interpretation by a lawyer, and the terms and conditions looked "too difficult" to read.[17]

That said, we are nowhere near a precise theory of exactly what format is the most effective. An approach that involves pilot projects and experimental testing to identify the most appropriate formatting options would probably work best.

Disclosure of Conflict of Interest

Received opinion is that advisers should disclose any potential conflicts of interest. But does this actually increase the welfare of the clients?

Research shows that when advisers disclose information that portrays them as self-interested, clients tend to use the information inappropriately and in counterintuitive ways. On the client's side, disclosure enhances trust, signals an adviser's professional standing, and confuses the client. When your wealth manager discloses that he is getting paid a commission by Bank ABC to recommend its funds, you might think, "Oh, that's really nice of him to disclose that – such an honest and upfront man!"

Perhaps the classic paradigm used for studying the effects of disclosure of a conflict of interest was developed by researchers Sunita Sah and her colleagues George Loewenstein and Daylian Cain.[18] Consider an experiment in which a participant can choose one of two dice to roll – the dice serve as a metaphor for different financial instruments in the sense that they represent different payoffs as a function of which number is rolled (i.e., each payoff has a probability of occurrence). Further, one of the dice (the blue die) dominates the other (the red die) in that its prizes, given the same exact probability distribution, are superior, but the consumer is not able to easily see the dominance. The consumer now has the ability to ask an adviser (who is privy to all the details of the prizes) about which die the adviser recommends. The adviser gets a commission each time she recommends the red (inferior) die, and the adviser always recommends the red die.

Under this basic paradigm, Sah and colleagues consider two scenarios – in one condition the adviser does not disclose her conflict of interest while in the other she does disclose it. The results are intriguing: 42 percent of participants chose the bad advice (i.e., agreed with the adviser and chose the red die) when there was no disclosure of conflict of interest. However, when the conflict of interest was disclosed, as many as 76 percent of the participants accepted the bad advice. Clearly, this was an example of the idea that disclosure reduces consumer welfare. While research on the disclosure of conflict of interest is in its infancy, these early results do raise some flags for mandating such disclosures. In the words of George Loewenstein and his colleagues, "disclosure does not live up to its protective promise."

Public Disclosure

What is public disclosure? In its most basic form, the idea is very simple. An authority (say a government, a regulatory body, or an industry association) wishes an entity, such as a firm, to comply with certain behaviors. For instance, a government wants companies to pay taxes and file reports on time; a regulatory body wants firms to install safety procedures to protect workers from risks; and an industry organization wants members to share data relevant to the industry as a whole. As with the intention-action gap for individuals, however, organizations might not wish to comply, for several reasons: it might be cheaper or easier not to comply, there might be other pressing priorities, or the firm might have reasons to believe that compliance would not be in its best interest.

The authority then introduces a public disclosure program. In particular, it decides to publish a list of offenders – firms that have failed to comply – on a quarterly basis. This list will be widely circulated and accompanied by a press release. How might this influence behavior?

If the entity were an individual, the individual might feel the pressure to comply because he or she would anticipate feeling guilt or shame. Both these emotions are aversive and can compromise the person's social relationships. But what happens when the entity is a firm? Firms don't feel shame, and firms don't have a social life.

But wait – they do have something even more valuable than emotions and social lives. They have reputations. And we know from a lot of research that a loss of reputation has consequences – real monetary consequences.[19] The reputation of a firm is a public signal of the quality of its products and services, strategies, plans, and future prospects. This allows the firm to charge a premium price for its products and also to get access to favorable partners in its going-to-market efforts. Further, individual and institutional investors rely on the reputation of the firm when making investment decisions, and so the ability of the firm to raise capital can be weakened by the loss of reputation. In addition, there are other social benefits that accompany reputation – benefits that increase engagement, cooperation, and citizenship behavior. It is not a surprise that firms will strive very hard to avoid any damage to their reputations. Public disclosures of failures to comply would do just that, and hence naming and shaming programs have become a relatively popular intervention in domains ranging from workplace safety, financial obligations, environmental pollution, sexual and other criminal offences, and human rights violations.[20]

While these arguments seem very compelling, is there anything we could do to be more behaviorally informed as we design a public disclosure program? There is a fascinating effect in psychology called the "What-the-hell" effect. It was first described by psychologists Winona

Cochran and Abraham Tesser,[21] who offered an example of a student who was striving to lose weight by keeping to strict caloric limits in his daily diet. One day he accidentally exceeded his limit and violated his goal. Rather than curbing his subsequent consumption, he responded by saying, "What the hell, I've already broken my limit, might as well indulge more." Amar Cheema and I conducted a number of experiments and found out that this effect does indeed occur in a number of domains; people who violate a weekly spending goal are likely to splurge for the rest of the week, and people who miss a deadline for submitting a piece of work are likely to procrastinate further.[22]

What does all of this mean for public disclosures? It means that when a reputation has already been destroyed by a "naming and shaming" process, there is not much else a firm can do about it. The firm may then have a "what-the-hell" response to the fact that its reputation is already in tatters and continue in its non-compliance.

Behavioral insights offer two specific pieces of advice for policymakers looking to design such programs. The first insight relates to the point we just made – a threat to reputation accompanied by the ability to comply with the request creates a strong motivation to act, but a public naming and shaming might not. Let's imagine that, two months before workplace safety reports need to be filed, a regulatory body sends a letter to firms that have still not acted on the request. The letter to the companies' CEOs says something like, "Dear CEO: You are one of a few firms that have not yet supplied us with the necessary information. Should we not have the information listed in the attachment [by the deadline], your company will be listed under the list of offending companies. The draft of a press release announcing the list is enclosed with this letter. Also attached is a step-by-step guide on submitting the information." This letter is likely to be effective because it does three things. First, it poses a threat to reputation. Second, in providing a draft of a press release, it makes the threat salient and very vivid. The threat could be made even more powerful by creating a belief that the list will be widely accessible and not simply buried in an obscure part of an annual report. Third, it gives the recipient a clear set of guidelines on what needs to be done, and sufficient time to do it.

The second insight has to do with the relative frequency of the offense. Let's imagine that we are in a domain where the majority of the firms offend, and compliance is a rarity. In such a situation, posting a list of offenders might not have any dramatic effects because – after all – a lot of people are on that list and hence it is not an unusual behavior at all. In such a circumstance, a praise list rather than a shame list might be more effective.

There is another story on disclosures to be told about mandated disclosures that were meant to be product risk disclosures but had effects similar to public disclosures. Because of psychological factors such as limited attention span, inattention to missing information, and so on, disclosure requirements are often not effective at changing consumer behavior as predicted. However, following disclosure, producers or disclosers often change behavior because they experience the equivalent of the spotlight effect from psychology. The spotlight effect refers to the phenomenon in which people tend to believe they are noticed more than they really are and hence change their behavior as if they are being watched.[23] As result of this tendency, disclosers may have an inflated sense of the level of scrutiny that the disclosed information is gathering, and may improve product performance to make the disclosed information look better.[24] Disclosure works by affecting the behavior of those whom the disclosure is about. This is evident in the instance where disclosure of car rollover ratings led to the production of safer vehicles.[25] Likewise, the disclosure of public hygiene grading cards in Los Angeles restaurants was associated with a 13.1 percent decrease in hospitalizations related to foodborne disease in the year following implementation of the program.[26]

What Makes a Disclosure Policy Effective?

While disclosure is a very popular policy intervention, not much is known about measures of effectiveness. When does one say that a disclosure program is effective? Based on my reading of the research, I can identify four factors that underlie disclosure effectiveness.

1. *Comprehension:* This indicator captures the answer to the question, "Do consumers understand the disclosed information?"
2. *Decision Making*: This indicator captures the response to the question, "Does the disclosed information change decisions to be more in line with the policy goal?"
3. *Experience*: This indicator captures the answer to the question, "Does the disclosure provide consumers with a better point-of-purchase experience?"
4. *Welfare*: This indicator captures the answer to the question, "Does the disclosure improve overall consumer welfare?"

Looking Forward

Now that we have looked through the disclosures landscape, I return to a question that is at the core of the last mile issue – what makes for an effective disclosure? Here is my checklist:

Simplicity – Use of simple language and clean visuals to convey key messages

Comprehensiveness – Good guidelines that are designed specifically to eliminate either outright failures of disclosure or failures due to shrouding and obfuscation

Consumer relevance – Disclosure of information on variables that are relevant to consumer decision making

Staging – Disclosure of content over time (at different stages of the application/purchasing process when the relevant information is most likely to be used), or across media (some information might be provided on an application form or prospectus, other disclosures might be made online)

Segmentation – Disclosure of core information supplemented by a series of additional disclosures targeted toward consumers that match a particular profile

These criteria notwithstanding, it is fair to conclude that when it comes to understanding disclosure effectiveness we do not know a whole lot! We have a number of generalizable principles (for instance, the format and timing of disclosures are as important as the content) but very little research that translates these principles into concrete implementation variables that are within the discloser's control. We also need to better understand the downsides of disclosures. Many of us assume that disclosure is always good – that providing consumers with more information can only help in improving their welfare over time. Recall that we used to say the same thing about choice – but we now know that too much choice can be paralyzing. Putting on my "behavioral theorist" hat, I sketch out three scenarios where disclosures might be harmful:

1. The research on the disclosure of conflict of interest suggests that disclosure increases trust and credibility. Extending that theorizing to the domain of financial disclosures, it is possible that the disclosure of negative attributes (say, a small fee) early in the disclosure

document enhances trust and makes consumers more likely to purchase inferior products.

2. A major psychological driver of decision making is *regret and antici-pated regret* about making the wrong choice. Many of the risks dis-closed in financial products are risks inherent in the product; however, it is possible that the explicit disclosure of these risks re-sults in their over-influencing consumers in their decision making. This would happen because the salience of the risk increases the potential for anticipated regret (as exemplified by an "I'd feel silly if the mutual fund didn't perform and I had been warned about it" response). Also, in the face of a negative outcome (e.g., a non-performing fund), investors might feel worse about their decision making.

3. It is well known that consumers are not very good at assessing what information is most relevant, and that they tend to incorpo-rate as much information as they can in their decision making. In general, this happens because consumers have an implicit belief that a rational actor would provide them with information if it is relevant to their decision making. Thus, it is possible that if a dis-closure provides information that is not relevant to every consum-er who receives it, these consumers might end up using irrelevant information.

These are speculations rather than known outcomes, but they cer-tainly seem plausible and I trust that one day someone will test these ideas out. But, as with my belief about a theory of decision making, I also doubt that we will ever have a complete theory of disclosure. What we should aim for instead is a culture of empirical testing.

A recent paper by Richard Thaler and Will Tucker also highlighted what might be the future of disclosure. According to these authors, "Repeated attempts to improve disclosure, including efforts to translate complex contracts into plain English, have met with only modest suc-cess." Further, they "believe, though, that a potent mix of modern tech-nology and new government policy is about to transform disclosure – and with it the workings of many parts of the economy. Increasingly, government-owned data and private-company disclosures will be made available in machine-readable formats, spurring the growth of new ser-vices we call 'choice engines' – technologies that interpret this data."[27]

In essence, Thaler and Tucker advocate a new form of disclosure that they call *smart disclosure*. Governments and organizations that collect data from individual consumers in machine-readable form could be obligated to release these data to the individual consumer (only the consumer's own data, not other consumers' data). Consumers could then use these data and analyze them using smartphone gadgets or web tools to make better decisions, to track their consumption, or to make better consumption tradeoffs. In the United Kingdom, the first step toward smart disclosure was taken through the launch of a voluntary program called Mi Data[28] that achieves precisely these objectives.

This argument can best be captured as follows: "Disclosure is only as effective as the tools consumers have at their disposal to help them use the disclosed data." More generally, in addition to improving disclosure effectiveness through consumer-friendly design, it is important to pay attention to the *overall ecosystem* by providing supports such as electronic choice engines and the expertise of "financial doctors" to help consumers evaluate the enhanced disclosures and make better choices.

13 Retailing

In chapter 13
You will find answers to questions such as:

1 *Why is price presentation as important as – or even more important than – price setting?*

2 *What can behavioral insights tell us about how best to present prices?*

3 *How do retailers make money?*

4 *How can behavioral insights help retailers win at the point of purchase?*

In my many years as an educator and consultant, a typical conversation I've had with managers goes something like this: "We have a fantastic product and our marketing is outstanding. People love our advertising. In concept testing, they value our product really highly, yet we don't sell as much as we think we should."

In the evolution of a product and its go-to-market strategy, retailing is the moment of truth for any business. Retailing is where actual transactions happen, when promise gets converted into purchases, and where consumers pay you money for the investments you have made in developing products and services. Retailing is the "last mile" for all tangible and, in many cases, intangible products and services.

How much do companies really think about the retailing effort? Over the last few months, I have worked with two University of Toronto students, Janice Cha and Lynda Liu,[1] to interview a number of managers of brands and services to ask them what they thought was the critical factor that influenced consumers' purchase decisions. In addition to citing the usual first mile components – such as advertising, branding, and product features – people told us most frequently that price is the biggest driver in influencing purchasing. In the words of one respondent, "Getting people to buy at retail is all about being priced right." However, behavioral insights from research tell us that an economic incentive is only one of many influences on decision making and sales.

Given the perceived importance of pricing in consumer decision making, I would like to do two things in this chapter. First, I want to talk a little bit about behavioral insights that influence how managers should think about presenting – not setting – prices. In this chapter, my goal isn't to focus on what the actual price should be, but rather to provide some ideas on how that price should be presented. I will make the simple claim that price presentation is often as important as (and perhaps even more important than) the actual price that you set for your product or service. In the second part of the chapter, I will present a broader framework for thinking through retail economics and asking questions such as "How does a retailer make money?" and "What can we learn from the world of behavioral economics to help retailers better convert promise into transactions?"

Prospect Theory and the Presentation of Prices

Let me start off with the world of behavioral pricing. Several years ago, a former PhD student, Maggie Liu, and I wrote a chapter summarizing the research in this area, and I refer readers who are interested in this area to that chapter.[2]

Chapter 4 in the present book presented a lot of research in the area of the psychology of money. In particular, it explored mental accounting and the idea that people treat money differently as a function of where it comes from.[3] It also discussed prospect theory, which is a model that predicts how consumers value monetary outcomes.[4] To repeat briefly, prospect theory has three very simple ideas. At its heart it argues that people don't have a very good internal mechanism to evaluate monetary outcomes. Instead, they are good at evaluating those outcomes in terms of a reference point. For example if a product is priced at $100, most people are not quite sure whether that is a good deal or a bad deal. But if they know that the average price is $150, and that on this occasion the product is available for $100, it now seems like a great deal.

What I've done here is evaluate the price in comparison to some internal standard, something that I've retrieved from my own brain. That something could be a previous price I've paid, or my knowledge of prices based on conversations with friends, or an advertised price, or the price I have paid for comparable items or services in the past. Prospect theory goes on to say that if the monetary outcome, in this case a price, is better than the reference point, human beings feel that they have gained in the transaction. On the other hand, if the reference point is worse, they feel they have lost in the transaction. Finally, prospect theory says that people's happiness at experiencing a gain is not equal to their sadness at experiencing a loss.

This is a fairly intricate concept. A good illustration of the concept is something that happened to me several years ago when I lived in Asia and was paid a visit by a traveling carpet salesman. He tried to convince me to purchase a handmade Indonesian carpet. Admittedly, while the carpet was absolutely beautiful, I was at the time not in a position to spend thousands of dollars on a carpet. So I politely declined.

My admiration for the carpet was clearly visible on my face. Right after I declined, the carpet salesman looked at me and said with a twinkle in his eye, "Sir, I have a proposal for you. Why don't I leave this particular carpet in your home for two weeks, with absolutely no strings attached, and at the end of the two weeks I will take it back if you still don't want to make a purchase."

Now I had been in situations like this before. Remember, this was a carpet salesman trying to sell an expensive product to a marketing professor, and I thought I knew it all. I pointed out to him that I expected him to come back in two weeks and make the claim that I had implicitly agreed to buy the product, or perhaps that he would point out a defect and suggest that I should then buy the product. But the carpet salesman was friendly. He was firm. He said that he would be willing to sign any piece of paper that absolved me of an obligation to make the purchase. To this date, I am not sure why I trusted him, but I did, and I kept the carpet for two weeks.

When he came back in two weeks, knocked at my door, and asked me if I still wanted to keep the carpet, I declined. I expected him to put up some sort of resistance. I expected that he would try and give me the hard sell, that he would try to convince me that the carpet was really good for me and that I should keep it. Instead, he simply said "okay" and proceeded to roll up the carpet, drape it over his shoulders, and leave. I was pleasantly surprised and thankful that I didn't have to deal with any further persuasive attempts. I thought to myself, "Dilip 1 – Salesman 0," shut the door behind him, turned back, and entered my living room.

It looked horrible. Just imagine your own living room without its rug or your mantelpiece without the painting that has adorned it for many years! For the past two weeks, the carpet had served as the centerpiece of my living room. I had put in cushions and throws to match the color of the rug, and now that the carpet had been taken away it suddenly seemed like a loss.

Notice what the carpet salesman had done through this intervention. By getting me to keep the carpet, he had managed to convert a potential gain for me into a potential loss. Two weeks ago when I was trying to purchase the carpet, I was balancing the gain that I would get from the carpet against its cost, which was a few thousand dollars. Today, I was now balancing the potential loss of the carpet with the same exact price tag. Since the value of a loss is significantly greater than the value of a gain, I now felt that I wanted to keep the carpet. The carpet salesman clearly knew his prospect theory well, or behaved as if he did. I almost walked out and purchased the carpet, but fortunately good sense prevailed and I did not.

This story illustrates the basic properties of prospect theory. If you start thinking about prospect theory and how it applies to pricing, there are a number of different implications. One particular implication of prospect theory is something called the "silver lining principle." It says that when consumers are presented with a big loss, for example a product with a high price, versus a small gain, perhaps a small discount or a gift, segregation of the loss and gain works better than integration of the two. In other words, it is better to present the loss and the gain as two separate items than it is to present them all as one integrated loss.

Here is an example. Many of us have had to go to a store to purchase car tires. Purchasing tires is perhaps the purest form of loss one can ever experience. Nobody plans to purchase car tires. Nobody looks forward to it. Typically, you only purchase tires when you have to, when your tire is damaged, or when you end up with a flat tire.

Let's imagine that a particular brand of tire costs $200 per tire, and that the seller is willing to offer a $10 discount on that particular product. How should the seller package that discount? In one world, the seller could say, "Look, my regular price is $200, and with a $10 discount I'm offering to sell you the tire for $190." In a second world, the seller might charge you $200 but then, after about a week or so, send you a check or a set of coupons for $10 as a way of delivering the promised discount. In which of these two worlds would you be happier? Research and anecdotal evidence suggests that you would be much happier in the second world, because now you have adapted to the loss of $200, and the $10 discount – or gift – shows up as a separate item. That makes you feel much happier. In the first world, there isn't much difference between the loss that you experience from spending $190 versus the loss from spending $200, and as a result you might be marginally happy about the discount but not all that happy. So a simple yet powerful implication of prospect theory for pricing is that if you have a big-ticket item and can offer a small discount on it, package the discount separately.

There is another way of packaging a large loss and a small gain differently, and that is to change the format of the small gain. In the tire example, the salesman was offering a $10 discount in the form of cash, but you could offer something else. For example, think about going to high-end stores to buy perfumes or cosmetics. These are fairly expensive products that come in extremely small bottles. If you're buying a tiny bottle of perfume for $100, would you be happy to receive a $10 discount or would you rather receive a gift, which is a little bag that you can use to carry the bottle of perfume along with some samples that would cost the seller about $10 dollars to manufacture? The cosmetics company is probably better off offering a gift rather than a discount because now it has unpackaged the benefit from the large loss.

Some recent research also examined the effects of partition pricing on consumer decision making. Let us imagine you have decided to purchase a $100 product. But on top of this base price, you have to pay a $20 tax, a $10 surcharge, and perhaps a $20 shipping and handling fee, so that the product ends up costing you $150 dollars. How might sellers best present these prices on their website? Should they say that the product costs $150, all expenses included, or should they say it costs $100 plus $20 plus $10 plus $20?

Research by Vicky Morwitz, Eric Greenleaf, and Eric Johnson[5] suggests that it is better to partition the prices and present them as $100 plus $20 plus $10 plus $20. The reason, they argue, is that people psychologically tend to anchor on the base price, in this case $100, and use that in the evaluation of the product rather than looking at all the additional items that are tacked on to the price.

A similar question is, "What is the best way of presenting a discount?" For example, if I have a product that I used to offer at $100 dollars and I offer a discount of $10 and then a second discount of $10, should I present the price as $100 minus $10 minus $10, or should I simply say that the price was $100 but now I'm offering a $20 discount? Behavioral insights seem to suggest that you are better off offering multiple smaller discounts because the consumer perceives this as getting several things rather than a single discount. As I said earlier, in many consumer decision-making scenarios, people tend to value the fact that they're getting a gift or a discount more than the actual dollar value of the gift or the discount.

My colleague Nina Mazar also did an interesting piece of research on a very powerful last mile pricing phenomenon. She and her colleagues studied consumers making a choice between a higher-quality, higher-priced product and a lower-quality, lower-priced product.[6] The easiest way to frame this decision is as the tradeoff between the extra quality one gains (say ΔQ) versus the extra price that needs to be paid for this (say ΔP). Of course, if ΔQ and ΔP are held constant, then the choice between the two options should not be altered. Not quite, say Nina and her colleagues!

In one of their (many) experiments, all participants faced a choice between a Lindt chocolate truffle and a Hershey chocolate. ΔQ was always the difference in quality between these two chocolates. ΔP for all participants was fourteen cents. However, this is where the similarity ended. In one condition, the expensive chocolate cost fifteen cents and the cheap one cost one cent. Thirty-six percent of participants bought Lindt, 14 percent bought Hershey, and 50 percent bought nothing. In a second condition, the expensive chocolate cost fourteen cents and the cheaper one cost nothing – it was free. Now the sales of Lindt went down to 19 percent, the sales of Hershey went up dramatically to 42 percent, and 39 percent bought nothing. Clearly, the "free" product added a lot more value than the ΔP of fourteen cents would suggest. The fact that the price of zero (or "free") is special has a number of last mile implications. For instance, it would suggest that rather than offering a 10 percent discount on products, it might make sense to offer one free after the purchase of ten!

Uncertainty in Prices and Discounts

When I was still working on my doctoral thesis, I got interested in a stream of research that is known as tensile pricing. I lived in Chicago then, and was struck by a fairly frequent form of sales promotion that I had seldom seen before. One of the most common kinds of sales promotion advertised, "Everything in the store is on sale at between 10% and 70% off." In this scenario, I was guaranteed to get a discount; I just didn't know how much the discount would be. Yet another form of promotion advertised "40–60% off on all items marked with a red dot"; here I was not only unsure of the magnitude of the discount, I was also unsure of the likelihood of getting the discount.

Sanjay Dhar, Claudia Gonzalez-Vallejo, and I studied situations where both the likelihood and the amount of the discount were uncertain.[7] Such unspecified discounts are called tensile discounts. In one experiment we worked with a campus store and offered what we called probabilistic discounts on candy bars. Every candy bar in the store had a sticker to be peeled off by the cashier on purchase; if the area under the sticker was a particular color, the consumer would get a discount. If it did not have the appropriate marking, there was no discount. Consumers knew they were playing a lottery to possibly get a discount.

Across different days in the store, we changed the *probability* of getting a discount (certain, high probability of 80 percent, or low probability of 25 percent) as well as the actual level of the discount (precise or tensile). We found that when the probability of getting a discount was low, people preferred the tensile pricing format. If the probability of getting the discount was high, the preference for the precise level of discount was great. Now – why was this happening? We figured this was happening because when the promotion became more like a gamble, people entered with a lottery mindset and tended to be very optimistic about the level of discount they were going to get. The discount would be seen as a gain, and people were optimistic in the domain of gains. On the other hand, when they were almost sure of getting a discount, then the tensile discounts opened up the possibility of a loss. The prescription from our findings was clear: when the likelihood of getting a deal was low, a tensile discount created more engagement and interest!

Fairness

Another behavioral variable that has a large impact on the profits that retailers and manufacturers can make as a function of their pricing strategy is something called fairness. Consumers will accept price differentials or price increases if they're considered fair but will reject them if they believe that those price increases are unfair. A natural question is, "What exactly is fairness?" It's one of those concepts that you can see when it is being violated but that is difficult to define.

A very early paper by Daniel Kahneman, Jack Knetsch, and Richard Thaler set up a number of experiments to try and identify inputs into the judgment of fairness.[8] For example, respondents might be told about a hardware store that was selling snow shovels for $15, but that increased the price to $25 after a big snowstorm. While this price increase was consistent with the laws of demand and supply and was economically perhaps a smart thing to do, most respondents reported that the price increase was unfair. In another experiment, the researchers told participants that a shortage had developed for a popular model of automobiles and customers must now wait some time for delivery. Rather than offering the cars at list price, the dealer advertised the model at $200 above the list price. In a second version, respondents learned about a shortage for the same popular model but were told that the dealer had been selling the cars at a discount of $200 but now was withdrawing the discount. The results show that participants thought that the price increase in the first version of the story was very unfair but that withdrawing a discount of the same amount in the second version was perfectly acceptable.

This finding is consistent with the prospect theory value function. When you increase your prices by $200 dollars, it is now a new loss, whereas if you remove a discount, it is a reduced gain, and since we know that losses have a bigger impact than gains, people feel more of a sense of unfairness when prices have been increased.

I was thinking about this research and made an interesting observation in a shopping center in Hong Kong where I found that many products – I'd say about 70 percent – were always sold at a discount. I spoke to the store manager about it and he shared with me an insight that was remarkably consistent with the experiments of Kahneman, Knetsch, and Thaler. He said it was very hard for him to increase prices over time because his customers did not like that and he would face a backlash. But if he reduced discounts, that was okay and his customers did not complain a whole lot about that.

In conjunction with the examples above, I believe that four factors drive the perception of price fairness and unfairness. First, a price increase is considered fair if it is justified by an increased cost. If you simply tell people that the raw material prices have gone up and that is why you need to increase prices, that is considered fair. But simply increasing the price of snow shovels because there's a snowstorm would be considered unfair. Second, a price increase is considered fair if it is accompanied by an improvement in the quality of service or product. Third, a price increase is more likely to be seen as fair if the customer has the ability to choose an alternative product. For example, you might increase a feature on a product but still allow consumers to choose the old product, the basic product, at the basic price, and that would be considered fair. But if you withdrew the basic product and simply forced everybody to buy the new and more expensive product, that might be considered unfair. Fourth, the palatability of a price increase is greater if it is framed as a reduced loss, as we just said, rather than an absolute price increase.

The Retail Store: A Basic Framework

Having waded through a number of useful last mile pricing phenomena, I would like to spend the next few pages taking a step back and looking at the bigger picture. I'd like to raise bigger questions such as, "How do retailers make money?" and "How can other non-price interventions help in improving the efficiency of the retail last mile?" The paragraphs below are based on observations and interviews with managers of real stores, but the names of the retailers have been changed to provide anonymity.

The basic revenue model in retail can best be illustrated by looking at the case of three hypothetical stores – T, C, and B.[9] Store T is a national drugstore franchise. Compared to other franchises in the area, Store T is achieving a monthly revenue that is 20 percent higher than average. Even while carrying the same product mixes as similar stores, Store T is more successful because of its frequently updated window display. As weekly flyers come in, Store T showcases relevant items that are on promotion for that week. Store T's relevant store display increases *traffic* in the store, thus increasing its overall revenue.

Store C is a local clothing boutique. The store looks like any other clothing retailer – clothes on hangers and shelves and mannequins that display a whole outfit. One key difference that gives Store C more sales is subtle but effective – beside each mannequin are a couple of photos and a chalkboard that give examples of occasions or places where people might wear the outfit. Each section of the store allows customers to envisage themselves wearing the outfit to a date night or a brunch. Store C is increasing the *conversion rate* of its customers by making it easy for them to imagine themselves wearing the outfit at a certain event.

Store B, a grocery store, was struggling with selling Brand A's two-liter milk carton. Even with a price discount on the two-liter size, customers continued to buy Brand A's one-liter milk carton. To solve this problem, Store B decided to re-shelve its dairy section. Instead of placing one-liter and two-liter cartons on the same level and the four-liter jug at the opposite end of the section, they placed the one-liter carton on the top shelf, the two-liter carton on a middle shelf, and the four-liter jug at floor level. They were put together in the same section but at different levels. Once the two-liter option was placed as the middle option between the one-liter size and the four-liter size, Brand A's two-liter milk cartons saw an immediate increase in sales. Store C increased sales not only by selling less popular items but also by increasing shopper *basket size*.

The revenue of any store is the product of the traffic, the conversion rate, and the basket size (see figure 13.1).

Traffic

Usually a store's traffic is driven by promotions, in-store ads, storefront attractiveness, online campaigns, and so on. But what about the shoppers who, originally with no intention to enter, casually stroll by your store? How will you get them to enter?

A bath soap store, Bubbly, offers great products at affordable prices. But how does it compete with other drugstore brands or luxurious premium brands? It comes down to Bubbly's personalized service. More and more consumers expect personalized service, from simple

Figure 13.1: The Building Blocks of Revenue

Traffic

Number of unique
visitors to a store

Conversion Rate

Percentage of visitors
who made a purchase

Basket Size

Dollar value per
transaction

Revenue = Traffic × Conversion Rate × Basket Size

greetings to appropriate product recommendations based on purchase history. As a local boutique, Bubbly offers personalized service by offering unique and relevant brands of soaps so that a sales associate can make truly customized suggestions for each customer's taste. This positive experience builds loyalty and attracts customers to come back to the store.

Therefore, two main drivers of traffic are relevant store displays (as mentioned in the Store T example above) and customized service. As a store manager, there are three specific questions I need to think about. First, are traffic efforts directed purposefully toward my specific *target segment*? For instance, if I am a local boutique, are my products relevant to the niche market? If I am a national franchise, are my window displays targeted toward the segment I want to visit my store? Second, can my product/service be framed as an *"experience"*? For instance, do I sell a car not for its parts and frame but for its family-friendly nature, or as a daredevil favorite or a business-must automobile! Customers are more likely to buy when they can visualize the experience derived from the product. And third, are *inventory and staffing* responding effectively to the current levels and nature of traffic? For instance, what time of the day requires the most attention from salespeople? Are my best-selling items always readily available?

Conversion Rate

Large bulks of sales fail to go through because of this key stage. To have a high conversion rate means that a high number of browsers become purchasers. As most shoppers are not quite sure what exactly they want, a clever integration of strategies in the right context will increase conversion and maximize sales revenue.

A furniture store called Blocks has been outperforming a national franchise in the same neighborhood. Blocks offers similar products as its competitors at similar or sometimes slightly lower prices. Instead of introducing its products at an aggregate price, the associates frame price as a *per month* rate, making it easier and less painful to accept for the customers. Furthermore, at the payment stage, Blocks informs customers about the various payment options available, emphasizing more transparent methods of payment such as by credit card or multi-month financing. By reframing the product's value, it makes consumers' mental accounting process easier and payments less painful. Especially for big-ticket purchases or products that have seasonality, helping customers to segment payments encourages them to make the purchase.

Many consumers are now looking for convenience and efficiency when shopping. This is why Pure Skin, a health and beauty products store, places unique product descriptions on its shelves. Instead of using promotional posters explaining obvious facts or proclaiming vague benefits, Pure Skin posts a comparative chart showing where the product plays in the current market in relation to similar products. These unique product descriptions make it easier for customers to find products that offer benefits that they are specifically looking for. In addition to the descriptions, Pure Skin carries a limited range of carefully selected products to make sure it does not overwhelm customers with too many choices.

No one likes to miss out. A national clothing retailer, Cotton, truly understands this psychology. To grab the attention of shoppers, in-store posters *frame* the promotion so that if customers choose not to buy sales items, they are losing the opportunity to save money. Making it very clear to customers that "by not buying this blazer now, you are losing money next time you go shopping for interview outfits" increases the conversion rate in Cotton stores.

To sum up, three drivers of conversion rate are (1) easy mental accounting, (2) streamlined decision making, and (3) the choice of framing. As a manager, there are three specific questions to think about. First, how is the shopper *navigating* the store – that is, what are the longest and shortest *browsing areas,* and am I strategically placing my products to reflect this? Second, which segment has the highest conversion rate? Are the products I wish to sell in this segment? And third, as discussed earlier in this chapter, what are the best ways to present prices and discounts to enhance conversion and purchase?

Basket Size

Think of a shopping basket. From a retail perspective, after getting the customer to put his first item into the basket, the goal is to have him add a second, a third, a fourth, and so on. Alternatively, the goal could be to get the consumer to upgrade to a higher quality (and presumably higher margin) version of a product. From a marketing perspective, a store can utilize methods such as bundling, discounts, and tiered selling, but I will explore other ways that stores can leverage to finish the last mile.

Merchandising, in particular the physical positions of products, is an important driver. Instead of simply putting all products of the same category together, Holly's House puts an assortment of products related to a particular activity together. For example, the store puts a high-end teapot set and a set of teaspoons together. This allows the store to put big-ticket items and smaller add-ons side by side. Purchase of a large item can easily lead to purchase of a smaller add-on, because of its contrast effect. Since the customer is already spending a large amount on an item, spending a few more dollars will not make a huge difference to her.

Heels, a premium shoe store, truly understands the power of choice architecture. When customers purchase a pair of shoes, they receive insoles for the new pair of shoes at the cashier. A customer may choose to opt out from purchasing the insoles, and pay less than what the associate originally told the customer. However, in most cases, if the choice already includes an add-on, and the previously communicated price includes this add-on, customers will not go through the extra step of opting out.

Overall, three main drivers of basket size include "magic" middle options (as mentioned in Store B), contrasting options, and opt-out framing.

As a manager, there are three specific questions to think about. First, what is the ideal *floor plan* layout of my store? Is a traditional vertical layout or a more creative "maze" layout (like that of Ikea) more likely to influence consumer decision making? Second, for an *online* store, have I strategically designed the layout so that the navigation process encourages consumers to make more purchases? Can return policies in physical stores (if applicable) encourage sales to be made through returns? And third, does product assortment provide too little, too much, or just the right amount of choice, keeping in mind that *choice overload* will lead consumers to refrain from making choices!

Where the Rubber Meets the Road

The retail store – be it brick and mortar or online – is a classic example of the last mile. In addition to being an area that is ripe for experimentation, given the sheer number of consumer interactions that a retailer has every day, retail is also a data-rich environment. In brick and mortar stores, modern electronic scanner systems mean that retailers have the ability to pull up and slice and dice a large volume of transactional data. Online, transactional data can also be supplemented by behavioral data. For instance, an online retailer could keep track of the number of pages visited, the time spent on each page, the sequence in which pages were visited, or even the specific widgets and tools that were used by the consumer. And finally, retailers get quick and unambiguous feedback on any changes they might make to the retail environment. For instance, changing the price presentation today will result in purchasing-pattern differences tomorrow, and changing a shelf location this week could influence the end-of-week market-share figures. The richness and breadth of behavioral phenomena, the richness of data, and the quick feedback make retailing perhaps one of the best laboratories in which to test behavioral interventions!

14 The Last Mile of the Last Mile

In chapter 14
You will find answers to questions such as:

1 *How have governments and other organizations embedded behavioral insights into their operations?*

2 *What does it mean to be an experimental organization?*

3 *What resources and capabilities does your organization need to build in order to truly embrace behavioral insights?*

4 *What do organizations that truly embrace behavioral insights do differently and do better?*

We are at the last mile of the last mile. Many chapters ago, I began this book with a plea to all of you to consider the last mile as seriously as you considered the first mile. In the world of business, I argued, the first mile represents the efforts that we make in designing strategy, designing products, and designing programs. The first mile is played out in the boardrooms, through research and development, and through extensive investment in both policy development and product development.

The last mile, on the other hand, focuses more on tactics. It focuses on the how and the when. It focuses on getting people to actually buy your products, or take up your services, or consume your offerings – in short, on getting your consumers and stakeholders to change their behavior in some desired fashion. The last mile is typically played out in retail spaces, on customer service locations, in your calling centers, on your web pages, and on your help lines, as well as in the interactions that your staff have with your customers.

I also made the claim in the book that all of us, whether a government, a for-profit organization, a not-for-profit organization, or even a little start-up venture, are fundamentally in the business of changing people's behavior. This is exactly what happens at the last mile. The science of the last mile is the science of behavior change. The last twelve chapters have covered a lot of ground about different approaches to the behavioral sciences. They have discussed behavioral theories and frameworks and the distinction between choice architecture approaches to influencing behavior versus decision crutches.

The last question is, "What do we need to do to make it happen?" Towards the end of chapter 1, I noted that an organization that strives to master the last mile needs to work on three sets of activities – *translation* (converting academic findings into managerially useful insights), *application* (auditing and monitoring the last mile interactions of the firm with its stakeholders), and *intervention* (developing behavior change interventions and testing them through controlled trials). This chapter will dig deeper into what organizations need to do to carry out these last three strategies (see figure 14.1).

Everything Matters

To make behavior change central to your operations and to your corporate philosophy, you need to keep two things in mind at the last mile: First, remember that everything matters. When your consumers make

Figure 14.1: Mastering the Last Mile

Mastering the Last Mile

Translation

Translating academic research into digestible insights

Coming up with prescriptive advice

Thinking through areas of application

Application

Auditing decision making

Monitoring efficiency of processes

Identifying bottlenecks and areas for improvement

Using tools from psychology to identify opportunities

Intervention

Designing nudging interventions

Piloting interventions and running controlled trials

Monitoring success

Iterating and identifying longer term success factors

a choice, they are influenced not only by the information you provide, the merits of your product, and the demerits of your competitors' products but also by the context and by their emotional state at the time. As the examples in this book have shown, consumers' decisions can be influenced by how your products are displayed, by the manner in which information is presented, by the consumers' state of mind, and by whether they are in a hurry or not. In fact, a multiplicity of things can play a role in consumer decision making.

In developing your own framework of the last mile, it is important to avoid approaching that last mile with a preconceived notion of what is or is not going to work. That said, there are some very simple guiding principles to follow. One principle, discussed in the chapter on decision points, is that inserting several decision points into the process can influence people to change their behavior, in particular their consumption behavior. Likewise, if you think about any particular behavior that you want people to adopt, your goal should be to make it as easy and as much fun as possible to engage in that behavior. Making it easy involves removing decision points and reducing the friction that consumers might experience in achieving a particular behavior. On the other hand, if there is some behavior that you want to discourage, then your goal would be to introduce a number of decision points for people engaging in that behavior. More generally, though, the second thing to keep in mind is the importance of collecting evidence on interventions through careful experimentation.

It could be argued that many corporations already use most of the ideas that I have talked about in this book to market and sell their products. I would be the first to agree with that proposition. At the same time, I wonder whether these corporations' success in selling or marketing their products is a function of a scientifically based framework they have developed for the last mile or whether it is due to the brilliance of a few individuals at the last mile.

At the level of governments or in the world of policy, there have been some examples of the success of choice architecture in helping citizens make better choices.[1] In the United Kingdom, for example, the government has centralized its behavioral initiatives with the formation of the Behavioural Insights Team, or BIT. It's also called the Nudge Unit. For several years, the Nudge Unit was a stand-alone government unit that worked with businesses, NGOs, and other government departments to develop and test interventions. It was formed in 2010, and since then the team has conducted numerous experiments in areas ranging from energy usage, debt and fraud, charitable donations, and tax compliance. Through its published reports and seminars, the team has helped educate and disseminate knowledge throughout the U.K. government on the application of behavioral economics to public policy and public welfare programs. Since its formation, the team has achieved much success, having identified a variety of behavior dimensions that have resulted in cost savings of over £300 million.

The success of its strategies has led the New South Wales and Australian governments to commission the team to assist them in applying behavioral economics to their public policy initiatives. The U.K. government recently privatized the Nudge Unit and made it part of an NGO called Nesta. This has given the team extra capacity and investment, increasing its potential to generate revenues for the government as well as for taxpayers.

In brief, the U.K. government has created a centralized internal consulting model that provides behavioral insights to help various government departments implement nudge-type interventions.

In the United States, Cass Sunstein, currently at the Harvard Law School, previously served as the administrator of the Office of Information and Regulatory Affairs (OIRA). During his appointment, Sunstein spearheaded many nudge initiatives, including the smart-disclosure initiative and the redesign of the U.S. Department of Agriculture (USDA) food pyramid and the fuel economy label. Following the success of the behavioral insights team, the U.S. government has formed its own social and behavioral science team to work with various government agencies to test and implement behavioral interventions.

In Canada, both the federal government and the Ontario provincial government recently announced behavioral insights initiatives in policy and welfare initiatives.

Elsewhere in the world, Denmark does not have a centralized unit for behavioral sciences, but several government departments are part of what is called the Danish Nudging Network. Other countries, including Singapore, the European Union, Canada, and India, are also working to incorporate behavioral interventions into their policies and welfare programs. It is therefore fair to say that, at least at the level of governments and public welfare organizations, there have been a number of instances of agencies adopting behavioral insights to improve the delivery of public programs and processes. The ecosystem has been strengthened further by the development of academic institutes (e.g., BEA@R at Toronto) and not-for-profits (e.g., ideas42) that support behaviorally informed policy and welfare programs.

Embracing Behavioral Insights

In thinking about what organizations need to do to fully embrace the culture of behavioral insights, there are two broad areas that I would like to touch on.

The first area relates to the outcomes that these organizations can achieve by adopting a full behavioral approach to the way they do business. The second area relates to *how* these organizations can do this. In other words, how can they fully embrace a behavioral approach to the last mile?

Let me focus first on what needs to be done. I would argue that there are three outcomes that a behavioral approach at the last mile could help organizations achieve. First, they could design products and policies that are more behaviorally informed. In other words, innovations often fail because the innovators have a flawed understanding of the psychology of the end user. Innovators tend to believe that the benefits of their product or service are obvious to the end user and that the end user or the consumer will overcome any obstacles they might face in order to purchase and use that product or service. Consumers, on the other hand, construct value as a function of the context and are not necessarily driven by purely rational considerations.[2] Keeping that simple insight in mind will encourage innovators to develop products and services that are more behaviorally informed.

How do you achieve behaviorally informed innovation? First, you need to articulate your intended value proposition before you produce and distribute the product. What is the product or service going to do for the consumer? Write that out in simple consumer language rather than focusing on the attributes of the product or service. Second, you need to think about using choice architecture approaches to nudge the consumer to purchase and to consume the product. Finally, it's important to integrate the innovation – the new product – into existing ecosystems of behaviors. If you have a product that requires a dramatic change in consumer behavior, then chances are good that the product will be rejected by your consumer base.

At the first level, a behavioral approach at the last mile will definitely help an organization improve the way it manufactures and markets its products. The second benefit of using a behavioral approach at the last mile is that it enables the organization to develop choice architecture and decision crutch approaches to steer consumers' decision making. If you are a for-profit organization, you want to steer consumers toward what is good for you. If you are a not-for-profit organization or a government, you want to steer consumers toward what is good for them. In all cases, you need to design interventions that will steer consumers toward what they think is good for them. This approach also allows the organization to develop a nuanced approach to designing nudges versus mechanisms like decision crutches that can help consumers incorporate more data and make better choices.

Third and last, adopting a behavioral approach at the last mile will enable the firm or organization to design products and services that are completely based on behavioral considerations. Earlier in the book we saw one example of this, the "Save More Tomorrow" savings plan, a simple behavioral program that outperformed many other programs.

A second example of such a product is Clocky, an alarm clock based on the simple idea that when all of us go to sleep we have every intention of waking up at 6:00 a.m., but when 6:00 a.m. arrives we are tempted to hit the snooze button. Clocky uses a simple technology that allows it to run away from anyone who tries to hit the snooze button. Shortly after the alarm has gone off, it runs away from its owner, using sensors that let it hide under the bed or in a corner. By the time the sleeper actually finds it and stops it, he is wide awake, and probably unable to go back to sleep.

Yet another example of a product or a program designed using a behavioral approach comes from a professor at the Wharton school, Katy Milkman. Katy and her collaborators designed a program that she calls *temptation bundling*.[3] The idea behind the program is simple. Temptation bundling works really well for the kind of consumers I called sophisticates earlier in the book – for example, consumers who wish that they exercised more but who lack the willpower to do so. The program further assumes that these consumers like a certain genre of novels – say, science fiction. But they also feel guilty wasting their time reading what other people might consider useless stuff.

Milkman and colleagues asked, "What if these consumers only allowed themselves to read science fiction novels while exercising at the gym?" This would encourage them to start craving trips to the gym to find out what's going to happen next in the story. Not only that, but they might enjoy both the workout and the novel more when they are combined, because they have less guilt about reading and a feeling of accomplishment from sticking to their exercise routine. If there is a way in which you can effectively combine what you *should* do with what you *want to do*, you have created temptation bundling.

In a study conducted at a gym to see if temptation bundling actually worked, Milkman and her colleagues randomly assigned a few hundred gym members to one of two groups. In one group (the temptation bundling group), participants received a loaned iPod and selected four audio novels from a list of books that a pre-test had shown were highly addictive. After choosing these novels, participants completed a workout while listening to the beginning of one of the novels. If they wanted to learn what happened next, they had to return to the gym and retrieve the iPod from the locker in order to continue with the story.

In a second group – the control group – participants again completed a thirty-minute workout at the beginning of the study, but instead of receiving an audio novel they got a gift certificate to a book store. The researchers found that, compared to the control group, the temptation bundling group showed a 50 percent increase in participants' exercise rate in the first seven weeks of their study!

Building Resources and Culture

Now let's focus on what the organization needs to do to become a behaviorally focused organization at the last mile. There are two broad questions to raise here. The first has to do with recognizing that the organization is in the business of changing behavior. In the last twenty years or so, I have worked with several for-profit and not-for-profit organizations, advising them on behavioral issues that relate to consumer adoption and the efficiency of their processes. All the organizations I've worked with have had an economic adviser, but very few have had a behavioral adviser. The first step in becoming behavioral at the last mile is to recognize the importance of behavior change.

In terms of how best to embed behavioral science into the organization, there are two broad approaches. As we saw with the example of the U.K. government's Nudge Unit, one approach is to create a centralized behavioral unit that can then act as an internal consultant and provide expertise to other units on how to develop experiments, design nudges, and test for the effectiveness of those nudges. The second approach is to embed behavioral expertise in various streams within the organization. If you think of your prototypical business organization, you might have a behavioral expert in your product development team, another behavioral expert in your sales and marketing team, and a third behavioral expert in your communications team. As long as these behavioral experts all meet from time to time and there is a shared understanding of the exact nature of the behavior that you're looking to change, either one of these two approaches might work for your organization.

It is also important for every organization to become what is called an "experimental organization." What does it mean for an organization to become an experimental organization? Simply being innovative doesn't make you an experimental organization. Likewise, simply trying new things from time to time does not make you an experimental organization. An experimental organization is one that is committed to the use of controlled trials to test the effectiveness of potential interventions.

What does an organization need to become an experimental organization? First, it needs the ability to generate small sub-samples of consumers, citizens, or constituents to experiment on. It is also important to be able to generate a control condition as well as the optimum number of treatment conditions needed to test a particular idea. You can generate such sub-samples by allocating consumers randomly across different groups. But it is also important for the groups to be segmentable. That is, you also need to be able to deliver a different intervention to each of these groups separately and in a cost-effective manner.

That delivery could happen in a number of ways. You could have a mailing that differs in relation to who will receive the mail. Or the product offering could be different depending on who is receiving that particular product. The key is to have the ability to generate various sample groups and treat them differently through either a different communication or a different product.

Next, you need a system for providing rapid feedback and rapid analysis of the data. The moment you generate an experiment and expose different consumer segments to different products or advertising messages, you need a process to help you quickly understand what effect that has had on the outcome variable that you are trying to measure. That outcome variable might be a change in choice, a change in attitude, or a change in the willingness to pay for your product.

Once you have the ability to collect that quick feedback, you also want to make sure that you can analyze the data effectively and that the analysis is then delivered to the people who might need to run follow-up experiments.

Stepping back, there are two qualities that are essential to make all of this happen. The first is the need for good process. In an earlier chapter, I talked a lot about developing processes for identifying and testing good nudging interventions. Organizations that truly want to embrace the behavioral approach need to embed these processes truly, deeply, and widely in the organization. It would be important to have the capability to automatically audit consumer decision making, for example, and make sure that bottlenecks in the process of decision making are routinely identified and reported back to people who can design interventions to clear those bottlenecks.

The second essential quality is a culture of empiricism – a belief in the value of concrete information. Organizations that wish to adopt a behavioral approach need to embrace data and accept that data can tell you about what is true as opposed to what is merely theoretical.

As yet, the theory of behavioral insights doesn't have as much vigor as the theory of classical economics does. That's easy to understand because the theory of classical economics deals with an artificial world, not a real world. It's also because behavioral science is young and because it is about human beings, and the number of things that affect the behavior of human beings is extremely large. For us to have a comprehensive theory of decision making, we would need to have a theory that embraces almost everything we see in the world around us.

That is going to take time. Until we get there it is important for those of us who work in this field to embrace the notion of evidence-based decision making. We need to be able to use evidence to inform policy, we need to be able to use evidence to inform new product introductions, and we need to be able to use evidence to deliver the most effective services to consumers and to citizens.

If we have a culture of evidence-based action, then we will be able to effectively use experiments meaningfully to improve processes, products, and policies.

Before I sign off, I want to discuss a number of questions that are often asked about issues like these. But here is one question that I will not debate: "Is nudging evil or is it ethical?" The reason I don't want to debate that question is that Richard Thaler and Cass Sunstein have already included an outstanding discussion of this question in their book *Nudge*. I will, however, offer a quick opinion on two levels. If people don't have an objection to influencing people's behavior using economic incentives or advertising, then neither should they have any objection to using choice architecture to influence people's behavior. Further, any choice architecture interventions that allow consumers to accomplish what they want to accomplish are by definition ethical and not evil. As long as we have a culture of transparency about how interventions are designed and what they are designed to achieve, I think we can benefit from using any and all of the tools at our disposal to engineer behavior change. Whether we like it or not, every decision that we make has a default. Every decision that we make has a context. Every decision that we make has information that is presented to us in a given manner.

These are all tools that businesses, policymakers, and deliverers of public services can use to help people make better choices. In my opinion, we should use them as effectively as possible, but with the appropriate checks and balances in place.

A Grand Unified Theory of Choice?

A question I am often asked concerns the difference between theory and practice. Think about the following specific form of the question:

"As a field, should we focus on developing a grand unified theory of decision making or should we simply focus on developing a culture of experimentation?"

There are a number of good arguments to be made for both sides of this debate. From an academic perspective, if we don't have a theory and we are simply experimenting then we don't do what we are supposed to do as academics. The goal of academia is to try and understand theoretically the drivers of behavior. Eventually, then, academics in the field of decision making behavior will seek to design a unified theory of decision making.

Having a good theory is important because theory guides us toward practice. Knowing what we are going to test and knowing why those particular effects are going to happen tells us a little bit more about what we should be doing to intervene and what sort of nudges we should be testing. Also, just because we will never have a perfect theory doesn't mean that we should stop trying to find a perfect theory. At the same time, however, there are practical things we need to do that are best tackled through experimentation. Theory can take us some way toward identifying what the right interventions would be, but theories are not very good at predicting which intervention is the most dominant or how big an effect it could have. That is why it is important for us as academics and as organizations to develop a culture of experimentation and let the data tell us what to do next.

Laboratory Experiments or Field Studies?

The second question I am often asked concerns the type of studies or experiments we should be running. Is the best insight developed from experiments where people in a laboratory setting make hypothetical decisions? Or is the best insight gained through field experiments? This question is particularly interesting to me because in 1993 it was one of the questions in the University of Chicago's comprehensive examinations for doctoral students (of which I was one).

I've obviously been thinking about this question for a number of years. I believe that the answer depends on which phase of research and discovery we are in. I believe that science, be it pure science or a social science, evolves through four phases. The first of those four phases is what I would call the discovery phase. This is where researchers go out and document new phenomena. For example, Itamar Simonson, many years ago, first documented the fact that people tend to choose the middle option when offered three alternatives. He did several ex-periments to confirm that hypothesis and has now developed a theory of what is called the compromise effect. Likewise, researchers went on and systematically observed phenomena such as the default effect, the duration heuristic, or even the pennies-a-day effect discussed in earlier chapters.

The second phase in research is theory testing. In this phase we try and understand why that particular phenomenon happened. Why do people choose the compromise option? Why do people go with the default? What is it about the pennies-a-day price that increases the likelihood that people will make a purchase? In this phase, the re-searchers are trying multiple iterations in order to rule out alternative explanations and to find process evidence for the underlying theory. If we have a good theoretical story to predict what's going to happen, we can then design careful experiments so that under certain conditions the theory makes one prediction. Under other conditions, it would make a different prediction.

The third phase in the context of engineering behavioral change would be the phase of nudge design. This is a phase in which we think through the process of what might be the best type of intervention if, in fact, we want to use that particular strategy to help people make better choices. We might think about a number of different interventions that we could possibly play with at a given point in time. We might want to try a few, perhaps five or six, to see which of them gives us consistent effects.

Finally, in phase four, we go through what is called an efficacy phase. This is a phase where we have decided on a particular nudge. We have decided what we want to do in order to try and change the behavior of our constituents. Now we want to experiment to see how big an effect that intervention will have.

In sum, there are four phases of research. I would make the argu-ment that *discovery* is best done in the field because, at the end of the day, we are looking for an effect that is empirically generalizable. Phenomena that we can see occurring in multiple places at multiple times across multiple cultures are the most robust. The field is a great setting to do that.

Testing theories is perhaps best done in a laboratory setting because at this stage we are looking to think through multiple explanations. We are looking to collect the kinds of data that give us insights into the psychology underlying these effects. We are looking to do experiments that require a very high degree of control. Control is not very easy to accomplish in the field, and therefore phase two is best done in the laboratory.

The last two phases, again, lend themselves nicely to field experiments. When you design a nudge, you've understood why the phenomenon happens. Now you know what you can control in terms of your interventions. You might think about randomized controlled trials as an approach to determining which of the different factors you have identified actually plays a role in the real world.

Finally, when you test for efficacy, again you want to test it in the field because that is exactly where you are going to use that intervention to improve decision making.

Nudging or Literacy?

The third question I am often asked is the following: "Which is better at improving welfare, nudging or literacy?" I don't think this is a debate at all. I think it is inappropriate to view nudging and literacy as competing strategies. Both have a role to play in helping to improve consumer welfare.

In fact, as I've argued before, I see welfare as a three-legged stool where one leg is a nudge. The second leg is literacy, and the third leg is motivation. When you think about designing any program in order to improve welfare you have three distinct tasks. The first task is to help people get started with the program. Nudging is a particularly effective tool for doing that.

The second task is to keep people engaged in the program – to keep them motivated to accomplish the end. Nudging might help here, as well, but there are other approaches that could be helpful. As discussed earlier, one of these is gamification. Finally, once consumers are in the program, they need to have a certain level of expertise in order to be successful at completing the program. For example, if it is a financial well-being program, they need to know what their own financial goals are and what the right mix of investments would be to help them accomplish that goal. In the case of a weight-loss program, they need to know what the right balance of healthy eating and exercise is to help them accomplish their goals.

When I talk about these three drivers as the legs of a three-legged stool, the metaphor is very vivid. If you take away one leg of a three-legged stool, the entire thing collapses. We need to view the equilibrium between nudging, literacy, and motivation strategies in pretty much the same way.

One Nudge at a Time

As I write this final paragraph, I realize that it's been over six years since Richard Thaler and Cass Sunstein published their book on nudging. Much has changed in those six years, but much still remains to be changed. Over the last six years the elephants that Thaler and Sunstein used on the cover of their book have come to be known as metaphors for nudging. Looking forward, there is a great deal more we need to do to successfully embed the science of behavioral insights into the DNA of both government and for-profit organizations. I hope we will be able to do it one nudge at a time.

Appendix 1
A Glossary of Behavioral Phenomena and Nudging Concepts

ACTIVE CHOICE AND ENHANCED ACTIVE CHOICE

Highlighting the fact that a decision needs to be made increases the attention paid to the decision-making process. This is especially useful for choices which are typically passive (e.g., getting a flu shot, renewing a health club plan, donating organs). Enhanced active choice refers to the presentation of options that highlight the cost of making a "no" choice.[1]

Example:

Rather than waiting for individuals to stop by a clinic to get a flu shot, they could be actively asked whether they intend to get one (active choice). Alternatively, they could be presented with two options: (a) Yes, I will get a flu shot and protect me and my family, or (b) No, I am willing to expose me and my family to the risk of disease. The likelihood of getting a flu shot should increase with active choice, and further increase with enhanced active choice.

ANCHORING

Numerical judgments tend to be influenced by prominent numbers that are available in the context. These prominent numbers – called anchors – need not even be relevant to the judgment.[2]

Example:

Two groups of people were asked to estimate the population of Perth, Australia. Before estimating, one group was asked whether they thought the population was greater or less than 50,000. The second group was asked whether they thought the population was greater or less than 10,000,000. The actual estimates provided by the second group were significantly higher.

Similarly, shoppers who encounter high-priced items early in their shopping trip are more likely to purchase cheaper items later.

ASYMMETRIC DOMINANCE/DECOY

Consider two options that vary on two attributes. A is better than B on attribute one, but not as good on attribute two. Adding a third option, B*, that is worse than B on both attributes shifts choices toward B. B* can be called a decoy because it is not really preferred, but shifts choices among the other two.[3]

Example:
A consumer cannot choose between two headphones. A has a sound quality index of 100 and a comfort rating of 50. B has a sound quality index of 50 and a comfort rating of 100. The addition of a third headphone B* with a sound quality index of 40 and a comfort rating of 90 will increase the likelihood of the consumer's choosing B.

AUTOMATIC ENROLLMENT

Automatically enrolling people in benefit programs or provident funds but giving them the option of withdrawing increases the likelihood that they will continue to participate.[4]

Example:
Company A requires all employees who want to participate in their benefits program to sign a form and send it to the human resources department. Company B automatically enrolls all employees into an identical benefits program but allows them to withdraw with no penalties by signing a form and sending it to the human resources department. In the long run, company B has a significantly higher participation rate in its benefits programs.

CHANNEL FACTORS

Features of the physical space and surroundings in a task-oriented environment can either facilitate or hinder the achievement of the task. Eliminating features that hinder the task will increase the likelihood of completion.[5]

Example:
Two groups of low-income consumers heard an (identical) seminar about the importance of opening bank accounts. At the end of the

seminar, one group was given the forms needed to open bank accounts, while the second was given forms as well as a map and directions to the bank. Significantly more people from the second group opened bank accounts.

CHOOSING VS. REJECTING
The manner in which people are asked to choose between two options can change the information they use in making the decision. In particular, asking people to choose between A and B results in their focusing on reasons to choose (positive aspects), while asking them to reject A or B results in their focusing on reasons to reject (negative aspects).[6]

Example:
A manager is looking to hire one of two job candidates. Mr. A is average on all four relevant attributes, while Ms. B is outstanding on two and weak on the other two. When the manager chooses between the two, B tends to be preferred over A (there are more reasons to choose B). When the manager is rejecting one of the two, B tends to get rejected more often (there are more reasons to reject B).

COMPROMISE EFFECT
When people choose between three options that vary along two dimensions, the option in the middle (which is average on both dimensions) tends to get chosen more often. Conversely, the likelihood that an option will be chosen can be increased by making it the "compromise" option. This effect is particularly strong for options where it is difficult to evaluate quality.[7]

Examples:
1. A gas station sold 89 and 91 octane petrol. The sales of 91 went up after they introduced a 94 octane grade, because 91 now became the "compromise" option.
2. In most coffee shops offering three sizes of beverages, medium is the most popular size.

CONSTRUAL LEVELS
When events are to happen in the future, people view them in light of their higher-level benefits. When the same event is to happen now, it is viewed in terms of concrete details. For events that have high levels of abstract benefits but involve a lot of concrete detail (effort), this results in a diminished attractiveness of the event as it comes closer in time.[8]

Example:
Neel was intrigued by the possibility of learning a new language and enrolled for Japanese classes that would happen in two months. After two months passed, the inconvenience of taking public transit, purchasing books, and giving up on leisure activities seemed too much, and he decided to cancel his registration.

DECISION POINTS

People often start consumption episodes with a decision to consume but then passively continue consumption until they hit a constraint. Inserting an opportunity to pause and think about the consumption in an active manner (a decision point) will increase vigilance and hence, the likelihood that consumption will stop. Decision points could take the form of reminders, small transaction costs, or physical partitions.[9]

Example:
Mr. X is given a large bucket of popcorn. Mr. Y has the same quantity of popcorn in four equal bags. Assuming that they are both conscious of the need to control consumption, Mr. Y will consume less than Mr. X.

DEFAULTS: OPT-IN VS. OPT-OUT

The default choice in any decision task refers to the outcome that would happen if the individual did not make a choice. If the likelihood that people will choose not to choose is high, making a desired outcome the default will increase the likelihood of its being chosen.[10]

Examples:
1. In Canada, citizens wishing to donate organs must follow a procedure to get registered. In France, the assumption is that everybody will donate organs, but citizens wishing not to donate can follow a procedure to get de-registered. Organ donation rates are significantly higher in France than in Canada.
2. In country A, credit card applicants must sign a consent allowing for their mailing address to be shared on a mailing list. In country B, applicants need to sign to prevent their addresses from being on a mailing list. The average citizen in country A receives a lot less junk mail than in country B.

EARMARKING

Money that is designated toward a particular cause is more likely to be spent on that cause. Earmarking can be achieved by physically segregating money.[11]

Example:
Labourers in India were given a savings target of rs. 40 per pay period. Some of them were encouraged to earmark rs. 40 by putting it in a separate envelope. These laborers were more likely to save.

FRAMING: GAIN VS. LOSS (LOSS AVERSION)

Presenting the same outcome as a loss has a greater psychological effect than presenting it as a gain.[12]

Examples:
1. When a 3% credit surcharge was framed as a cash discount, the price difference between paying by credit cards and cash was seen as more acceptable.
2. In one neighborhood, employees of a utility company tried to convince households to purchase energy-efficient appliances by saying, "If you use these appliances, you will save $10 per month." In a second neighborhood, this statement was changed to "If you fail to use these appliances, you will lose $10 per month." The likelihood of purchasing was significantly greater in the second neighborhood.

FRAMING: PENNIES A DAY

Presenting a large dollar amount as an equivalent number of dollars per day could increase the acceptability of this expense. However, this effect reverses if the per-day expense is very large.[13]

Example:
A charity asked individuals to donate $350 toward a certain cause. Subsequently, they changed their request and framed the money as "less than a dollar a day." Donations increased significantly.

GOAL VISIBILITY

When people are in the middle of a goal-oriented task, they work harder toward accomplishing the goal when it is in sight.

Consequently, reminding people of their goal or making the goal more salient or visible increases motivation.[14]

Examples:
1. Competitive swimmers swim faster on laps in which they face the end point of the race, and slower when they are swimming away from the endpoint.
2. Putting photographs of children on savings envelopes increased the saving rate of parents who were saving for their children's education.

HEDONIC EDITING

People either integrate or segregate monetary outcomes in order to maximize their psychological impact. In particular:
- A single loss is preferred to multiple losses.
- In situations where there is a large loss and a small gain, the gain should be separated from the loss (the silver lining principle). Multiple gains are preferred to a single gain.[15]

Example:
A tire shop that charged $200 for tire replacement offered a $10 discount. This small benefit was lost in the context of the large price tag. A second tire shop instead mailed their patrons a $10 gift certificate two weeks after they had their tires replaced. By separating this small gain, they made its psychological value much higher.

MINDSET: CHOICE VS. EVALUATION

A mindset refers to the style with which the human brain processes information. When a person has made a large number of choices, they are more likely to view incoming (unrelated) information as a choice problem.[16]

Example:
One group of people was asked "Which of the following is more prototypical of birds?" by making choices between a large number of pairs of birds (e.g., "Crow or penguin?"). A second group was asked to evaluate (not choose) the prototypicality of a large number of birds on a scale. Both groups were shown purchase opportunities where they could choose Product A, Product B, or not choose at all. People who had chosen among birds were more likely to choose, and hence make a purchase, than people who merely evaluated.

MINDSET: DELIBERATIVE VS. IMPLEMENTAL
A mindset refers to the style with which the human brain processes information. When a person has approached a large number of events with a view to getting them done (rather than merely thinking about them), he is more likely to get the next event done.[17]

Example:
Ms. A and Ms. B both faced a job that was due in three weeks and were asked when they planned to start working on it. Prior to this, Ms. A was asked about the value of five other jobs she had done, while Ms. B was asked how she accomplished five other jobs that she had done. Ms. B was more likely to start working on the new job sooner.

PAIN OF PAYMENT AND PAYMENT TRANSPARENCY
In addition to the negativity of paying a certain amount, the manner in which the payment is made can create further negativity. Certain methods of payment that are extremely transparent (e.g., cash or check) feel more painful than others that are not as transparent (e.g., electronic or direct debit). The pain of payment determines the willingness to spend.[18]

Examples:
1. When a laundromat shifted from accepting cash to accepting prepaid cards, the number of people running multiple loads of laundry increased.
2. When a cafeteria in Hong Kong moved from accepting cash to accepting the Octopus (a prepaid electronic card), the sales of desserts and beverages increased.

PARTITIONING/BRACKETING
Partitioning multiple objects into separate categories increases the nature of the choice process between those alternatives.[19]

Example:
A mutual fund company sorted its offering of mutual funds by the country of origin. As a result, their customers diversified by trying to purchase funds from different countries. When the same set of mutual funds was sorted by industry type, diversification by country decreased while diversification by industry increased.

PAYMENT DEPRECIATION
The pain of payment decreases as time passes after the payment. As a result, the strength of the sunk cost effect (a pressure to consume events that have been prepaid) decreases with time.[20]

Example:
The attendance rates at a physical fitness center gradually decline from the time of making an annual membership payment. On the other hand, patrons who make monthly payments show a more stable attendance rate as a function of time.

PEER PROGRAMS AND SOCIAL COMPARISONS
Making a commitment in the presence of peers increases the likelihood that the commitment will be followed by appropriate action. Also, the presence of peers who have high levels of accomplishment increases the motivation to similarly increase accomplishment.[21]

Examples:
1. Members of a self-help group savings program increased their savings rate when their peers routinely met to discuss progress and outcomes.
2. Households in the United Kingdom were sent letters encouraging them to pay taxes on time. When these letters included a statement of peer performance (e.g., "9/10 of people in the United Kingdom pay their taxes on time") the letters were more effective.

PERCEIVED PROGRESS
People in a goal-oriented task are more motivated to accomplish the task when they receive feedback about the progress they have made. Their motivation is driven not only by actual levels of progress, but also by their perception of progress.[22]

Examples:
1. People waiting in a long queue were more likely to continue waiting when the queue took the form of a line that moved as some people were being served, rather than a take-a-number-and-wait queue.
2. Two groups of people were given 400 lines of text to proofread. The first group received 20 pages of 20 lines each; the second group received 40 pages of 10 lines each. Members of the second group found themselves flipping through pages faster, had a

greater perception of progress, and were hence more likely to finish the task.

PRECOMMITMENT

When people view events that are in the future, they are more likely to be rational and wise about their choices. When the same events are in the present, people act impulsively and make foolish choices. Therefore, the best way of nudging people to make wise choices is to ask them to commit to making those choices for the future.[23]

Example:
Employees in an organization were asked if they would like to increase their savings rate in the future. Most agreed, and committed to setting aside a proportion of their future salary increase into a separate savings account. Those people who were asked to save more saved significantly more than people who worked with a traditional financial adviser.

SELF-AWARENESS/ IDENTITY

Any intervention that increases people's sense of identity as "virtuous persons" increases the likelihood that they will make virtuous choices. However, it is important that the intervention happens before the choices have to be made.[24]

Example:
People often misreport (cheat) in domains ranging from tax forms to insurance claims. In most of these situations, people have to sign and declare that the contents of the form are true – but the declaration is made at the end of the form, after all the reporting has been done. When the declaration is made prior to the reporting, the extent of misreporting and cheating significantly declines.

SINGLE-STAGE VS. MULTIPLE-STAGE DECISIONS

Presenting the same choice as a multiple-stage decision rather than a single-stage decision can change the outcome of the choice task.[25]

Examples:
1. One group of people (A) were told they would play in a lottery which offered a 25% chance of going to the second round. At this round, they were asked to choose between:

Option 1A: Get $300 for sure
Option 2A: 80% chance of winning $450, otherwise nothing
   A second group (B) were offered a choice between two gambles:
Option 1B: 25% chance of winning $300, otherwise nothing
Option 2B: 20% chance of winning $450, otherwise nothing
   Option 1A is identical to 1B, and 2A is identical to 2B. Yet people in group A prefer 1A over 2A (there is an illusion of certainty) while people in group B prefer 2B to 1A (now $450 appears larger than $300, while the difference between 20% and 25% doesn't seem as large). Hence, presenting a gamble as a two-stage decision could create an illusion of certainty and change choice.

2. A group of friends are deciding which restaurant to go to for dinner. In one version, they are asked to choose between Chinese, Italian, or Thai cuisines. In a second version, they are first asked if they would like Chinese, and if not, whether they would like Thai or Italian. The likelihood of choosing Chinese is significantly greater in the second version.

SUNK COST EFFECT
People who have prepaid for a consumption opportunity are driven to consume so that they can satisfactorily close their mental account without a loss. The drive to consume will be greater when the amount prepaid is higher.[26]

Example:
Jack and Jill both had rink-side seats for a basketball game. On the day of the game, there was a heavy snowstorm and the game was being shown on TV. Jill decided to stay home, while Jack braved the treacherous conditions to attend the game. Jill had received her ticket as a gift, while Jack had paid $100 for it.

TEMPTATION BUNDLING
Creating a mechanism where people can only consume an indulgence while they consume a virtuous product will increase the likelihood that the virtuous product is consumed.[27]

Example:
Two groups of people were encouraged to exercise more often. One of the groups was allowed to watch their favorite TV show only in the gym room, while the other had no such constraint. People in the first

group exercised more because they could bundle their temptation along with the exercise.

TRANSACTION DECOUPLING
The strength of the sunk cost effect can be weakened if the physical form of a transaction makes it difficult to associate a price tag with every unit of consumption.[28]

Example:
Jack and Jill both had season tickets for their favorite basketball team. While they paid the same amount, the physical formats of the season tickets were different. Jack's tickets took the form of a booklet of coupons – one coupon for each game. Jill's ticket took the form of a membership card which she showed every time she entered the stadium. On the day of one of the games, there was a heavy snowstorm, but the game was being shown on TV. Jill decided to stay home, while Jack braved the treacherous conditions to attend the game. The physical format of his ticket made it easier to realize that he would be "wasting" money by not attending.

Appendix 2
Tools for the Choice Architect

TOOL 1: A CHECKLIST FOR AUDITING THE DECISION

Properties of the Decision
1. Is the decision important to the individual or does it receive little attention?
2. What moments or events motivate an individual to act on the decision?
3. Is this an active or an automatic, passive choice?
4. How many options are available? What is the default option if an individual decides to do nothing?
4. Is feedback available, and is it received immediately?
5. What are the incentives? Which ones are most prominent? Which ones are less prominent?
6. What are the associated costs (financial, social, psychological)?

Information Sources
1. What knowledge or expertise is needed to make a decision?
2. How is information or knowledge communicated to the individual (visually, verbally, in text)?
3. Does the information flow sequentially? What information is presented first? Presented last?

Features of the Individual Mindset
1. Are the benefits of making a good decision delayed or experienced immediately?
2. Is the decision usually made when the individual is in an emotional state?

3. Does the decision require exertion of willpower or self-control (such as in the domains of smoking, dieting, exercising)?

Environmental Factors
1. Is the decision made in isolation or in a social environment?
2. Is the decision influenced by what is presented in the media or by expert opinions?
3. Are peers a major source of information?
4. Is there an application process, and is it difficult to navigate?

TOOL 2: QUESTIONS TO ASK IN DESIGNING NUDGES

Heuristics for Nudge Design
1. Are the individuals aware of what they need to do but unable to accomplish it, or does a desired behavior/action need to be activated?
   Yes: Think about self-control devices.
   No: Increase salience of desired behavior.
2. Are they motivated enough to impose a nudge on themselves?
   Yes: Develop products/services that sophisticated consumers might adopt.
   No: Think about context changes that might be seen by all (defaults, auto-enrollment, information-presentation strategies, etc.) but be especially effective for those who are motivated.
3. Is the action more likely to be taken with increased cognition, or are individuals currently hampered by cognitive overload?
   Yes: Provide relevant information in the most compelling manner.
   No: Simplify information and provide decision aids.
4. Is the desired action not being accomplished because of a competing action, or due to inertia? Consequently, should we aim to discourage the competing action or encourage the target action?
   Yes: Target on the competing behavior and nudge to discourage it.
   No: Target on the focal behavior and nudge to achieve it.

Notes

1. The Last Mile

1 "The Big Dig – Highway Division," *The Big Dig – Highway Division.* Accessed on 23 September 2014. Available at: http://www.massdot.state .ma.us/highway/thebigdig.aspx.
2 J.-P. Rodrigue, C. Comtois, and B. Slack, "The 'Last Mile' in Freight Distribution," in *The Geography of Transport Systems*, 2nd ed. (London: Routledge, 2009), 212.
3 "Bicycles." *Bicycles.* Toronto Transit Commission. Accessed on 24 September 2014. Available at: https://www.ttc.ca/Riding_the_TTC/Bicycles.jsp.
4 N. Potter, "City Car: Hiriko Electric Fold-Up Car for Crowded Cities," *ABC News*, ABC News Network (31 January 2012). Accessed on 29 October 2014. Available at: http://abcnews.go.com/Technology/citycar-hiriko-fold-car-future/story?id=15472566#.TylPoRxNM4Q.
5 *Roboscooters.com.* Accessed on 24 September 2014. Available at: http:// www.roboscooters.com/.
6 D. Yoney, "MIT GreenWheel: Simply an Electric Bicycle Revolution," *AutoblogGreen* (19 February 2009): n.p. Accessed on 24 September 2014. Available at: http://www.autoblog.com/2009/02/19/ mit-greenwheel-simply-an-electric-bicycle-revolution/.
7 J. Schneider and J. Hall, "Why Most Product Launches Fail," *Harvard Business Review* (April 2011): 1–4.
8 L. Brown, "Canada Learning Bond Helps Low-Income Families," *Toronto Star*, 26 June 2011. Downloaded 15 September 2014. Available at: http:// www.thestar.com/life/parent /2011/06/26/canada_learning_bond_ helps_lowincome_families.html.

9   D. Weil, A. Fung, M. Graham, and E. Fagotto, "The Effectiveness of Regulatory Disclosure Policies," *Journal of Policy Analysis and Management*, 25(1) (2006): 155–81.

10 D. Soman, "Option Overload: Dealing with Choice Complexity," *Rotman Magazine* (Fall 2010): 43–7.

11 S. Mullainathan, "Solving Social Problems with a Nudge." Presentation given at the TED conference in India, 7 November 2009. Accessed from https://www.youtube.com/watch?v=XBJQENjZJaA on 31 August 2014.

12 R.H. Thaler and C.R. Sunstein, *Nudge: Improving Decisions about Health, Wealth, and Happiness* (New Haven, CT: Yale University Press, 2008).

13 E. Johnson and D. Goldstein, "Do Defaults Save Lives?" *Science*, 302(5649) (21 November 2003): 1338–9.

14 S.T. Fiske and S.E. Taylor, *Social Cognition*, 2nd ed. (New York: McGraw-Hill, 1991).

15 I. Simonson, "Choice Based on Reasons: The Case of Attraction and Compromise Effects," *Journal of Consumer Research*, 16(2) (September 1989): 158–74; see also A. Tversky and S. Itamar, "Context-Dependent Preferences," *Management Science*, 39(10) (October 1993): 1179–89.

16 B. Crowell, *Light and Matter*, especially at Section 4.2, *Newton's First Law*, Section 4.3, *Newton's Second Law*, and Section 5.1, *Newton's Third Law* (2011). Available at: http://www.lightandmatter.com/.

17 B. Wansink, *Mindless Eating: Why We Eat More Than We Think* (New York: Bantam Dell, 2006).

18 A. Burroughs, *Magical Thinking* (New York: St. Martin's Press, 2004).

19 Ibid., p. 110.

20 P. Gollwitzer, "Mindset Theory of Action Phases," in P.A.M. Van Lange, A.W. Kruglanski, and E.T. Higgins (Eds.), *Handbook of Theories of Social Psychology*, 526–45 (London: Sage, 2012).

21 D. Kahneman, *Thinking, Fast and Slow* (London: Penguin Books, 2011).

2 Choice Architecture and Nudging

1   J. Colvin, "New York Soda Ban Approved: Board of Health Oks Limiting Sale of Large-Sized, Sugary Drinks," *Huffington Post* (13 September 2012). Retrieved 30 November 2012. Available at: http://www.huffingtonpost.com/2012/09/13/new-york-approves-soda-ban-big-sugary-drinks_n_1880868.html.

2   J. Poterba, "Tax Policy to Combat Global Warming: On Designing a Carbon Tax," National Bureau of Economic Research (March 1991).

Accessed on 28 September 2014. Available at: http://www.nber.org/papers/w3649.

3 R.H. Thaler and C.R. Sunstein, *Nudge: Improving Decisions about Health, Wealth, and Happiness* (New Haven, CT: Yale University Press, 2008), 6.

4 K. Ly, N. Mazar, M. Zhao, and D. Soman, *A Practitioner's Guide to Nudging*. Research Report Series: Behavioural Economics in Action (Rotman School of Management, University of Toronto, 2013). Accessed on 28 September 2014. Available at: http://www-2.rotman.utoronto.ca/facbios/file/GuidetoNudging-Rotman-Mar2013.ashx.pdf.

5 K.L. Katz, B.M. Larson, and R.C. Larson, "Prescriptions for the Waiting-in-Line Blues: Entertain, Enlighten and Engage," *Sloan Management Review*, 32 (Winter 1991): 44–53.

6 J.J. Kellaris and R.J. Kent, "The Influence of Music on Consumers' Temporal Perceptions: Does Time Fly When You're Having Fun?" *Journal of Consumer Psychology*, 1(4) (1992): 365–76.

7 N. Prabhu, *Foundations of Queuing Theory* (Boston, MA: Kluwer, 1997). (A discussion on optimal queuing systems.)

8 K. Ly and D. Soman, *Nudging around the World*. Research Report Series: Behavioural Economics in Action (Rotman School of Management, University of Toronto, 3 September 2013). Accessed on 29 September 2014. Available at: http://inside.rotman.utoronto.ca/behaviouraleconomicsinaction/files/2013/12/Nudging-Around-The-World_Sep2013.pdf.

9 A. Carey, "Facebook to Require New Timeline Profile," *ABC News*, ABC News Network (25 January 2012). Accessed on 29 September 2014. Available at: http://abcnews.go.com/Technology/facebook-require-timeline-profile-users/story?id=15440189.

10 U. Khan and R. Dhar, "Licensing Effect in Consumer Choice," *Journal of Marketing Research*, 43(2) (May 2006): 259–66; and N. Mazar and Chen-Bo Zhong, "Do Green Products Make Us Better People?" *Psychological Science: A Journal of the Association for Psychological Science*, 21 (2010): 494.

11 V. Tiefenbeck, T. Staake, K. Roth, and O. Sachs, "For Better or for Worse? Empirical Evidence of Moral Licensing in a Behavioral Energy Conservation Campaign," *Energy Policy*, 57 (2013): 160–71.

12 R. Catlin and W. Yitong, "Recycling Gone Bad: When the Option to Recycle Increases Resource Consumption," *Journal of Consumer Psychology*, 23(1) (2013): 122–7.

13 "Organ Donation Bid to Target New Drivers," *BBC News* (31 December 2010). Retrieved 1 March 2013. Available at: http://www.bbc.co.uk/news/health-12097225.

14 P.A. Keller, B. Harlam, G. Loewenstein, and K.G. Volpp, "Enhanced Active Choice: A New Method to Motivate Behavior Change," *Journal of Consumer Psychology*, 21(4) (October 2011): 376–83.

15 L. Shu, N. Mazar, F. Gino, D. Ariely, and M.H. Bazerman, "Signing at the Beginning Makes Ethics Salient and Decreases Dishonest Self-Reports in Comparison to Signing at the End," *Proceedings of the National Academy of Sciences*, 109(38) (18 September 2012): 15197–200.

16 E.P. Bettinger, B.T. Long, P. Oreopoulos, and L. Sanbonmatsu, "The Role of Simplification and Information in College Decisions: Results from the H&R Block FAFSA Experiment," National Bureau of Economic Research Working Paper No. 15361 (2009). Retrieved 28 February 2013. Available at: http://www.nber.org/papers/w15361.

17 T. Hossain and J.A. List, "The Behavioralist Visits the Factory: Increasing Productivity Using Simple Framing Manipulations," *Management Science*, 58(12) (2012): 2151–67.

3 Choice

1 J. Von Neumann and O. Morgenstern, *Theory of Games and Economic Behavior* (Princeton, NJ: Princeton University Press, 1994).

2 M. Allais, "Rational Man's Behavior in the Presence of Risk: Critique of the Postulates and Axioms of the American School," *Econometrica*, 21(4) (1953): 503–46; D. Ellsberg, "Risk, Ambiguity, and the Savage Axioms," *Quarterly Journal of Economics*, 75 (1961): 643–99; also D. Kahneman and A. Tversky, "Subjective Probability: A Judgment of Representativeness," *Cognitive Psychology*, 3 (1972): 430–54.

3 H.A. Simon, "A Behavioral Model of Rational Choice," *The Quarterly Journal of Economics*, 69(1) (1955): 99–118.

4 U.S. Karmarkar, "Subjectively Weighted Utility: A Descriptive Extension of the Expected Utility Model," *Organizational Behavior and Human Performance*, 21(1) (1978): 61–72.

5 D. Kahneman and A. Tversky, "Prospect Theory: An Analysis of Decision under Risk," *Econometrica*, 47(2) (1979): 263–91.

6 C.H. Coombs and D. Beardslee, "On Decision-Making under Uncertainty," in R.M. Thrall, C.H. Coombs, and R.L. Davis (Eds.), *Decision Processes*, 255–86 (New York: Wiley, 1954).

7 D.E. Bell, "Risk Premiums for Decision Regret," *Management Science*, 29(10) (1983): 1156–1166.

8 Ellsberg, "Risk, Ambiguity, and the Savage Axioms."

9 D. Soman, "Framing, Loss Aversion, and Mental Accounting," in D.J. Koehler and N. Harvey (Eds.), *Blackwell Handbook of Judgment and Decision Making,* 379–98 (Malden, MA: Blackwell Publishing, 2004).

10 R. Thaler, "Mental Accounting Matters," *Journal of Behavioral Decision Making, 12* (1999): 183–206.

11 A. Tversky, "The Intransitivity of Preferences," *Psychological Review, 76* (1969): 31–48.

12 C.R. Sunstein and R. Thaler, *Nudge: Improving Decisions about Health, Wealth, and Happiness* (New Haven, CT: Yale University Press, 2008).

13 Goldstein and Hogarth, chapter 1, "Judgment and Decision Research: Some Historical Context," in W.M. Goldstein, and R.M. Hogarth (Eds.), *Research on Judgment and Decision Making: Currents, Connections, and Controversies* (Cambridge: Cambridge University Press, 1997).

14 A. Tversky and D. Kahneman, "Extensional versus Intuitive Reasoning: The Conjunction Fallacy in Probability Judgment," *Psychological Review, 90*(4) (1983): 293.

15 Allais, "Rational Man's Behavior in the Presence of Risk"; and M. Machina, "Choice under Uncertainty: Problems Solved and Unsolved," *The Journal of Economic Perspectives, 1*(1) (1987): 121–54.

16 J.W. Payne, J.R. Bettman, and E.J. Johnson, *The Adaptive Decision Maker* (Cambridge: Cambridge University Press, 1993); and J.W. Payne, J.R. Bettman, E. Coupey, and E.J. Johnson, "A Constructive Process View of Decision Making: Multiple Strategies in Judgment and Choice," *Acta Psychologica, 80*(1) (1992): 107–41.

17 Payne et al., *The Adaptive Decision Maker.*

18 Simon, "A Behavioral Model of Rational Choice."

19 G. Gigerenzer, *Gut Feelings: Short Cuts to Better Decision Making* (London: Penguin Books, 2008); and D. Kahneman, "Maps of Bounded Rationality: Psychology for Behavioral Economics," *American Economic Review* (2003): 1449–75.

20 R.M. Hogarth, "Beyond Discrete Biases: Functional and Dysfunctional Aspects of Judgmental Heuristics," *Psychological Bulletin, 47* (1981): 116–31.

21 G.L. Allport, "The Historical Background of Social Psychology," in G. Lindsay and E. Aronson (Eds.), *The Handbook of Social Psychology, 50* (New York: McGraw Hill, 1985).

22 J. Levine and R. Moreland, "Small Groups," in D. Gilbert, S. Fiske, and G. Lindzey (Eds.), *The Handbook of Social Psychology,* 4th ed., vol. 2, 415–69 (Boston: McGraw-Hill, 1998).

23 S. Asch, "Opinions and Social Pressure," *Scientific American, 193* (1955): 35.

24 I. Simonson, "Choice Based on Reasons: The Case of Attraction and Compromise Effects," *Journal of Consumer Research*, 16 (1989): 158–74.

25 D. Ariely and J. Levav, "Sequential Choice in Group Settings: Taking the Road Less Traveled and Less Enjoyed," *Journal of Consumer Research*, 27 (2000): 279–90.

26 Ibid., 288.

27 F. Kast, S. Meier, and D. Pomeranz, "Under-Savers Anonymous: Evidence on Self-Help Groups and Peer Pressure as a Savings Commitment Device," No. w18417 (National Bureau of Economic Research, 2012); also L. Goette, D. Huffman, and S. Meier, "The Impact of Group Membership on Cooperation and Norm Enforcement: Evidence Using Random Assignment to Real Social Groups," *The American Economic Review* (2006): 212–16.

28 D. Kahneman, *Thinking, Fast and Slow* (London: Penguin Books, 2011).

29 D. Ariely, *Predictably Irrational* (New York: HarperCollins, 2008).

30 S. Iyengar, *The Art of Choosing* (New York: Twelve, 2011).

31 B. Schwartz, *The Paradox of Choice: Why More Is Less* (New York: Harper Perennial, 2005).

32 G. Loewenstein, *Choice over Time* (New York: Russell Sage Foundation, 1992).

33 D. Kahneman and A. Tversky (Eds.), *Choices, Values, and Frames* (Cambridge: Cambridge University Press, 2000).

34 A. Tversky and D. Kahneman, "Availability: A Heuristic for Judging Frequency and Probability," *Cognitive Psychology*, 5(2) (1973): 207–32.

35 Tversky and Kahneman, "Extensional versus Intuitive Reasoning," 297.

36 A. Tversky and D. Kahneman, "Judgment under Uncertainty: Heuristics and Biases," *Science*, 185(4157) (1974): 1124–31.

37 B.M. Barber and T. Odean, "All That Glitters: The Effect of Attention and News on the Buying Behavior of Individual and Institutional Investors," *Review of Financial Studies*, 21(2) (2008): 785–818.

38 G.B. Northcraft and M.A. Neale, "Experts, Amateurs, and Real Estate: An Anchoring-and-Adjustment Perspective on Property Pricing Decisions," *Organizational Behavior and Human Decision Processes*, 39(1) (1987): 84–97.

39 U. Simonsohn and G. Loewenstein, "Mistake #37: The Effect of Previously Encountered Prices on Current Housing Demand," *The Economic Journal*, 116(508) (2006): 175–99.

40 D. Ariely, G. Loewenstein, and D. Prelec, "'Coherent Arbitrariness': Stable Demand Curves without Stable Preferences," *Quarterly Journal of Economics*, 118(1) (2003): 73–106.

41 J. Huber, J.W. Payne, and C.P. Puto, "Adding Asymmetrically Dominated Alternatives: Violations of Regularity and the Similarity Hypothesis," *Journal of Consumer Research*, 10 (1982): 31–44.

42 Simonson, "Choice Based on Reasons."

43 D. Prelec, B. Wernerfelt, and F. Zettelmeyer, "The Role of Inference in Context Effects: Inferring What You Want from What Is Available," *Journal of Consumer Research*, 24(1) (1997): 118–26.

44 J.T. Gourville and D. Soman, "Overchoice and Assortment Type: When and Why Variety Backfires," *Marketing Science*, 24(3) (2005): 382–95.

45 S.S. Iyengar and M.R. Lepper, "When Choice Is Demotivating: Can One Desire Too Much of a Good Thing?" *Journal of Personality and Social Psychology*, 79 (2000): 995–1006.

46 H. Cronqvist and R.H. Thaler, "Design Choices in Privatized Social-Security Systems: Learning from the Swedish Experience," *American Economic Review* (2004): 424–8.

47 S.S. Iyengar, G. Huberman, and W. Jiang, "How Much Choice Is Too Much? Contributions to 401 (k) Retirement Plans," in O.S. Mitchell and S. Utkus (Eds.), *Pension Design and Structure: New Lessons from Behavioral Finance*, 83–95 (Oxford: Oxford University Press, 2004).

48 D. Soman, G. Ainslie, S. Frederick, X. Li, J. Lynch, P. Moreau, A. Mitchell, D. Read, A. Sawyer, Y. Trope, K. Wertenbroch, and G. Zauberman, "The Psychology of Intertemporal Discounting: Why Are Distant Events Valued Differently from Proximal Ones?" *Marketing Letters*, 16(3, 4) (2005): 347–60.

49 W. Mischel, Y. Shoda, and M.L. Rodriguez, "Delay of Gratification in Children," *Science* 244 (1989): 933–8; and W. Mischel, E.B. Ebbesen, and A. Raskoff Zeiss, "Cognitive and Attentional Mechanisms in Delay of Gratification," *Journal of Personality and Social Psychology*, 21(2) (1972): 204–18.

50 R. Strotz, "Myopia and Inconsistency in Dynamic Utility Maximization," *The Review of Economic Studies*, 23(3) (1955): 165–80.

51 D. Soman, "The Illusion of Delayed Incentives: Evaluating Future Effort-Money Transactions," *Journal of Marketing Research*, 35(4) (1998): 427–37.

52 G. Zauberman and J.G. Lynch, Jr., "Resource Slack and Discounting of Future Time versus Money," *Journal of Experimental Psychology: General*, 134(1) (2005): 23–37.

53 S. Benartzi, *Save More Tomorrow: Practical Behavioral Finance Solutions to Improve 401(k) Plans* (London: Penguin Group, 2012).

4 Money

1 *Merriam-Webster Online Dictionary and Thesaurus*. Merriam-Webster, Incorporated. Retrieved 22 August 2014. Available at: http://www.merriam-webster.com/.

2 R.H. Thaler, "Toward a Positive Theory of Consumer Choice," *Journal of Economic Behavior and Organization, 1*(1) (1980): 39–60; R.H. Thaler, "Mental Accounting and Consumer Choice," *Marketing Science, 4* (1985): 199–214; and R.H. Thaler, "Saving, Fungibility and Mental Accounts," *Journal of Economic Perspectives, 4* (1990): 193–205.

3 S. O'Curry, *Income Source Effects*. Working paper, Marketing Department, DePaul University (1997).

4 D. Kahneman and A. Tversky, "Prospect Theory: An Analysis of Decision under Risk," *Econometrica, 47*(1979): 263–91.

5 D. Prelec and G. Loewenstein, "The Red and the Black: Mental Accounting of Savings and Debt," *Marketing Science, 17* (1998): 4–28.

6 H.R. Arkes, "The Psychology of Waste," *Journal of Behavioral Decision Making, 9* (September 1996): 213–24.

7 H.R. Arkes and C. Blumer, "The Psychology of Sunk Cost," *Organizational Behavior and Human Performance, 35* (February 1985): 124–40.

8 D. Soman and J.T. Gourville, "Transaction Decoupling: How Price Bundling Affects the Decision to Consume," *Journal of Marketing Research, 38*(1) (February 2001): 30–44.

9 J. Gourville and D. Soman, "Payment Depreciation: The Behavioral Effects of Temporally Separating Payments from Consumption," *Journal of Consumer Research, 25*(2) (1998): 160–74.

10 O. Zellermayer, "The Pain of Paying." Unpublished PhD dissertation, Carnegie Mellon University, 1996.

11 H. Helson, *Adaptation-Level Theory* (Oxford: Harper and Row, 1964).

12 J. Gourville and D. Soman, "Pricing and the Psychology of Consumption," *Harvard Business Review* (September 2002): 90–6.

13 V. Zelizer, *The Social Meaning of Money: Pin Money, Paychecks, Poor Relief, and Other Currencies* (New York: Basic Books, 1994).

14 P. Henderson and R. Peterson, "Mental Accounting and Categorization," *Organizational Behavior and Human Decision Processes, 51* (1992): 92–117.

15 C. Heath and J.B. Soll, "Mental Accounting and Consumer Decisions," *Journal of Consumer Research, 23* (1996): 40–52.

16 D. Soman, "Effects of Payment Mechanism on Spending Behavior: The Role of Rehearsal and Immediacy of Payments," *Journal of Consumer Research, 27* (March 2001): 460–74.

17 E. Hirschman, "Differences in Consumer Purchase Behavior by Credit Card Payment System," *Journal of Consumer Research, 6* (1979): 58–66; and R.A. Feinberg, "Credit Cards as Spending Facilitating Stimuli: A Conditioning Interpretation," *Journal of Consumer Research, 13* (December 1986), 348–56.

18 D. Prelec and D. Simester, "Always Leave Home without It: A Further Investigation of the Credit Card Effect on Willingness to Pay," *Marketing Letters, 12* (2001): 5–12.

19 Soman, "Effects of Payment Mechanism on Spending Behavior."

20 S. Liu, Y. Zhuo, D. Soman, and M. Zhao, *The Consumer Implications of the Use of Electronic and Mobile Payment Systems.* Financial Consumer Agency of Canada, Research Report Series: Behavioural Economics in Action (Rotman School of Management, University of Toronto, 2012); and S. Trites, C. Gibney, and B. Levesque, *Mobile Payments and Consumer Protection in Canada* (Research Division, Financial Consumer Agency of Canada, 2013).

21 D. Soman and V. Lam, "The Effects of Prior Spending on Future Spending Decisions: The Role of Acquisition Liabilities and Payments," *Marketing Letters, 13* (2002): 359–72.

22 D. Soman, *The Effect of Payment Transparency on Consumption: Quasi-Experiments from the Field* (Boston: Kluwer Academic Publishers, 2003).

23 D. Aslett, *The Cleaning Encyclopedia* (New York: Dell Publishing Co., 2001).

24 H. Weisbaum, "Do You Really Need to Separate Colors from Whites?" KOMOnews.com (2011). Accessed on 22 October 2014. Available at: http://www.komonews.com/news/consumer/122836809.html.

25 E. Shafir, P. Diamond, and A. Tversky, "Money Illusion," *Quarterly Journal of Economics, 112* (1997): 342–74.

26 K. Wertenbroch, D. Soman, and A. Chattopadhyay, "On the Perceived Value of Money: The Reference Dependence of Currency Numerosity Effects," *Journal of Consumer Research, 34*(1) (2007): 1–10.

27 B. Pelham, T. Sumarta, and L. Myaskovsky, "The Easy Path from Many to Much: The Numerosity Heuristic," *Cognitive Psychology, 26* (1994): 103–33.

5 Time

1 R.W. Emerson, *Early Lectures of Ralph Waldo Emerson, Volume 2* (Cambridge, MA: Harvard University Press, 1964), 317.

2 B. Fredrickson and D. Kahneman, "Duration Neglect in Retrospective Evaluations of Affective Episodes," *Journal of Personality and Social Psychology, 65* (1993): 45–55.

3 See also D. Kahneman, B.L. Fredrickson, C.L. Schreiber, and D.A. Redelmeier, "When More Pain Is Preferred to Less: Adding a Better End," *Psychological Science, 4* (1993): 401–5; and D.A. Redelmeier and D. Kahneman, "Patients' Memories of Painful Medical Treatments: Real-Time and Retrospective Evaluations of Two Minimally Invasive Procedures," *Pain, 68* (1996): 3–8.

4 D. Ariely, D. Kahneman, and G. Loewenstein, "Joint Comment on When Does Duration Matter in Judgment and Decision Making?" *Journal of Experimental Psychology: General, 129* (2000): 524–9; quotation at 524.

5 R.A. Block, "Models of Psychological Time," in R.A. Block (Ed.), *Cognitive Models of Psychological Time*, 1–30 (Hillsdale, NJ: Lawrence Erlbaum Associates, 1990); J. Glicksohn, "Temporal Cognition and the Phenomenology of Time: A Multiplicative Function for Apparent Duration," *Consciousness and Cognition, 10* (2001): 1–25; and M. Treisman, "Temporal Rhythms and Cerebral Rhythms," *Annals of the New York Academy of Sciences, 423* (1984): 542–65.

6 H.-K. Ahn, M. Liu, and D. Soman, "Memory Markers: How Consumers Remember Experiences," *Journal of Consumer Psychology, 19*(3) (2009): 508–16.

7 See R.S. Wyer and T.K. Srull, "Human Cognition and Its Social Context," *Psychological Review, 93* (1986): 322–59; and R.S. Wyer and T.K. Srull, *Memory and Cognition in Its Social Context* (Hillsdale, NJ: Lawrence Erlbaum Associates, 1989).

8 This is consistent with the findings of J. Kellaris and R. Kent, "The Influence of Music on Consumers' Temporal Perceptions: Does Time Fly When You're Having Fun?" *Journal of Consumer Psychology, 1* (1992): 365–76.

9 W. James, *The Principles of Psychology*, vol. 1, ch. 15 (New York: Holt, 1980), 624.

10 G. Zauberman, J. Levav, K. Diehl, and R. Bhargave, "1995 Feels so Close Yet so Far: The Effect of Event Markers on the Subjective Feeling of Elapsed Time," *Psychological Science, 21*(1) (2010): 133–9.

11 See D. Soman, "The Mental Accounting of Sunk Time Costs: Why Time Is Not Like Money," *Journal of Behavioral Decision Making, 14* (July 2001): 169–85.

12 Y. Tu and D. Soman, "The Categorization of Time and Its Impact on Task Initiation," *Journal of Consumer Research, 41*(3) (2014): 810–22.

13 Adapted from A. Mishra and H. Mishra, "Border Bias: The Belief That State Borders Can Protect against Disasters," *Psychological Science, 21*(11) (2010): 1582–6.

14 N. Prabhu, *Foundations of Queuing Theory* (Boston: Kluwer, 1997).

15 M. Hui and D. Tse, "What to Tell Consumers in Waits of Different Lengths: An Integrative Model of Service Evaluation," *Journal of Marketing, 60* (April 1996): 81–90; see also S. Taylor, "Waiting for Service: The Relationship between Delays and Evaluations of Service," *Journal of Marketing, 58* (April 1994): 56–69.

16 T. Meyer, "Subjective Importance of Goal and Reactions to Waiting in Line," *Journal of Social Psychology, 134* (December 1994): 819.

17 G.S. Becker, "A Theory of the Allocation of Time," *Economic Journal, 75* (September 1965): 493–517.

18 J. Hornik, "Subjective vs. Objective Time Measures: A Note on the Perception of Time in Consumer Behavior," *Journal of Consumer Research, 11* (June 1984): 615–18.

19 K. Katz, B. Larson, and R. Larson, "Prescriptions for the Waiting-in-Line Blues: Entertain, Enlighten, and Engage," *Sloan Management Review, 32* (Winter 1991): 44–53.

20 D. Soman and M. Shi, "Virtual Progress: The Effect of Path Characteristics on Perceptions of Progress and Choice Behavior," *Management Science, 49(9)* (September 2003): 1229–50.

21 M. Zhao, L. Lee, and D. Soman, *The Effects of Virtual Boundaries on Task Commitment.* Working paper (Rotman School of Management, University of Toronto, 2011).

22 S. Mullainathan and E. Shafir, "Savings Policy and Decision Making in Low-Income Households," in M. Barr and R. Blank (Eds.), *Insufficient Funds: Savings, Assets, Credit, and Banking among Low-Income Households,* 121–45 (New York: Sage, 2009).

23 L. Festinger, "A Theory of Social Comparison Processes," *Human Relations, 7* (1954): 117–40; and P. Gilbert, J. Price, and S. Allan, "Social Comparison, Social Attractiveness and Evolution: How Might They Be Related?" *New Ideas in Psychology, 13* (July 1995): 149–65.

24 R. Zhou and D. Soman, "Looking Back: Exploring the Psychology of Queuing and the Effect of the Number of People Behind You," *Journal of Consumer Research, 29* (March 2003): 517–30.

25 P.M. Gollwitzer, "Action Phases and Mind-Sets," in E.T. Higgins and R.M. Sorrentino (Eds.), *The Handbook of Motivation and Cognition: Foundations of Social Behavior,* vol. 2, 53–92 (New York: Guilford, 1990); and P. Gollwitzer, "Mindset Theory of Action Phases," in P.A.M. Van Lange, A.W. Kruglanski, and E.T. Higgins (Eds.), *Handbook of Theories of Social Psychology,* 526–45 (London: Sage, 2012) .

26 J.K. Rowling, *Harry Potter and the Goblet of Fire* (New York: Scholastic, 2002).

27 Ibid., 434.

28 J.G. Lynch and G. Zauberman, "When Do You Want It? Time, Decisions, and Public Policy," *Journal of Public Policy and Marketing, 25* (2006): 67–78; E. Pronin, C. Olivola, and K.A. Kennedy, "Doing unto Future Selves as You Would Do to Others: Psychological Distance and Decision Making," *Personality and Social Psychology Bulletin, 34* (2008): 224; and H.E. Hershfield, "Future Self-Continuity: How Conceptions of the Future Self Transform Intertemporal Choice," *Annals of the New York Academy of Sciences, 1235* (2011): 30–43.

29 H.E. Hershfield, D.G. Goldstein, W.F. Sharpe, J. Fox, L. Yeykelvis, L.L. Carstensen, and J. Bailenson, "Increasing Saving Behavior·through Age-Progressed Renderings of the Future Self," *Journal of Marketing Research*, 48 (2011): S23–S27. Quotation at S24.

30 D.M. Bartels and L.J. Rips, "Psychological Connectedness and Intertemporal Choice," *Journal of Experimental Psychology-General*, 139(1) (2010): 49–69.

31 "Face Retirement and Meet the Future You," *Face Retirement*. Accessed on 22 October 2014. Available at: <http://faceretirement.merrilledge.com/>.

6 A Theory of Decision Points

1 T. O'Donoghue and M. Rabin, "Doing It Now or Later," *American Economic Review*, 89(1) (1999): 103–24.

2 R.H. Thaler and H.M. Shefrin, "An Economic Theory of Self-Control," *Journal of Political Economy*, 89(2) (April 1981): 392–406.

3 G. Loewenstein and J. Elster (Eds.), *Choice over Time* (New York: Sage, 1992).

4 See, for example, an outstanding book on the role of mindlessness in eating: B. Wansink, *Mindless Eating: Why We Eat More Than We Think* (New York: Random House, 2010).

5 See, for example, D. Kahneman, *Thinking, Fast and Slow* (London: Penguin Books, 2011); S.A. Sloman, "The Empirical Case for Two Systems of Reasoning," *Psychological Bulletin*, 119 (1996): 3–22; F. Strack and R. Deutsch, "Reflective and Impulsive Determinants of Social Behavior," *Personality and Social Psychology Review*, 8(3) (2004): 220–47; and A. Dijksterhuis and L.F. Nordgren, "A Theory of Unconscious Thought," *Perspectives on Psychological Science*, 1 (2006): 95–109.

6 A. Cheema and D. Soman, "The Effect of Partitions on Controlling Consumption," *Journal of Marketing Research*, 45(6) (2008): 665–73.

7 "'I Love Lays Potato Chips' – An Amazing Story of Human Experience," *Experience Project*. Accessed 29 October 2014. Available at: http://www.experienceproject.com/stories/Love-Lays-Potato-Chips/323495.

8 A.B. Geier, B. Wansink, and P. Rozin, "Red Potato Chips: Segmentation Cues and Consumption Interrupts Frame Portion Sizes and Reduce Food Intake," *Health Psychology*, 31 (2012): 398–401.

9 T. Rogers, H. Schofield, and S. Mullainathan, *Structural Facilitation: Small Structural Changes Can Lead to Unexpectedly Large Behavior Shifts*. Working paper (Harvard University, 2010).

10 D. Karlan, M. McConnell, S. Mullainathan, and J. Zinman, "Getting to the Top of Mind: How Reminders Increase Saving." Discussion Paper 988,

Economic Growth Center, Yale University (New Haven, CT: Yale University Press, 2010).

11 D. Soman and A. Cheema, "Earmarking and Partitioning: Increasing Saving by Low-Income Households," *Journal of Marketing Research, 48* (Special) (2011): S14–S22.

7 Experiments and Trials

1 G. Gamow, *One Two Three… Infinity: Facts and Speculations of Science* (Mineola, NY: Dover Publications, 1988).

2 D. Kahneman and A. Tversky, "Choices, Values, and Frames," *American Psychologist, 39*(4) (1984): 341–50; and D. Kahneman and A. Tversky, "Prospect Theory: An Analysis of Decision under Risk," *Econometrica, 47*(2) (1979): 263–91.

3 J.T. Gourville, "Pennies-a-Day: The Effect of Temporal Reframing on Trans-action Evaluation," *Journal of Consumer Research, 24*(4) (March 1998): 395–408; and J.T. Gourville, "The Effect of Implicit versus Explicit Comparisons on Temporal Pricing Claims," *Marketing Letters, 10*(2) (May 1999): 113–24.

4 A. Agresti, *Categorical Data Analysis,* 3rd ed. (Hoboken, NJ: Wiley, 2012); R. Gonzalez, *Data Analysis for Experimental Design* (New York: Guilford Press, 2008); and A. Agresti, *Statistical Methods for the Social Sciences,* 4th ed. (London: Pearson, 2008).

5 D. Kenny, "Mediation" (2014). Accessed on 8 October 2014. Available at: http://davidakenny.net/cm/mediate.htm; and K.J. Preacher and A.F. Hayes, "SPSS and SAS Procedures for Estimating Indirect Effects in Simple Mediation Models," *Behavior Research Methods, Instruments, and Computers, 36* (2004): 717–31.

6 D. Soman, "The Effect of Payment Transparency on Consumption: Quasi Experiments from the Field," *Marketing Letters, 14*(3) (2003): 173–83.

7 D. Prelec and D. Simester, "Always Leave Home without It: A Further Investigation of the Credit-Card Effect on Willingness to Pay," *Marketing Letters, 12* (2001): 5–12.

8 D. Soman, "Effects of Payment Mechanism on Spending Behavior: The Role of Rehearsal and Immediacy of Payments," *Journal of Consumer Research, 27* (2001): 460–74.

9 C.F. Camerer, L. Babcock, G. Loewenstein, and R. Thaler, "Labor Supply of New York City Cabdrivers: One Day at a Time," *Quarterly Journal of Economics, 112* (1997): 407–41.

10 E. Cannon and G. Cipriani, "Euro-Illusion: A Natural Experiment," *Journal of Money, Credit and Banking, 38*(5) (2006): 1391–1403.

11 D. Soman and A. Cheema, "Earmarking and Partitioning: Increasing Saving by Low-Income Households," *Journal of Marketing Research, 48* (Special) (2011): S14–S22.

12 M. Bertrand, D.S. Karlan, S. Mullainathan, E. Shafir, and J. Zinman, "What's Psychology Worth? A Field Experiment in the Consumer Credit Market." Discussion paper 918, Economic Growth Center, Yale University (New Haven, CT: Yale University Press, 2005).

8 Understanding Preferences and Judgments

1 P.J. Hoffman, "The Paramorphic Representation of Clinical Judgment," *Psychological Bulletin, 57* (March 1960): 116–31.

2 E. Brunswik, *The Conceptual Framework of Psychology* (Chicago: University of Chicago Press, 1952); and E. Brunswik, *Perception and the Representative Design of Psychological Experiments,* 2nd ed. (Berkeley, CA: University of California Press, 1956).

3 The more formal term for the "judgment machine" is "judgment bootstrapping"; see C. Camerer, "General Conditions for the Success of Bootstrapping Models," *Organizational Behavior and Human Performance, 27* (1981): 411–22.

4 R.M. Dawes, "A Case Study of Graduate Admissions: Application of Three Principles of Human Decision Making," *American Psychologist, 26* (1971): 180–8; R.M. Dawes, "The Robust Beauty of Improper Linear Models in Decision Making," *American Psychologist, 34* (1979): 571–82; R.M. Dawes and B. Corrigan, "Linear Models in Decision Making," *Psychological Bulletin, 81* (1974): 95–106; and Camerer, "General Conditions for the Success of Bootstrapping Models."

5 Camerer, "General Conditions for the Success of Bootstrapping Models."

6 L.R, Goldberg, "Five Models of Clinical Judgment: An Empirical Comparison between Linear and Nonlinear Representations of the Human Inference Process," *Organizational Behavior and Human Performance, 6* (1971): 458–79.

7 A.H. Ashton, R.H. Ashton, and M.N. Davis, "White-Collar Robotics: Levering Managerial Decision Making," *California Management Review, 37* (1994): 83–109.

8 M. Newborn, *Kasparov versus Deep Blue: Computer Chess Comes of Age* (New York: Springer, 1997).

9 K.R. Hammond, *Human Judgment and Social Policy: Irreducible Uncertainty, Inevitable Error, Unavoidable Injustice* (New York: Oxford University Press, 1996), 60.

10 R.M. Hogarth, *Educating Intuition* (Chicago: University of Chicago Press, 2001), 14.

11 P. Lindsay, *Human Information Processing: Introduction to Psychology* (New York: Academic Press Inc., 1977).

12 S.J. Hoch and D.A. Schkade, "A Psychological Approach to Decision Support Systems," *Management Science*, 42(1) (1996): 51–64.

13 S. Lichtenstein, B. Fischhoff, and L.D. Phillips, "Calibration of Probabilities: The State of the Art to 1980," in D. Kahneman, P. Slovic, and A. Tversky (Eds.), *Judgment under Uncertainty: Heuristics and Biases*, 306–34 (Cambridge: Cambridge University Press, 1982).

14 P. West, C. Brown, and S. Hoch, "Consumption Vocabulary and Preference Formation," *Journal of Consumer Research*, 23 (2 September 1996): 120–35.

9 Choice Repair

1 H. Simon, "A Behavioural Model of Rational Choice," *The Quarterly Journal of Economics*, 69(1) (1955): 99–118.

2 "OECD-FCAC Conference on Financial Literacy: Partnering to Turn Financial Literacy into Action" (OECD: N.p., n.d.). Accessed 26 October 2014. Available at: http://www.oecd.org/canada/oecd-fcacconference onfinancialliteracy.htm.

3 D. Fernandes, J.G. Lynch, and R.G. Netemeyer, "Financial Literacy, Financial Education and Downstream Financial Behaviors," *Management Science*, 60(8) (August 2014): 1861–83.

4 R. Thaler and B. Shlomo, "Save More Tomorrow: Using Behavioural Economics to Increase Employee Saving," *Journal of Political Economy*, 112(1) (2004): part 2.

5 A. Lusardi, *Overcoming the Saving Slump: How to Increase the Effectiveness of Financial Education and Saving Programs* (Chicago: University of Chicago Press, 2009).

6 S. Lichtenstein, B. Fischhoff, and L.D. Phillips, "Calibration of Probabilities: The State of the Art to 1980," in D. Kahneman, P. Slovic, and A. Tversky (Eds.), *Judgment under Uncertainty: Heuristics and Biases*, 306–34 (Cambridge: Cambridge University Press, 1982).

7 See R.P. Larrick, "Debiasing," in D. Koehler and N. Harvey (Eds.), *Handbook of Judgment and Decision Making*, 316–38 (Oxford: Blackwell Publishing, 2004); and D. Soman and M.W. Liu, "Debiasing or Rebiasing? Moderating the Illusion of Delayed Incentives," *Journal of Economic Psychology*, 32 (2011): 307–16.

8 S. Oskamp, "Overconfidence in Case-Study Judgments," *The Journal of Consulting Psychology* (American Psychological Association), 2 (1965): 261–5; and A. Koriat, S. Lichtenstein, and B. Fischhoff, "Reasons for

Confidence," *Journal of Experimental Psychology: Human Learning and Memory, 6*(2) (1980): 107–18.

9 S. Benartzi, *Save More Tomorrow: Practical Behavioral Finance Solutions to Improve 401(k) Plans* (New York: Penguin, 2012).

10 This table is adapted from Soman and Liu, "Debiasing or Rebiasing?"

11 C. Yeung and D. Soman, "The Duration Heuristic," *Journal of Consumer Research, 34* (September 2007): 315–26.

12 B. Shiv, Z. Carmon, and D. Ariely, "Placebo Effects of Marketing Actions: Consumers May Get What They Pay For," *Journal of Marketing Research, 42*(4) (2005): 383–93.

13 T. Mussweiler, "The Malleability of Anchoring Effects," *Experimental Psychology, 49* (2002): 67–72.

14 P. Sedlmeier, *Improving Statistical Reasoning: Theoretical Models and Practical Implications* (Hillsdale, NJ: Lawrence Erlbaum Associates, 1999).

15 C. Camerer, L. Babcock, G. Loewenstein, and R. Thaler, "Labor Supply of New York City Cab Drivers: One Day at a Time," *Quarterly Journal of Economics, 112*(2) (1996): 407–41.

16 D. Soman, "Effects of Payment Mechanism on Spending Behavior: The Role of Rehearsal and Immediacy of Payments," *Journal of Consumer Research, 27*(4) (2001): 460–75.

17 D. Soman, "The Mental Accounting of Sunk Time Costs: Why Time Is Not Like Money," *Journal of Behavioral Decision Making, 14*(3) (2001): 169–85.

18 R.M. Dawes and N.B. Corrigan, "Linear-Models in Decision-Making," *Psychological Bulletin, 81*(2) (1974): 95–106.

19 C. Gonzalez-Vallejo and E. Moran, "The Evaluability Hypothesis Revisited: Joint and Separate Evaluation Preference Reversal as a Function of Attribute Importance," *Organizational Behavior and Human Decision Processes, 86*(2) (2001): 216–33.

10 Choice Architecture: A Process Approach

1 E. Lyons and J. House, *Towards a Taxonomy of Nudging Strategies*. Research Report (Rotman School of Management, University of Toronto, 2012).

2 R. Thaler and S. Benartzi, "Save More Tomorrow Program™: Using Behavioral Economics to Increase Employee Saving," *Journal of Political Economy, 112*(1) (2004): 164–87.

3 "Clocky," *Clocky* (N.p., n.d.). Retrieved 26 October 2014. Available at: http://alumni.media.mit.edu/~nanda/projects/clocky.html.

4 A.S. Gerber and T. Rogers, "Descriptive Social Norms and Motivation to Vote: Everybody's Voting and So Should You," *The Journal of Politics, 71*(1) (2009): 178–91.

5 S.M. Jespersen, "Green Nudge: Nudging into the Litter Bin," *iNudgeyou. com* (16 February 2012). Retrieved 6 February 2013. Available at: http:// inudgeyou.com/green-nudge-nudging-litter-into-the-bin/.

6 S. Johnson, "Harvard Grads Turn Gym Business Model on Its Head: Fitness Plan Members Pay More if They Don't Work Out." Boston.com (24 January 2011)..Retrieved 6 February 2013. Available at: http://www .boston.com/business/articles/2011/01/24/gym_pact_bases_fees_on_ members_ability_to_stick_to_their_workout_schedule/?p1=Upbox_links.

7 "Gyms and Behavioral Economics – 10 Questions for the Gym-Pact Duo," *Nudge Blog* (18 May 2011). Retrieved 8 March 2013. Available at: http:// nudges.org/2011/05/18/ gyms-and-behavioral-economics-gym-pact-answers-your-questions.

8 "Gym-Pact – Never Miss Another Workout" (n.d.). Retrieved 6 February 2013. Available at: http://www.gym-pact.com.

9 F. Kast, M.S. Felipe, and D. Pomeranz, "Under-Savers Anonymous: Evidence on Self-Help Groups and Peer Pressure as a Savings Commitment Device," Harvard Business School Working Paper No.12-060 (2012). Retrieved 2 February 2013. Available at: http://www.hbs.edu/faculty/ PublicationFiles/12-060_4073be1c-88ba-4d5e-9fca-d5275baf3355.pdf.

10 "Waterpebble – Your Little Water Saver" (n.d.). Retrieved 30 March 2015. Available at: http://www.boa-waterpebble.com/.

11 S. Benartzi and R. Thaler, "Behavioral Economics and the Retirement Savings Crisis," *Science, 339*(6124) (March 2013): 1152–3.

12 G.D. Carroll, J.J. Choi, D. Laibson, B.C. Madrian, and A. Metrick, "Optimal Defaults and Active Decision," *Quarterly Journal of Economics, 124*(4) (2009):1639–74.

13 R. Thaler, "Watching Behavior before Writing the Rules," *New York Times*, 7 July 2012. Retrieved 15 February 2013. Available at: http://www. nytimes.com/glogin?URI=http://www.nytimes.com/2012/07/08/ business/behavioral-science-can-help-guide-policy-economic-view.html.

14 S. Weinburg, *Dreams of a Final Theory: The Scientist's Search for the Ultimate Laws of Nature* (New York: Vintage, 1994).

11 Decision Crutches

1 R. Herrnstein and D. Prelec, "Melioration: A Theory of Distributed Choice," *Journal of Economic Perspectives, 5*(3) (1991): 137–56. Quotation at 137.

2 D. Soman, "The Effects of Prior Spending on Future Spending Decisions: The Role of Acquisition Liabilities and Payments," *Marketing Science, 17*(1) (2002): 4–28.

3 *WeightWatchers.com – Official Site* (N.p., n.d.). Retrieved 24 October 2014. Available at: https://welcome.weightwatchers.com/.

4 "Fitbit" (N.p., n.d.). *Fitbit® Official Site: Flex, One & Zip Wireless Activity & Sleep Trackers.* Retrieved 26 October 2014. Available at: http://www.fitbit.com/ca.

5 "SleepBot" (N.p., n.d.). *SleepBot.* Retrieved 26 October 2014. Available at: https://mysleepbot.com/.

6 "Toyota" (N.p., n.d.). *Toyota.* Retrieved 26 October 2014. Available at: http://www.toyota.com/prius-family/.

7 S. Lichtenstein, B. Fischhoff, and L.D. Phillips, "Calibration of Probabilities: The State of the Art to 1980," in D. Kahneman, P. Slovic, and A. Tversky (Eds.), *Judgment under Uncertainty: Heuristics and Biases,* 306–34 (New York: Cambridge University Press, 1982); and A. Koriat, S. Lichtenstein, and B. Fischhoff, "Reasons for Confidence," *Journal of Experimental Psychology: Human Learning and Memory,* 6(2) (1980): 107–18.

8 J. Russo and P. Schoemaker, "Managing Overconfidence," *Sloan Management Review, 33*(2) (1992): 7–17; and S. Russo, *Decision Traps: Ten Barriers to Brilliant Decision-Making and How to Overcome Them* (New York: Simon and Schuster, 1990).

9 This is a small-scale version of a phenomenon that was made popular by J. Surowiecki's book *The Wisdom of Crowds* (New York: Anchor, 2005).

10 R.P. Larrick, A.E. Mannes, and J.B. Soll, "The Social Psychology of the Wisdom of Crowds," in J.I. Krueger (Ed.), *Frontiers of Social Psychology: Social Psychology and Decision Making* (Philadelphia: Psychology Press, 2012); and J.B. Soll and R.P. Larrick, "Strategies for Revising Judgment: How (and How Well) People Use Others' Opinions," *Journal of Experimental Psychology: Learning, Memory, and Cognition, 35* (2009): 780–805.

11 D. Kahneman and D. Lovallo, "Timid Choices and Bold Forecasts: A Cognitive Perspective on Risk Taking," *Management Science, 39*(1) (1993): 17–31.

12 S. Hoch and D. Schkade, "A Psychological Approach to Decision Support Systems," *Management Science, 42* (1996): 51–64.

13 R.C. Blattberg and S.J. Hoch, "Database Models and Managerial Intuition: 50% Model and 50% Manager," *Management Science, 36*(8) (1990): 887–99.

12 Disclosures

1 D. Weil, A. Fung, M. Graham, and E. Fagotto, "The Effectiveness of Regulatory Disclosure Policies," *Journal of Policy Analysis and Management,* 25(1) (2006): 155–81.

2 G. Loewenstein, D. Cain, and S. Sah, "The Limits of Transparency: Pitfalls and Potential of Disclosing Conflicts of Interest," *American Economic*

Review, *101*(3) (2011): 423–8; and S. Sah, G. Loewenstein, and D. Cain, "The Burden of Disclosure: Increased Compliance with Distrusted Advice," *Journal of Personality and Social Psychology*, *104*(2) (2013): 289–304.

3 I.A. Razaq, M. Zhao, and D. Soman, *A Behavioural Analysis of Public Disclosure Programs*. Working Paper, Behavioural Economics in Action (Rotman School of Management, University of Toronto, 2014).

4 "Departments," *Nova Scotia Canada*. Retrieved 26 October 2014. Available at: http://novascotia.ca/lae/dept/.

5 "Employer Records," *Alberta*. Retrieved 30 March 2015. Available at: work. alberta.ca/occupational-health-safety/employer-records-search.asp.

6 "Toxics Release Inventory (TRI) Program," *Toxics Release Inventory (TRI) Program*. U.S. Environmental Protection Agency. Retrieved 26 October 2014. Available at: http://www2.epa.gov/toxics-release-inventory-tri-program.

7 D. Kahneman, *Thinking, Fast and Slow* (London: Penguin Books, 2011); R.H. Thaler and C.R. Sunstein, *Nudge: Improving Decisions about Health, Wealth, and Happiness* (New Haven, CT: Yale University Press, 2008).

8 R. Pitofsky, "Beyond Nader: Consumer Protection and the Regulation of Advertising," *Harvard Law Review*, *90*(4) (1977): 661–701; and M.S. Shapo, "A Representational Theory of Consumer Protection: Doctrine, Function and Legal Liability for Product Disappointment," *Virginia Law Review*, *60*(7) (1974): 1109–1388.

9 X. Gabaix and D. Laibson, "Shrouded Attributes, Consumer Myopia, and Information Suppression in Competitive Markets," *Quarterly Journal of Economics*, *121*(2) (2006): 505–40; and J. Brown, T. Hossain, and J. Morgan, "Shrouded Attributes and Information Suppression: Evidence from the Field," *Quarterly Journal of Economics*, *125*(2) (2010): 859–76.

10 G. Ellison and S.F. Ellison, "Search, Obfuscation, and Price Elasticities on the Internet," *Econometrica*, *77*(2) (2009), 427–52; and C.R. Sunstein, "Empirically Informed Regulation," *University of Chicago Law Review*, *78*(4) (2011): 1349–1429.

11 Weil, Fung, Graham, and Fagotto, "The Effectiveness of Regulatory Disclosure Policies."

12 J. Beshears, J. Choi, D. Laibson, and B. Madrian, "How Does Simplified Disclosure Affect Individuals' Mutual Fund Choices?" in D.A. Wise (Ed.), *Explorations in the Economics of Aging*, 75–96 (Chicago: University of Chicago Press, 2010).

13 J. Lee and J. Hogarth, "Returns to Information Search: Consumer Mortgage Shopping Decisions," *Financial Counseling and Planning*, *10*(1) (1999): 1–67.

14 J. Davis, "Protecting Consumers from Overdisclosure and Gobbledygook: An Empirical Look at the Simplification of Consumer-Credit Contracts," *Virginia Law Review*, *63*(6) (1977): 841–920.

15 B. Fischhoff, N. Brewer, and J. Downs (Eds.), *Communicating Risks and Benefits: An Evidence-Based User's Guide* (Washington, DC: Food and Drug Administration, 2011): 242. Retrieved 30 March 2015. Available at: http://www.fda.gov/downloads/AboutFDA/ReportsManualsForms/Reports/UCM268069.pdf.

16 I.M. Lipkus and J.G. Hollands, "The Visual Communication of Risk," *Journal of the National Cancer Institute Monographs, 25* (1999): 149–63.

17 Financial Consumer Agency of Canada, "Qualitative Testing of Proposed MasterCard Plain Language Application Form" (2008). Retrieved 30 March 2015. Available at: http://www.fcac-acfc.gc.ca/Eng/resources/researchSurveys/Pages/Qualitat-Testqual.aspx.

18 Loewenstein, Cain, and Sah, "The Limits of Transparency: Pitfalls and Potential of Disclosing Conflicts of Interest"; and Sah, Loewenstein, and Cain, "The Burden of Disclosure."

19 G. Dowling, *Creating Corporate Reputations: Identity, Image, and Performance* (Oxford: Oxford University Press, 2002).

20 J. Meernik, R. Aloisi, M. Sowell, and A. Nichols, "The Impact of Human Rights Organizations on Naming and Shaming Campaigns," *Journal of Conflict Resolution, 56*(2) (2012): 233–56.

21 W. Cochran and A. Tesser, "The 'What the Hell Effect': Some Effects of Goal Proximity and Goal Framing on Performance," in L. Martin and A. Tessler (Eds.), *Striving and Feeling: Interaction among Goals, Affect, and Self-Regulation, 99*–120 (Hillsdale, NJ: Lawrence Erlbaum Associates, 1996).

22 D. Soman and A. Cheema, "When Goals Are Counter-Productive: The Effects of Violation of a Behavioral Goal on Subsequent Performance," *Journal of Consumer Research, 31*(1) (June 2004): 52–62.

23 T. Gilovich, V.H. Medvec, and K. Savitsky, "The Spotlight Effect in Social Judgment: An Egocentric Bias in Estimates of the Salience of One's Own Actions and Appearance," *Journal of Personality and Social Psychology, 78*(2) (2000): 211–22.

24 G. Loewenstein, C. Sunstein, and R. Golman, *Disclosure: Psychology Changes Everything.* Harvard Public Law Working Paper No.13-30 (2013), 42.

25 A. Fung, M. Graham, and D. Weil, *Full Disclosure: The Politics and Perils of Transparency Policies* (West Nyack, NY: Cambridge University Press, 2007).

26 G.Z. Jin and P. Leslie, "The Case in Support of Restaurant Hygiene Grade Cards, *Choices, 20*(2) (2005): 97–102.

27 R.H. Thaler and W. Tucker, "Smarter Information, Smarter Consumers," *Harvard Business Review* (January-February 2013): 3–11. Quotation at 4.

28 See https://www.gov.uk/government/news/the-midata-vision-of-consumer-empowerment. Retrieved 30 June 2014.

13 Retailing

1 J. Cha, L. Liu, and D. Soman, *Going the Extra Mile in Retailing*. White paper (Rotman School of Business, University of Toronto, 2015).
2 D. Soman and W. Liu "The Psychology of Pricing," in C.P. Haugtvedt, P.M. Herr, and F.R. Kardes (Eds.), *Handbook of Consumer Psychology*, 659–81 (Society for Consumer Psychology) (Oxford: Psychology Press, 2008).
3 See also R.H. Thaler, "Toward a Positive Theory of Consumer Choice," *Journal of Economic Behavior and Organization*, 1(1) (1980): 39–60; R.H. Thaler, "Mental Accounting and Consumer Choice," *Marketing Science*, 4 (1985): 199–214; and R.H. Thaler, "Saving, Fungibility and Mental Accounts," *Journal of Economic Perspectives*, 4 (1990): 193–205.
4 D. Kahneman and A. Tversky, "Prospect Theory: An Analysis of Decision under Risk," *Econometrica*, 47 (1979): 263–91.
5 V.G. Morwitz, E.A. Greenleaf, and E.J. Johnson, "Divide and Prosper: Consumers' Reactions to Partitioned Prices," *Journal of Marketing Research*, 35(4) (1998): 453–63.
6 K. Shampanier, N. Mazar, and D. Ariely, "Zero as a Special Price: The True Value of Free Product," *Marketing Science*, 26(6) (2007): 742–57.
7 See S. Dhar, C. Gonzalez-Vallejo, and D. Soman, "Brand Promotions as a Lottery," *Marketing Letters*, 6(3) (1995): 221–33; and S. Dhar, C. Gonzalez-Vallejo, and D. Soman, "Modeling the Effects of Advertised Price Claims: Tensile versus Objective Claims," *Marketing Science*, 18(2) (1999): 221–33.
8 D. Kahneman, J. Knetsch, and R.H. Thaler, "Experimental Tests of the Endowment Effect and the Coase Theorem," *Journal of Political Economy* 98(6) (1990): 1325–48.
9 See also D. Soman and S.N. Marandi, *Managing Customer Value: One Stage at a Time* (Singapore: World Scientific Publishing, 2009).

14 The Last Mile of the Last Mile

1 K. Ly and D. Soman, *Nudging around the World*. Research Report Series: Behavioural Economics in Action (Rotman School of Management, University of Toronto, 3 September 2013).
2 See J. Gourville, "Eager Sellers and Stony Buyers: Understanding the Psychology of New Product Adoption," *Harvard Business Review* (June 2006): 99–106.
3 K.L. Milkman, J.A. Minson, and K.G.M. Volpp, "Holding the Hunger Games Hostage at the Gym: An Evaluation of Temptation Bundling," *Management Science*, 60(2) (2014): 283–99.

Appendix 1

1 P.A. Keller, B. Harlam, G. Loewenstein, and K.G. Volpp, "Enhanced Active Choice: A New Method to Motivate Behavior Change," *Journal of Consumer Psychology*, 21(4) (October 2011): 376–83.

2 A. Tversky and D. Kahneman, "Judgment under Uncertainty: Heuristics and Biases," *Science*, 185(1124) (1974): 1128–30.

3 Ibid.

4 B.C. Madrian and D.F. Shea, *The Power of Suggestion: Inertia in 401(k) Participation and Savings Behavior,* National Bureau of Economic Research Working Paper No. 7682 (May 2000).

5 S. Mullainathan and E. Shafir, "Savings Policy and Decision-Making in Low-Income Households," in M. Barr and R. Blank (Eds.), *Insufficient Funds: Savings, Assets, Credit and Banking among Low-Income Households,* 121–45 (New York: Russell Sage Foundation Press, 2009).

6 E. Shafir, "Choosing versus Rejecting: Why Some Options Are Both Better and Worse Than Others," *Memory & Cognition*, 21 (1993): 546–56.

7 I. Simonson, "Choice Based on Reasons: The Case of Attraction and Compromise Effects," *Journal of Consumer Research*, 16 (September 1989): 158–74.

8 Y. Trope and N. Liberman, "Temporal Construal," *Psychological Review, 110* (2003): 403–21.

9 D. Soman, J. Xu, and A. Cheema, "A Theory of Decision Points," *Rotman Magazine* (Winter 2010).

10 E. Johnson and D. Goldstein, "Do Defaults Save Lives?" *Science* 302(5649) (21 November 2003): 1338–9.

11 D. Soman and A. Cheema, "Earmarking and Partitioning: Increasing Saving by Low-Income Households," *Journal of Marketing Research, 48* (Special) (2011): S14–S22.

12 D. Kahneman and A. Tversky, "Prospect Theory: An Analysis of Decision under Risk," *Econometrica, 47*(2) (1979): 263–91.

13 J.T Gourville, "Pennies-a-Day: The Effect of Temporal Reframing on Transaction Evaluation," *Journal of Consumer Research 24*(4) (March 1998): 395–408.

14 A. Cheema and R. Bagchi, "Goal Visualization and Goal Pursuit: Implications for Individuals and Managers," *Journal of Marketing, 75* (March 2011): 109–23.

15 R.H. Thaler, "Mental Accounting Matters," *Journal of Behavioral Decision Making, 12* (1999): 183–206.

16 A.J. Xu and R.S. Wyer, Jr., "The Comparative Mind-Set: From Animal Comparisons to Increased Purchase Intentions," *Psychological Science, 19* (2008): 859–64.

17 P. Gollwitzer, "Implementation Intentions: Strong Effects of Simple Plans," *American Psychologist, 54* (July 1999): 493–503.

18 D. Soman, "Effects of Payment Mechanism on Spending Behaviour: The Role of Rehearsal and Immediacy of Payments," *Journal of Consumer Research, 27* (March 2001): 460–74.

19 C.R. Fox, R.K. Ratner, and D. Lieb, "How Subjective Grouping of Options Influences Choice and Allocation: Diversification Bias and the Phenomenon of Partition Dependence," *Journal of Experimental Psychology: General, 134*(4) (2005): 538–51.

20 J. Gourville and D. Soman, "Payment Depreciation: The Behavioural Effects of Temporally Separating Payments from Consumption," *Journal of Consumer Research, 25*(2) (1998): 160–74.

21 F. Kast, S. Meier, and D. Pomerantz, *Under-Savers Anonymous: Evidence on Self-Help Groups and Peer Pressure as a Savings Commitment Device,* Working Paper (Columbia University, 2011).

22 R. Zhou and D. Soman, "Looking Back: Exploring the Psychology of Queuing and the Effect of the Number of People Behind You," *Journal of Consumer Research, 29* (March 2003): 517–30.

23 R.H. Thaler and S. Benartzi, "Save More Tomorrow: Using Behavioral Economics to Increase Employee Saving," *Journal of Political Economy, 112* (2004): 164–87.

24 L.L. Shu, N. Mazar, F. Gino, D. Ariely, and M.H. Bazerman, "Signing at the Beginning Makes Ethics Salient and Decreases Dishonest Self-Reports in Comparison to Signing at the End," *Proceedings of the National Academy of Sciences (PNAS), 109*(38) (2012): 15197–200.

25 Kahneman and Tversky, "Prospect Theory: An Analysis of Decision under Risk."

26 Thaler, "Mental Accounting Matters."

27 K.L. Milkman, J.A. Minson, and K.G.M. Volpp , "Holding the Hunger Games Hostage at the Gym: An Evaluation of Temptation Bundling," *Management Science* (2014).

28 D. Soman and J. Gourville, "Transaction Decoupling: How Price Bundling Affects the Decision to Consume," *Journal of Marketing Research, 38* (February 2001): 30–44.

Index